53-13

Self-determination in social work

a collection of essays on self-determination
and related concepts by philosophers
and social work theorists

The International Library of Welfare and Philosophy

General Editors

Professor Noel Timms
*School of Applied Social Studies,
University of Bradford*

David Watson
*Department of Moral Philosophy,
University of Glasgow*

Self-determination in social work

a collection of essays on self-determination
and related concepts by philosophers
and social work theorists

Edited by

F. E. McDermott

Department of Philosophy
University of Sheffield

Routledge & Kegan Paul
London and Boston

First published in 1975
by Routledge & Kegan Paul Ltd
Broadway House, 68-74 Carter Lane,
London EC4V 5EL and
9 Park Street,
Boston, Mass. 02108, USA
Set in 10/12 pt English
and printed in Great Britain by
The Lavenham Press Ltd

ISBN 0 7100 7980 x (c)
       0 7100 7981 8 (p)
Library of Congress Catalog Card No. 74-84171

Contents

Part II Self-determination, freedom and related concepts

Notes on the contributors

Father F. P. Biestek is a Professor in the School of Social Work, Loyola University of Chicago. Among his publications are *The Principle of Client Self-Determination in Social Casework* and *The Casework Relationship*.

Saul Bernstein is Professor Emeritus of the Boston University School of Social Work.

Alan Keith-Lucas is Alumni Distinguished Professor in Social Work, University of North Carolina. Among his publications are *Decisions about People in Need* and *Some Casework Concepts for the Public Welfare Worker*.

David Soyer is Director of Community Services for the Jewish Association for Services for the Aged (JASA), an affiliate of the Federation of Jewish Philanthropies of New York, and has contributed to several social work journals.

Helen Harris Perlman is Samuel Deutsch Distinguished Service Professor Emeritus, in the School of Social Service Administration, University of Chicago. Among her publications are *Social Casework: A Problem-Solving Process* and *Perspectives on Social Casework*.

Colin Whittington is a Fellow in Advanced Studies at the University of Keele, and is engaged in research on social work and the sociology of organizations.

R. F. Stalley is a Lecturer in Moral Philosophy at the University of Glasgow.

F. E. McDermott is a Lecturer in Philosophy at the University of Sheffield.

Sir Isaiah Berlin is President of Wolfson College, Oxford. Among his publications are *Karl Marx* and *Four Essays on Liberty*.

H. J. McCloskey is Professor of Philosophy at La Trobe University. Among his publications are *Meta-Ethics and Normative Ethics* and *John Stuart Mill: A Critical Study*.

Iring Fetscher is Professor of Political Science at the University of Frankfurt-am-Main. Among his publications are *From Marx to Soviet Ideology* and *Rousseau's Political Philosophy*.

H. L. A. Hart is Principal of Brasenose College, Oxford. Among his publications are *Law, Liberty and Morality* and *Punishment and Responsibility*.

John Wilson, formerly Director of the Farmington Trust Research Unit, is now at the University of Oxford Department of Educational Studies. Among his publications are *Reason and Morals* and *Philosophy and Educational Research*.

A. I. Melden is Professor of Philosophy at the University of California, Irvine. Among his publications are *Rights and Right Conduct* and *Free Action*.

Stanley I. Benn is a Senior Fellow in Philosophy in the Institute of Advanced Studies, Australian National University, Canberra. Among his publications is *Social Principles and the Democratic State,* of which he is the joint author with R. S. Peters, and he is currently preparing a book to be called *Freedom and Autonomy*.

Acknowledgments

I wish to express my thanks to all the authors who have allowed me to use their papers, or extracts from their books, in this collection; and to the general editors of the series for their help and encouragement in its preparation. My thanks are also due to the publishers and copyright holders for permission to reprint. Specific acknowledgments are given at the beginning of each selection.

F. E. McDermott

Introduction

It would, I believe, be agreed by anyone acquainted with social work theory, that the principle of client self-determination has been rather under a cloud in recent years. With the increasing emphasis on the place of authority in social work, its position as possibly the 'single concept without which modern casework simply could not exist',[1] has come to look decidedly precarious. It is true that the principle still evokes the verbal genuflexions due to its traditional status, and continues to be accorded a place in lists of fundamental social work values; but, as the articles by Alan Keith-Lucas and Colin Whittington in this collection indicate, its practical significance is in some dispute, and such practical significance as it might have is not always regarded as beneficial. Indeed, one critic of the principle, finding it the source of 'complex exercises in ethical duplicity and professional double-talk', suggests that:[2]

> If caseworkers put aside this idealistic, and in my estimation unrealistic, notion of self-determination it may become plainer to them that much of the lip service paid to the notion amounts to little more than an argument about whether seduction is a more effective way of inducing behavioural change than direction!

There would be nothing remarkable in all this if the principle were a merely technical one, having to do solely with questions of means towards some given social work end. For technical principles have their roots in specialized fields of knowledge which may be expected, in the course of their development, to require modifications and changes in the principles derived from them. But the principle of client self-determination is of an entirely different order. Over and above any instrumental value that self-determination may possess, it owes its status in social work to its importance in the hierarchy of values to which we, as an avowedly liberal society, subscribe. Far from being a mere means to any goal, the individual's right to make his own decisions and choices in matters affecting him, has long been regarded as one of the cornerstones of the moral framework to which democratic western societies are committed; a framework determining both the goals that may be justifiably pursued, and the means that may be chosen to attain them.

What we seem to be faced with, therefore, is a conflict between the professional outlook of many who are involved in social work, and the professed values of the societies in which they practise. A situation which neither social workers and social administrators, nor philosophers—not to mention the layman in whose name and for whose benefit the services of the profession are offered—can afford to take lightly or ignore. The deep divisions and conflicts of conscience it is likely to create cannot but detract from the effectiveness of the social work profession; and the persistence of such a conflict must raise doubts about the adequacy of current philosophical analyses of the values involved. It is for this reason that the articles and extracts in this volume, some by social workers and social work theorists, and others by philosophers, but all concerned in one way or another with self-determination as a value, have been brought together under one cover. With their common interest in trying to understand and resolve the apparent conflict between self-determination as a general moral or social principle, and the values that seem to be dictated by circumstances peculiar to social work, or perhaps to the 'helping' professions generally, there is everything to be said for each group's becoming more fully aware of the relevant work being done by the other in their respective fields.

The collection has been divided into two parts. The first part contains articles representing a wide spectrum of views on the principle of client self-determination. The first six of these are drawn from social work literature, and are presented in the sequence in which they first appeared. The remaining two are previously unpublished papers by philosophers with an interest in social work theory. The second part of the collection comprises philosophical articles and extracts of a more general nature on self-determination, freedom and related concepts. One of the main criteria used in the selection of these articles has been their relevance to certain key issues arising out of current interpretations of the principle of client self-determination. It may, therefore, be useful, by way of introduction, to outline them briefly.

Negative and positive freedom

The first of these issues is the meaning of the words 'self-determination' and 'freedom'. It is not unusual for these words to be used interchangeably, nor is the practice without some justification; but it carries the risk of perpetuating certain ambiguities that have played havoc in moral and political thought. There are many senses in which the word 'self-determination' may be used, many more than those outlined below. These, however, seem to be the ones most in need of being distinguished from each other, if its meaning in social work is to be clarified.

Self-determination—its ordinary or literal meaning Interpreted literally, the word 'self-determination' refers to that condition in which an agent's behaviour emanates from his own wishes, choices and decisions. In this sense of the word, most human beings have a capacity for self-determination—they are capable of making their own choices and decisions, foolish though these may sometimes be. It is perhaps because of this that we do not normally use the word descriptively: it would after all add nothing to the description of a man—nothing to distinguish him from other men—to describe him as self-determining. When we do use it, it is usually to express our commitment to it as a value.

Self-determination as negative freedom If the capacity for self-determination, in the ordinary sense of the word, is part of the common endowment of mankind, to value it would be to desire not something one lacks so much as the removal of obstacles in the way of one's exercising a capacity one has. It would be to demand that others refrain from coercing or imposing their will upon one; that they should, in other words, leave one free. Because the analysis of freedom, in this sense of the word, is given in negative terms, that is to say, in terms of the absence of constraints, it has been characterized in philosophical thought as a 'negative' form of the concept of freedom. It is for these reasons that the demand for self-determination may be equated with the demand for negative freedom.

The paradigm case of the denial or curtailment of self-determination in this sense of the word, is confinement behind prison bars. But the exercise of self-determination can also be prevented by the imposition of legal penalties, by threats, and by various forms of psychological control and pressure; all of which, therefore, are usually included among those constraints, the absence of which is regarded as constituting negative freedom. There is a case, however, for extending the concept of freedom to cover not only the absence of such overt controls exercised by some people over others, but also those that arise from economic and social systems in so far as these are subject to human choice and control. For instance, although a man may not be physically or legally prevented from obtaining adequate nourishment for himself, he may, because of the social position to which he has been relegated, be too poor to afford it. Such poverty it is argued, particularly by socialists, is as much a curtailment of his freedom—his freedom to obtain what he needs— as any physical or legal restrictions might be.

Because the emphasis in examples like this is on what the individual wants to do, rather than on what he wants to avoid; and perhaps because the remedy for the situation requires positive political action rather than the avoidance by others of some overt form of coercion; the freedom sought in such cases is sometimes characterized as 'positive' freedom. But it is questionable whether this is justified. If the reason why poverty is to be regarded as a deprivation of freedom (for the case against doing so see Berlin, p. 143 below) is that it prevents a man's obtaining what he needs and doing what he wants to, it is still negative freedom—the absence of constraints—that is involved. The only difference between a pauper and a prisoner, so far as their freedom is concerned, is in the kind of constraint that affects them and, consequently, the things they are prevented from doing. But that they suffer such constraints is what constitutes their lack of freedom; and it is a lack of freedom in the same sense that is involved in both cases.

Self-determination as positive freedom Although most human beings are capable of self-determination, their capacity to exercise it rationally and constructively varies from person to person, and from time to time in the life of the same person. It is possible, therefore, to evaluate self-determination in terms of these and other criteria, and to form in this way an ideal of self-determination on which one puts the highest possible value. Strictly speaking, this is to value self-determination not for itself, but for qualities such as rationality that characterize it in this ideal form. Nevertheless, it is as an ideal of self-determination that it has been discussed in social work and in philosophy.

Like its more humble counterpart, this concept of self-determination is also regarded as a form of freedom. To be self-determining in this sense, it is argued, is to be liberated from the bonds of ignorance, prejudice and passion (the Idealist view), or from the crippling and distorting effects of a repressive economic and social system (the Marxist view). Because it consists, however, not merely in the notion of the absence of constraints and impediments, but in a positive ideal of human behaviour as rational, constructive and socially co-operative—these being among the qualities thought to be characteristic of liberated human beings—it is regarded as a positive concept of freedom. Of the two interpretations of positive freedom mentioned, it is that of the Idealists that has dominated social work thought; though there is an obvious affinity between the Marxist view of freedom and the tradition of opposition to a wholly casework orientated, as opposed to reformist or radical, conception of social work.

Although this idealized concept of self-determination as a rational, constructive and socially co-operative mode of existence is often presented as a perfectly natural extension of self-determination in its ordinary sense, it has implications that have seemed to many liberal thinkers to put it in opposition to the values embodied in self-determination as negative freedom. The most important of these is the fact that since one may not always be inclined to behave in accordance with the ideal of positive freedom, and constraint may be the only way to ensure that one does, commitment to this ideal could be used by others to justify the curtailment of one's freedom in the negative sense of the word. And although one has, with others, to accept some restraints in the name of freedom, it is questionable whether it is one's freedom that is being protected when the supposed enemy is one's own inclinations.

In an article that has attracted considerable attention, [3] G. C. MacCallum has argued that the distinction between negative and lositive freedom is for the most part a spurious one preventing the positive freedom is for the most part a spurious one preventing the freedom. Freedom, he suggests, is a triadic relation. In its paradigm sense, freedom is the freedom of x, from y, to do or become z. And unless the values of all three variables are specified, its meaning cannot be fully understood. Thus to suggest that freedom is essentially freedom from something, as those who advocate the negative interpretation do, or that it is in its fullest sense freedom to do something, as their adversaries do, is to misunderstand the logical structure of the concept of freedom.

Now I do not wish to deny that freedom is a triadic relation, or that the distinction between being free from something and being free to do something is a more or less spurious one. But I am not convinced that MacCallum's formula shows that freedom is not essentially a negative concept. As an analysis of freedom it needs to be amended so as to eliminate the concept of which it is supposed to be an analysis. When one tries to do this one is obliged, it seems to me, to fall back on the notion of the absence of constraints, impediments or preventing conditions; that is to say, one is obliged to analyse x's freedom as his *not* being prevented by y from doing z. It is true that this still expresses a triadic relation: any statement satisfying this formula would be about an agent, something he wished to do or become, and something that might bar his way. But what it would assert about them is the negative point that whatever might have prevented the agent from doing or becoming is in fact absent. Thus the acceptance of the view that freedom is a triadic relation would not seem to be incompatible with the view that freedom is essentially a negative concept. However, this is an issue that obviously requires fuller consideration.

The debate on negative and positive freedom is represented in this collection by the extract from Isaiah Berlin's 'Two Concepts of Liberty', H. J. McCloskey's 'A critique of the ideals of liberty' and Iring Fetscher's 'Marx's concretization of the concept of freedom'. Berlin's famous inaugural lecture provides a defence of a 'negative' interpretation of liberty against a wide range of 'positive' interpretations which, he argues, tend to burgeon into ideals that are diametrically opposed to the 'truer and more humane ideal' embodied in the concept of negative liberty. McCloskey, on the other hand, unconvinced by the claims put forward on behalf of negative liberty, considers a number of alternative interpretations and reaches the conclusion that a concept resembling the Idealist notion of positive freedom is the only one which expresses a genuine, ultimate and irreducible ideal. Fetscher's article provides a critique of both the liberal as well as the idealist conceptions of freedom from a Marxist point of view.

Turning to social work theory one finds that each of the concepts outlined above is employed in it; but that the failure to distinguish between them leads to considerable confusion about the import of the principle of client self-determination.

The dominant conception of the value of client self-determination is that of its being a condition of, or a means towards the development of the client. In Florence Hollis's eloquent words,[4]

Why do we put all this stress on self-direction? Because we
believe it is one of the greatest dynamics of the whole
casework approach. Because we believe that the soundest
growth come from within. Because we want to release the
individual's own life energy to take hold of his situation . . . .
But for this growth from within to occur there must be
freedom—freedom to think, freedom to choose, freedom from
condemnation, freedom from coercion, freedom to make
mistakes as well as to act wisely.

It is clear that the self-determination or self-direction being written
about here is not some elevated standard of human conduct, but the
exercise in very ordinary, and perhaps even foolish ways of the
powers of deliberation and choice the client already possesses. And
that there is great value in client self-determination in this sense of
the expression is a common thread running through all the articles
in Part I of this collection.

Commitment to the value of self-determination in promoting the
development of the client leads naturally, as in the quotation from
Hollis, to the demand that the client be accorded freedom in the
negative sense of this word. But whether the obligation to refrain
from coercing or manipulating the client should be regarded as
stemming from a fundamental right of the client as a human being,
or merely as a pragmatic or technical principle for achieving certain
social work goals is the point at which controversy breaks out. And
the issue is further complicated by the fact that those who acknowledge that the client has a right to self-determination tend to
disagree on whether it is a right to self-determination in the ordinary
sense of this word or some idealized version of the concept. Thus, to
relate these points to some of the articles in Part I of this collection,
although F. P. Biestek as well as David Soyer may be regarded as
championing the client's right of self-determination, it is only Soyer
who uses the word 'self-determination' consistently in its ordinary
sense. The sort of self-determination to which Biestek regards the
client as having a right is much more closely akin to the ideal
embodied in the concept of positive freedom.

Generally speaking, however, those who identify the concept of
self-determination with that of positive freedom tend to play down
its status as a right, and to emphasize its role as an ideal or end to be
pursued in the casework process. Although they share the view that
self-determination in the ordinary sense of the word is valuable in

promoting the client's development, they regard its value as subordinate to that of self-determination in the sense of positive freedom, and needing on occasion to be denied in the pursuit of the latter ideal. This approach is exemplified in the article by Saul Bernstein, and to a lesser extent in that of Helen Harris Perlman.

My own article may be regarded as a contribution to this issue in that it is an attempt to identify some of the factors that tend towards the interpretation of self-determination as positive freedom in social work theory, and to present arguments against such interpretations.

The right of self-determination

Whatever view one may take of the meaning of 'self-determination', one thing that is reasonably clear is that it is only in so far as it is interpreted in what I have called the ordinary or literal sense that self-determination as a right would have much significance in social work. It is not when clients are self-determining in the sense that they are behaving rationally, constructively and in a socially acceptable manner that they are likely to need protection from possible coercion or manipulation by social workers. A right to self-determination in this sense of the word would be virtually redundant. It is only the right to make his own choices and decisions, however foolish and self-defeating they may seem, that would be likely to affect the treatment of the client in any important way. Yet it is precisely this right that has been the main target of those who are critical of the principle of client self-determination.

Their views, which are represented in this collection by Alan Keith-Lucas and Colin Whittington, may be summarized in the following points: (i) that the recognition of such a right is incompatible with the authority vested in social workers and the controlling function they are required to exercise; (ii) that any serious attempt to implement it in practice would be unworkable (which implies, of course, that in so far as social work is 'working' at present, it is because the client's right of self-determination is accorded no more than lip service); and (iii) that all that is valuable in self-determination either as a means towards the client's development, or as an end towards which he is to be led, so that the notion of the client's having a right to self-determination is, any case, superfluous.

The opposition to these arguments in social work, in so far as there is any, seems to be rather muted. It is not that the right is not affirmed but that it tends to be hedged round with so many qualifications and limitations as to deprive it of much of its practical significance. Even David Soyer's 'The right to fail', which expresses one of the most unreserved commitments to client self-determination in the ordinary sense of this word in social work literature, is based on the essentially pragmatic argument that in the long run the results of such a policy may be expected to be beneficial. This is no doubt a very sensible and sound argument, so far as it goes; but it leaves one wondering how secure the right would be if the prognosis, for some clients at least, happened in fact to be much less reassuring. Besides, if the main justification for client self-determination is a pragmatic or utilitarian one, this seems only to reinforce the position of the 'revisionists' who argue that the vocabulary of 'rights' and 'obligations' is otiose in this field—a merely rhetorical icing to a cake of wholesome pragmatic reasons.

The contrast when one turns to contemporary analytic philosophy is marked. Whereas the social work approach is predominantly teleological in character, with the value of self-determination being interpreted in terms of its relation to some end, whether of a Thomist, Idealist or Utilitarian variety; one of the main trends in recent analytic philosophy has been towards what has been called a 'mixed deontological system':[5] one in which morality is seen not simply as the promotion of certain intrinsically desirable ends, but as the promotion of these within a normative framework arising out of the requirements of justice. To put it another way, what morality has to do with, according to this view, is not the ends that are pursued so much as the relationship between human beings in their pursuit of those ends. It has to do, for instance, with whether that relationship is a manipulative and exploiting one, or one based on mutual trust and fairness. On this view, whatever value self-determination may have as a means to some desirable end, its more fundamental place in morality lies in its being one of the rights that go to form the normative framework within which the pursuit of any end would have to remain to be morally justifiable. In stressing the independence of this framework from considerations of utility, and in giving pride of place in it to the right of self-determination or negative freedom, those who adopt this approach are, of course, reviving basic elements in the moral philosophy of Immanuel Kant.

The philosophers in this collection who are most closely identified with this approach are H. L. A. Hart and A. I. Melden, though it is only Hart's paper that is concerned directly with the question whether freedom or self-determination should be regarded as having the status of a fundamental human right. Hart's argument in its essentials is that since the having of a right of any kind is the having of a justification for limiting another's freedom, any morality such as our own which employs the concept of a right must presuppose the existence of a basic right to freedom, the interference with which calls for justification. The form of his argument is Kantian in the sense that it proceeds from generally accepted moral beliefs and distinctions to the presuppositions that render them intelligible. By contrast, the extract from John Wilson's *Equality* begins with certain facts about human beings, rather than accepted moral beliefs, and explores the possibility of grounding a belief in their equal status as 'choosers and creators of value', and their equal right to self-determination, on these facts.

Now if there is any validity in the view that a rationally defensible moral system must presuppose the equal right of all human beings to self-determination or freedom, we should have to examine very carefully the attacks on the right of self-determination in social work; for it is most unlikely that it should have no place for so fundamental a right. It would not do, for instance, for such critics to complain that the recognition of such a right would be incompatible with the authority vested in social workers. For if the right is as fundamental as many philosophers have claimed it to be, then it is the right which would determine the moral acceptability of social institutions and practices and not the other way round. In other words, the question should be not whether the recognition of the client's right of self-determination would be compatible with the authority vested in social workers, but whether such claims to authority are compatible with the right. And if it is argued that this is unrealistic, since the nature of social institutions is not determined by moral and philosophical criteria, the answer must be that their moral justification is. And that this is a question which social workers with any conscience cannot ignore, whatever 'society' may be supposed to require of them.

Rights and obligations

The suspicion that a right of self-determination scrupulously observed would prove unworkable or harmful seems to stem, in part at least, from certain assumptions about the practical implications of such a right which need to be scrutinized more closely. The first of these is that the right of self-determination has to be something like an absolute right before it can be any good at all. This manifests itself in arguments to the effect that since it is continually liable to be subordinated to other claims in social work, it cannot be regarded as a genuine right; or if it is regarded as a genuine right then social workers would have to be convicted of paying it only lip service. Although there is some truth in this—a right which made no difference to how a man was treated would indeed be illusory—it is a truth that needs to be stated rather carefully.

It is a widely appreciated fact of moral life that duties and obligations which are in themselves perfectly genuine do often come into conflict with each other, and that to try to fulfil all one's obligations in all circumstances would be not only morally dis-astrous, but impossible. So, just as the fact that one is sometimes obliged to break a promise does not impugn the authenticity of the promise's right to its being kept; the fact that social workers are sometimes obliged to go against their clients' wishes need cast no doubt on the validity of their right of self-determination, or on the seriousness with which it is regarded by social workers. What would call this into question would be a willingness to subordinate the right to relatively trivial counterclaims, and a tendency to do so without the least sign of regret or compunction. These questions are discussed in the extract from Melden's *Rights and Right Conduct,* in which he is concerned to clarify the distinction between recogniz-ing and acknowledging a right, and deciding in a particular situation whether the claims stemming from it are decisive. Also relevant to this issue is Hart's paper which discusses the various grounds on which one individual may be justified in restricting the freedom of another.

Self-determination and persuasion

The other source of scepticism about the right of self-determination is a tendency to confuse it with other concepts such as value neutrality, permissiveness and non-directiveness, the adoption of which as social work principles would indeed tend to leave the social worker an impotent spectator of his client's troubles. This tendency stems from the assumption that any form of influence or persuasion upon the client resulting from his contact with a social worker constitutes a diminution in the scope of his self-determination. Thus the mere fact that the behaviour and attitudes of some clients are altered in directions approved of or congenial to the social workers helping them is sometimes taken as evidence of some loss of self-determination on the part of those clients.

This is, of course, far too simple a view of the matter. To be given information by others is no doubt to have one's future behaviour influenced by them. But the acquisition of such knowledge does not make one less self-determining; on the contrary, it is likely to help one achieve one's own goals more effectively. Similarly, to be persuaded into seeing a situation in a new light by someone is not necessarily to have his will imposed upon one, nor need it make one's subsequent behaviour any the less self-determined. In other words, there are a great many different kinds of persuasion and influence, and it is not until the ethically significant differences between them have been systematically examined that the requirements of the principle of client self-determination can be properly understood.

The main contribution to the subject in this collection of articles is Stanley I. Benn's 'Freedom and persuasion'. Though concerned mainly with methods of mass persuasion, it elucidates the sort of problems that are likely to be involved in attempting a similar analysis of the ethics of persuasion in the more intimate setting of social casework.

Self-determination and determinism

Finally, there is the issue of determinism versus free-will, which is too important and relevant to be ignored, yet too large a subject to be adequately represented in a collection of this kind. Its importance lies in the fact that all discussion of self-determination as a value presupposes that at least some of the actions and activities of the individual are his own; that is to say, that they are actions he has chosen 'of his own free will', and can therefore be held responsible for. Increasingly, however, what Helen Harris Perlman describes as our 'prefabricated, preplanned, preorganized, predetermined social order' (p. 65 below) seems to mock such pretensions towards individual responsibility for the course of events. Moreover, the development of modern science, and in particular the sciences of psychology and sociology has appeared to strengthen and lend greater plausibility to the philosophical doctrine of determinism: the doctrine that, to put it in its simplest form, every event is uniquely determined by the combination of events and circumstances preceding it. Consequently, many philosophers as well as laymen have been led to question the coherence of the framework of ideas and beliefs within which alone principles of freedom and self-determination can retain their significance.

Perlman's 'Self-determination: reality or illusion?' is an attempt to show, through an analysis of the way in which critical stages in their development are experienced by human beings, that despite the pressures that militate against it, most human beings do, or can be helped to, acquire that sense of self as cause which, she suggests, is the essence of self-determination, and the foundation of their self-respect and dignity as human beings. Her reliance, however, on subjective experience of choice as evidence of self-determination raises old philosophical doubts about the relevance and force of subjective experience and conviction in these matters. It is well known, for instance, that individuals acting under post-hypnotic suggestion, do not necessarily lose their sense of self as cause, and will give what appear to them perfectly genuine reasons for doing what they are in fact compelled to do under hypnosis. Could it not be that similar convictions in other contexts are just as illusory?

To try to answer this question is to become involved in the philosophical problem of determinism. It is to this problem that R. F. Stalley's paper is addressed. It provides a useful introduction to recent discussions of the topic in philosophy, and the outlines of a possible solution which would be compatible with commitment to the principle of client self-determination.

Now the focus of this volume is mainly on the place of client self-determination in the casework relationship. Consequently, the role of the social worker in alleviating the pressures and constraints that emanate from the client's economic and social circumstances does not receive the attention it deserves. The decision to limit its scope in this way was due primarily to two factors: my original brief to compile a small(!) collection of articles on self-determination in social work, and my concern at the apparent decline in the status of the principle of client self-determination in its traditional stonghold, social casework. Since I regard adherence to this principle as essential to the respect for human personality on which not only social work, but morality itself, is founded, it seemed a sufficiently important topic to which to devote the whole of the collection; thus ensuring the representation of the fullest possible range of views within social work, as well as some scope for philosophical contributions on the various issues involved.

This will no doubt displease those who, conscious of the limitations of social casework in meeting the more fundamental needs of clients, would like to see much more attention paid by social workers to the repressive features of the client's economic and social environment, than to preserving what can in their view be no more than a semblance of self-determination in the casework relationship. But as much as I agree with such critics in regarding the economic and social system as itself the source of pressures and constraints immeasurably more powerful and enduring than any that are likely to arise in the casework context, this does not seem to me to warrant the dismissal of the latter as of little consequence. It is precisely because of the severity of the pressures to which clients are already subject, that the greatest care needs to be taken to ensure that they receive the respect they deserve as human beings. And this cannot be done without the most scrupulous regard for their right of self-determination.

Notes

1 H. H. Aptekar, *The Dynamics of Casework and Counseling,* Boston, Mass., 1955, pp. 11-12.
2 Neil Leighton, 'The myth of self-determination', *New Society,* no. 230, February 1967, p. 276.
3 G. C. MacCallum, Jr,'Negative and positive freedom', *Philosophical Review,* vol. 76, 1967.
4 Florence Hollis, 'Principles and assumptions underlying casework practice' in *Social Work and Social Values.* Eileen Younghusband (ed.) London, 1967, p. 26.
5 William K. Frankena, *Ethics,* Englewood Cliffs, N.J., 1963, p.35.

Part one　　　　**The principle of client self-determination**

1   Client self-determination *

Felix P. Biestek

Caseworkers are not philosophers by profession and seem to have little inclination in that direction. However, since they enter people's lives in a very practical and intimate way, they necessarily become involved in issues which have an inescapable connection with the philosophy of human living. [1]

> Social workers are precipitated into philosophical considerations that take on practical importance when we consider of what it is that our practice consists. Questions about the nature of the self and other selves, the nature of reality, of consciousness, of determinism, of science, of reason, and of the function of the will cannot be evaded, because we are technicians who work with people and people live in a social world, in a world of change, of continuity, and of habit.

Today one of the firmest convictions of the profession of social work is that the person has an innate ability for self-determination and that a conscious, willful violation of the client's freedom by a caseworker is an unprofessional act which transgresses the client's natural right and impairs casework treatment or makes it impossible. This conviction slowly developed over a period of more than thirty years.

By 1920 the casework profession had long since renounced the attitude of the English poor laws toward the client. However dependent he may have been, he was recognized as a human being with certain God-given and inalienable rights to live his own life.

From 1920 to 1930 there was a growing awareness that the client had a right and a need to participate actively in the decisions and choices in the casework process. This awareness was born of the

*Reprinted with the permission of the author and Loyola University Press, from *The Casework Relationship* by Felix P. Biestek, Loyola University Press, 1957, pp. 100-19. Available in Great Britain in an edition published by Allen & Unwin, 1961.

belief that all men are free agents by nature; it was nurtured by the concept of democratic living; and it was confirmed by the pragmatic observation that casework treatment was truly effective only when the client made his own choices and decisions. The cultural residue of the old attitudes to the client, however, did not disappear completely. The 'participation' of the client in treatment plans was the expression of the highest ideal regarding client freedom in this era. Not all caseworkers subscribed to this ideal. Others professed it, but for various reasons found it difficult or impossible to apply in practice. The socio-economic conditions, especially the large number of illiterate immigrants, the economic depression of the early thirties, and the general public's lack of understanding of the casework process complicated the application of the democratic ideal. Client participation made the casework process slower, while the condition of the times called for speed. Also, since the ideal was comparatively new in welfare work, the realistic modifications of client freedom had not yet been worked out on a practical level by over-burdened supervisors and caseworkers.

From 1930 to 1940 the concept of client freedom was slowly purified and many of the practical problems arising from it were clarified. The right of the client was seen as extending beyond mere 'participation'; such phrases as 'self-help' and 'making his own plans and decisions' indicated that the chief responsibility for plan making was shifted from the caseworker to the client. In this era a number of trends in casework aided the growth and development of client freedom. The emphasis in casework changed from diagnosis to treatment, and the client's ability to make his own choices and formulate his own plans were considered both a means and a goal of treatment, an aid to personality maturity and a test of it. The vigorous new interest in the casework relationship contributed to the advancement of client self-determination, because the latter was considered an essential ingredient of the former. Finally the advent of new types of clients, including indigents during the great depression who came from the same social and economic strata as the caseworker and other clients who could pay for casework services, emphasized as never before the necessity and practicality of client self-determination.

The interest in client freedom at this time manifested itself less in connection with the theory and more in connection with the practical aspects. The function of the caseworker in reference to client freedom was more concretely detailed. Perhaps the greatest contribution was the balancing of the ideal with the realities of the casework situation. The principle of self-determination, it was now recognized, had to be individuated to the ability of clients; not all clients were equally capable of making their own decisions. The limitations to client freedom arising from civil and moral law, and from the function of the agency, were discussed at considerable length in casework literature. This was an era of self-criticism. Caseworkers copiously recorded in their literature the shortcomings and failures of practitioners in regard to client freedom. As in the previous decade, there was a gap between the ideal and the actual practice; but there were indications that the gap was not so large and that it was rapidly diminishing.

From 1940 to 1950 the trend to incorporate the ideal into daily practice continued. The literature of social work contained discussions of how caseworkers applied the ideal to a variety of casework settings, in public and private agencies, in authoritative and nonauthoritative agencies. The compatibility of the concept of authority with client self-determination was discussed at considerable length. Progress was made in spite of the fact that the casework profession, like the world at large, was undergoing many and serious disturbances. The war and its aftermath called for rapid readjustments in casework service. The influence of psychology and psychiatry, however, counterbalanced the disturbing elements and allowed the principle of client self-determination to maintain and even advance the status which it had won during the previous two decades. Currently, it is understood in the following terms:

> The principle of client self-determination is the practical
> recognition of the right and need of clients to freedom in
> making their own choices and decisions in the casework
> process. Caseworkers have a corresponding duty to respect that
> right, recognize that need, stimulate and help to activate that
> potential for self-direction by helping the client to see and use
> the available and appropriate resources of the community and
> of his own personality. The client's right to self-determination,
> however, is limited by the client's capacity for positive and
> constructive decision making, by the framework of civil and
> moral law, and by the function of the agency.

Throughout a thirty-year history the highest possible value has been placed upon the principle of client self-determination in casework; it would be difficult to imagine how its value could be assessed any higher. Client freedom was said to be (1) a necessary, fundamental right of the client flowing from his essential dignity as a human being; (2) a necessarily fundamental right of all individuals in a democratic society; (3) necessary for the effectiveness of casework service and treatment; and (4) an essential principle in casework philosophy. It is called a principle, a basic premise, a key concept, a foundation stone of social casework in all agencies and settings.

The right and the need of the client

Like every human being, the client has the responsibility of living his life in such a manner as to achieve his life's goals, proximate and ultimate, as he conceives them. And since every responsibility is accompanied with corresponding rights, he is endowed by the Creator with a fundamental, inalienable right to choose and decide the appropriate means for the attaining of his own personal destiny.

As he receives the services of a social agency he has no intention, under ordinary circumstances, of surrendering either his basic right to freedom or any of its derivates. He comes to a social agency because he wants assistance with a need or problem. He believes that the social caseworker, because of his professional competence, can help him mobilize his own capacities and acquaint him with the resources in the community. He wants to know what choices are available to him and will welcome the caseworker's evaluation of each alternative. Although he may feel inadequate to meet his problems and although he may need the caseworker's psychological support in the process, he wants to remain free to make his own decisions.

The exercise of responsibility is one of the principal sources of personality growth and maturity. Only through the exercise of responsibility in free decisions can the client strive toward the maturity of his personality, intellectually, socially, emotionally, and spiritually. Specifically as a client, he needs freedom to make his own choices of the available means in order to make casework help effective. Social workers can give abundant testimony from long experience of the futility of casework when plans are superimposed upon the client. Social responsibility, emotional adjustment, and personality development are possible only when the person exercises his freedom of choice and decision.[2]

The role of the caseworker

The caseworker is the person who is primarily responsible for applying the principle of client self-determination in practice. His understanding of his own role in the casework situation, and how he carries it out, manifest his attitude to client freedom. Presupposing that the client is capable of constructive self-determination and that he is contemplating decisions that are within the civil and the moral law and within the agency function, the caseworker's role can be stated positively and negatively. Positively, the following activities are considered to be in accord with the principle of client self-determination:

1 *To help the client see his problem or need clearly and with perspective.* The caseworker's diagnostic study and thinking, his acceptance of the client and identification with him, will help the client work through the emotional disturbance which the problem created and which deprived the client of clarity in seeing himself and his problem.[3]

2 *To acquaint the client with the pertinent resources in the community.* If there are alternatives in the available resources, the client is helped to see the significance of each choice. The caseworker expresses his own evaluation of each choice and offers suggestions, but in such a way that the client does not feel obliged to accept the caseworker's evaluation and follow his suggestions.

The role of the worker is a delicately balanced activity and passivity. The passivity consists of restraint in doing things for and to the client, thus helping the client to express himself as fully and as freely as he wishes. The remote activity consists in acquiring a knowledge of personality patterns which will be used in gaining an understanding of the particular personality of the client. The worker is active in observing and evaluating the words, actions, and emotions of the client, learning his strengths and weaknesses, enriching his inner and outer resources, and stimulating the client to his own activity.[4]

3 *To introduce stimuli that will activate the client's own dormant resources.* These stimuli consist in helping the client to free himself from fears and tensions, in giving him whatever support he may need, and in helping him grow through the interaction of personalities in the worker-client relationship.[5]

4 *To create a relationship environment in which the client can grow and work out his own problems.* The caseworker combines a

listening, receptive attitude with active participation in which the client is helped to gain a deeper realization of his own person and his problems. The client, using his inner resources and the resources of the community, grows in the potential to work out his own problems, to move along at his own speed and in his own way.[6]

To summarize the role of the caseworker in a figure of speech, the caseworker opens doors and windows to let in air, light, and sunshine, so that the client can breathe more easily and see more clearly. The aim is to help him gain a better insight into his problem, and develop strength to help himself.[7]

Negatively, the following activities of a caseworker are considered to be at variance with the principle:

1 *To assume the principal responsibility for the working out of the problem and to allow the client to play only a subordinate role.* The extreme of this would be to determine the treatment plan and then superimpose it upon the client.

2 *To insist on a minute scrutiny of the social or emotional life of every client, regardless of the service he requests.* A disproportionate diagnosis, as some caseworkers have expressed it, reveals the total responsibility and the implied omniscience which the caseworker is assuming. The supposition seems to be that, if the caseworker knows all, he can remedy all.[8]

3 *To manipulate, directly or indirectly.* By manipulation is meant the activity of maneuvering the client to choose or decide modes of action in accordance with the caseworker's judgment in such a way that the client is not aware of the process; or if he is aware of it, he feels 'moved about' against his will.

4 *To persuade in a controlling way.* Such persuasion is understood to do more than put the client in possession of the facts to make his decision; it means to urge him to accept the caseworker's decision, in such a way as to weaken his freedom of choice and decision. This is equivalent to making the decisions and allowing the client the subordinate role of 'participating' or 'cooperating.'

Summarizing the positive and negative activities, the principle of client self-determination does not narrow the scope of the caseworker's activity, except in the area of the client's choices and decisions. It encourages every other casework activity that can help the client help himself. The caseworker is urged to increase constantly his knowledge of personality structures which helps him to understand each client better. The caseworker is encouraged to develop skills in observing and understanding the meaning of the client's feelings and behavior in the interview sessions. In brief, the case-worker is very active in self-preparation for the role of a helping person, is zealous for the acquisition of the best thinking that is produced in casework and in the allied sciences, and develops proficiency in the best casework skills and techniques.

Illustrations

The following brief summaries illustrate the role of the caseworker in relatively uncomplicated cases. In each instance the client is free to choose from two or more alternatives.

Myrna, aged 17, raised from infancy in one foster home, under care of a private welfare agency, was found to be in need of vocational planning. Aptitude and psychological tests were administered to assist in the planning. The results indicated that Myrna had potentiality for general office work and for the operation of power sewing, and some ability in the field of commercial art. She was always considered by her very dominating foster mother to be a dull, physically weak child. Actually, she was neither: she scored in the average range in the Stanford-Binet Form L; a physical examination showed that she was healthy. Outwardly Myrna was docile, dependent, and had little initiative. She herself felt that she was 'dumb.' She expressed no particular preference about the types of employment suggested, nor about any other kind of job. The caseworker's function was to explore the advantages and disadvantages of the different available jobs, stimulate Myrna's interest, give her psychological support and encourage her in thinking independently, build up some confidence, and eventually select a job in which she would be comfortable.

Mrs Allen, after a brief period of hospitalization, required several weeks of nursing care either in her own home or in a nursing home. The family agency was asked to help with the planning. There are three children, all of school age. The eldest, a high-school girl of 17, has been taking care of the two younger children after school and helping her mother with the housework and meal preparation. The family is on a marginal income, and the family agency would have to pay for either the nursing-home care or for the housekeeper. There would be little difference in cost. The function of the caseworker is to help Mrs Allen evaluate the choices. Should she choose the services of a housekeeper, she would have the comforts and the pleasant atmosphere of her own home. It would be comforting to the children to have their mother at home, even though bedridden. The children have been somewhat threatened by Mrs Allen's illness, and the youngest has expressed fears of being deserted by the mother. On the other hand, if she chose a nursing home, she might get better physical care, where a trained nurse would be in attendance. Recovery would probably be speeded because there would be less responsibility for Mrs Allen. Moreover, the housekeeper would not live with the family, and Mrs Allen needs some assistance during the night. Since both plans have advantages and disadvantages, and diagnostically they are both possible and workable, the role of the caseworker would be to help Mrs Allen explore her feelings and to support her in whatever decision she finally made.

Miss Clark, an unwed mother, 20 years old, came to the attention of the agency after the birth of her child. She was faced with making a plan for herself and the baby. Her family, well known in the community, gave some thought to keeping the child; it could provide financial support, but it feared the community gossip. Her sister could adopt the child, but that would mean that the child would be raised in the same community. The child strongly resembles the mother, and there is fear that in time the people of the community would notice this resemblance. Miss Clark's third alternative is to release the child for adoption, but she has strong negative feelings about doing this. The function of the caseworker was to assist the client in examining the possible plans and in helping her to evaluate them realistically. Throughout this relationship the caseworker's sensitivity to feelings of the mother were vital. She was stimulated to talk out her feelings and to clarify her own mind. It became quite obvious that the first two possibilities had too many difficulties, and that adoption was the most realistic choice. The client was able to work through her guilt feelings about adoption, and with the support of the caseworker decided upon that course of action.

Limitations to self-determination

The principle of client self-determination can become a meaningless cliché, however, if the client's right is not balanced realistically with the limitations to that right. A person's freedom to choose and decide is not synonymous with license. The rights of one individual are circumscribed by the rights of other individuals in society. The right of the individual is accompanied by the duty to respect the right of others. Human freedom is a means, not a goal in itself; it is a means for attaining the legitimate proximate and ultimate goals in life. It cannot, therefore, sanction self-injury or injury to others.

Specifically related to social casework, the client's right to self-determination has four limitations:

1 *The client's capacity for positive and constructive decision making.* No method or principle can be applied rigidly with universal sameness to every client and to every problem. Just as casework generally is individualized in accordance with the differentials in the client's personality, his need, the function of the agency, and the competence of the worker, so also the principle of client self-determination is individually applied. The ideal of each clients's being fully self-determined must be modified by the realities in each individual instance. Since the capacity to make decisions varies from client to client, the worker is aware of the client's mental and physical capacity to act for himself and does not force him to self-determination beyond his capacity. The incapacity of the client, however, is not freely presumed by the worker. Rather, the assumption should be that the client is capable of making his own constructive plans and decisions. This assumption is sustained until the worker has clear evidence, or at least a prudent doubt, concerning the client's capacity for decision making. The capacity of the client has degrees. The evaluation of this capacity is one of the more important skills in casework.

Some clients are able to keep the full responsibility for the direction of their own situations. Others are too weak to assume full responsibility and need the active support of the caseworker. Temporarily, the caseworker may have to share some of the responsibility in the case of some clients. This, however, is done only to the degree that the client is incapacitated.

Caseworkers have differed in their evaluation of the capacity of unmarried mothers, as a group, to make sound decisions.[9] Some feel that the unmarried mothers are so damaged emotionally that they are incapable of arriving at a good decision themselves. These caseworkers have expressed the conviction that they must guide, 'steer,' and 'take sides in' the final decision. Other caseworkers seem to have a higher evaluation of the ability of unmarried mothers for self-determination. Both agree, however, that each unmarried mother's ability should be individually evaluated. The function of the caseworker is to study the mother's social, cultural, economic, and psychological pattern, to help the mother work through her emotional problems, to acquaint her with the resources available to her, to help her consider realistically the factors in the possible choices and plans, and thus to help her make a decision about her child.

In casework with children, adolescents, the aged, and the mentally retarded the caseworker may have to be more or less active, depending upon the capacity of each client.[10] Plans may have to be made for the client. In some cases the caseworker may have to assume an authoritative or executive role in order to protect the client from the very probable results of his own confused planning. In such instances, however, the caseworker continues to seek the client's participation by interpreting what is being done and why.

A few clients may be so impaired in their ability for adjustment that they need to be treated as socially sick persons. In extreme instances, in emergencies, the caseworker may have to act as quickly 'as an ambulance surgeon,' especially in the case of 'the very ill or ignorant or inarticulate'; but these instances may be rare and will be recognized by the caseworker who generally follows the principle of client self-determination.[11] Refusal to share the responsibility with such clients would be equivalent to a refusal of service.

Mrs M had two children, 2 and 4 years old, in foster care for six months with a private agency. Now she wanted to remove the children from the foster home, where they were making an excellent adjustment, and take them to live with her in an apartment. Mrs M was an alcoholic. In one of the episodes, about seven months ago, the father had taken the children and left the home. He had obtained a divorce and physical custody of the children but was willing to allow Mrs M to arrange for their care. Mrs M was very upset. She was filled with guilt feelings because of her behavior, unhappy at being separated from her children; she wanted a reconciliation with her husband. She was physically and emotionally run down, and on regular occasions drank heavily. Diagnostically, it was quite clear that Mrs M was not ready to assume the care of her children and that the children should remain in the foster home for a while longer. The role of the caseworker was to help Mrs M accept foster care for the time being, while assisting the mother with her personal problems.

Mr R was brought to a V.A. hospital following an alleged suicide attempt. At the time of admission he said that the suicide attempt followed rejection by a girl friend. He also told that, when he was in the Army, while driving with his fiancée, he had an accident in which she was killed and he suffered a fractured back. During the first interview the patient said he wanted to be a policeman and asked whether his hospitalization in a mental hospital would interfere with this. The caseworker said he did not know, but suggested that, in order to plan wisely, it might be good to discuss what work the client did in civilian and Army life, what he liked to do, why he wanted to be a policeman, and whether there were other things he might want to do. This was agreeable to him, but he kept returning to the topic of being a policeman. Before the next interview a review of the claims folder revealed that the accident had involved four servicemen returning from a furlough, that the patient had not been driving the car, and that no one else was injured in the accident. The Rorschach, TAT, and other psychological tests indicated no suicidal, homicidal, or schizophrenic tendencies, but a basically immature, dependent, and emotionally unstable personality. The psychiatrist thought it unwise and unrealistic to participate in any plan toward the patient's becoming a policeman, both because of the patient's own limitations and because of the hospital's responsibility toward society. The caseworker continued to see the client, and the topic of becoming a policeman continued to be discussed with a therapeutic goal rather than for actual social planning.

2 *Limitation arising from civil law.*[12] Authority and law are realities of organized society. During the last twenty years caseworkers have discussed the relationship of the concept of authority with client self-determination and generally have agreed upon the compatibility of the two. Caseworkers are primarily interested in the skills whereby the clients are helped to accept and adjust to the limitations of personal freedom arising from law and authority. The general purpose of law is to prevent the individual from abusing or misusing his liberty and to protect society from such abuse. The experience of caseworkers has been that normally clients are willing to accept and adjust to the limitations set down by legitimate authority. Some of the socially and mentally ill have a neurotic or psychotic aversion to any form of authority, and these need special care. Others have a hostility, not to authority itself, but rather to the authoritative *attitude* of those who administer it. An authoritative attitude is described as a rigid, emotional, domineering manner wherein the person of the administrator of the authority is made to appear as the only basis of the authority. Such an attitude in a social caseworker is destructive.

The authoritative approach, however, is sometimes necessary and useful in casework, but it must be delicately and skillfully used. The authoritative approach is described as the use of a legitimate, objectively existing civil law or ordinance. In those public agencies where the caseworker is actually or equivalently a public officer, the authoritative approach may be frequent. In private agencies and in public nonauthoritative agencies the authoritative approach may seldom be used, except as a last resource in circumstances of imminent serious danger to the client himself or to other people. The function of using coercive force to compel submission to authority is avoided by caseworkers and delegated to licensed public servants.

In using the authoritative approach the spirit, the manner, and the attitude of the caseworker are all-important. The use of authority is individualized and related to the capacity of the client and to the realities in each case. In agencies exercising a protective function, as in probation and parole, and in child-placing agencies there are certain areas in which the client's choices and decisions are defined by law; there remain, however, many areas in which the client is free to make his own decisions. In a public assistance agency the law determines the eligibility requirements which the applicant must meet in order to receive financial assistance. The client's freedom in this area is limited in the sense that he must give evidence that he is eligible. Beyond that limitation, the client has the right to determine for himself fully. The caseworker considers authority as an item in the client's reality situation, and by means of the casework skills and techniques helps the client to accept and adjust to the requirements established by law.

Mr and Mrs A separated. She had been given temporary custody of their child pending the divorce proceedings. At the time of the preliminary hearing Mrs A testified that her husband had been abusive to her; she obtained an order restraining him from visiting the home and from seeing the child until the divorce hearing took place. Mr A told the caseworker at the family agency that his wife's charges were untrue, that he had not been abusive, and that his wife was negligent in caring for the child. Despite the restraining injunction he planned to go to the home, abduct the child, and leave the state. In so doing he would make himself liable for contempt of court and for kidnapping, if he took the child out of the state. Mr A stated that the child was his as well as his wife's, and that the court could not tell him what was best for his child's welfare, since he loved the child and would do what was best. Mr A felt free to express his hostile feelings toward his wife and toward the authorities. In helping Mr A to talk through his feelings and his problem, the caseworker was able to get him to the point where he was able to accept and adjust to the limitations of his personal freedom arising from law and to consider other plans of action. The caseworker acquainted Mr A with community resources available for help with problems such as his. He was referred to Legal Aid, which assigned an attorney to plead his case in an effort to gain permanent custody of the child. He saw his problem more clearly and in so doing he was able to conclude that his initial plan was not a good one for himself or for his child.

Mrs B, an ADC recipient with two young children, requested to be removed from the ADC rolls. She was deserted by her husband three years ago and has not heard from him since; the marriage has not been legally dissolved. She has never been able to accept the idea of public assistance. She was asked how she intended to support the children. She could go to work, she explained, but she did not want to leave the children during the day, nor does she want housekeeping service. She has extra rooms in her home which could be rented, but she objects to strangers in her home. Recently she received a proposal of marriage from a stable, dependable man. She told this man that her first husband died. In order to be removed from the ADC payroll, and because she really cares for this man, although she said that she did not feel she loved him, she is willing to commit bigamy and marry him. Throughout the weekly interviews, which lasted over a period of many months, the caseworker by means of a good relationship helped Mrs B to express and clarify her feelings, to avoid entering into a bigamous union, and to remain on the ADC roll, a more realistic plan for herself and her children.

3 *Limitation arising from the moral law.* The natural right to make choices and decisions about one's own life does not extend to moral evil; a person might have the physical power to make such a choice, but he has no real right to do so. Ordinarily, the choices confronting the client in most casework situations are within the framework of moral good, but cases do arise in which the client is inclined to a course of action which is immoral. A caseworker who operates within a well-integrated philosophy of social work does not assume an air of indifference in such a situation, but helps the client to avoid such a decision. The realistic worker knows that a morally out-of-bounds decision may be a source of future problems, perhaps worse than the one which is being avoided by illicit means. Such situations may raise perplexing problems, especially when the

caseworker and the client subscribe to different standards and codes of morality. These problems need to be faced and resolved on the basis of principle rather than by an amoral expediency.

Many of the commonly accepted moral laws, such as those prohibiting stealing and murder, are covered by the civil law. In some cases, such as divorce, sterilization, and abortion, the civil law may legislate some restrictions while the church contributes additional restrictions. Some moral laws are a part of the church's legislation only.

The caseworker, especially when he is of a different religion than the client, must respect the conscience of the client and help the client make choices and decisions which are within the boundaries of that conscience. If the client violates the moral law and acts contrary to his conscience, he does spiritual harm to himself. This not only produces psychological difficulties for the client, such as guilt feelings, but it also does spiritual damage. The caseworker needs to have a real conviction about the ontological reality of spiritual values. The caseworker is not promoting the total welfare of the client if he helps the client to solve a social or emotional problem by means which are contrary to the client's philosophy of life.

The case of a client who is considering remarriage after a divorce from a valid marriage can serve as an illustration of this difficult area. There are three possible situations: (1) both the client and the caseworker are of the same religion, which prohibits such a marriage; (2) the remarriage is contrary to the client's religious beliefs but not to the caseworker's; and (3) it is contrary to the caseworker's religion but not to the client's. In each of these situations the caseworker needs to be clear about his role in regard to client self-determination.

In the first situation, in which remarriage is contrary to the religious beliefs of both, the role of the caseworker is to help the client avoid the immoral action by helping him to solve the problem in some other way. The caseworker helps the client to express his feelings, to clarify them, to develop insight into the full meaning of remaining within his own moral code, and to explore alternative plans. The caseworker refrains from any activity which would be equivalent to cooperation in the violation of the moral law. In most instances a referral to a clergyman may be indicated.

In the second situation, in which remarriage is contrary to the religious beliefs of the client but not of the worker, the caseworker helps the client remain within his code, because for the client his religious beliefs are a reality in his environment. An early referral to a clergyman may be imperative. To help the client remain true to himself in times of stress, when he is tempted to violate his own principles, is a great service to him. The long-view welfare of the client is thus promoted. If the client eventually decides on the immoral course of action, the caseworker does not help in implementing the decision, for this would be a disservice rather than a service to the client.

In the third situation, in which remarriage is contrary to the religious beliefs of the caseworker but not of the client, a few basic principles of human conduct need to be considered. The principles are these: the client has a right to follow his conscience; the caseworker does not impose his own standards upon the client; the caseworker has a right to his own conscience and his own integrity, and therefore he has the right to refrain from cooperating in that which he believes to be wrong. In practice, therefore, the caseworker helps the client to discuss and clarify the decision. But if the client decides to remarry, the caseworker cannot cooperate in implementing the decision, because by so doing the caseworker would be cooperating in something which he considers wrong.

4 *Limitations arising from the agency function.* Each social agency, whether public or private, has been established to perform a more or less specifically defined function in the community. To achieve its purpose the agency has the right and the need to establish limitations to its services. These boundaries are incorporated into agency function and are concretely expressed in rules, standards, eligibility requirements, and kinds of services offered.

The client has a corresponding duty to respect this right of the agency. If he wishes to use its services, he is obliged to remain within the framework of the agency function. He has no right to services or assistance which are beyond the scope of the agency's function or for which he is not eligible. If his application for service is a voluntary one (that is, not required by law), he is free to terminate his contact with the agency that does not offer the service he desires and to seek that service elsewhere. Referral aid, of course, would be offered to him.

Notes

1 Lucille Nickel Austin, 'The evolution of our social case work concepts,' *Family* 20,43, April 1939.

2 Helen C. White, 'Activity in the case work relationship,' *Family* 14,208-14, October 1933; Hamilton, 'Helping people—the growth of a profession,' pp. 294-5.

3 Mary Hester, 'Field teaching in a private family agency,' *Family* 22,14-20, March 1941; Harriett M. Bartlett, 'Emotional elements in illness: responsibilities of the medical social worker,' *Family* 21,42, April 1940.

4 Eleanor Neustaedter, 'The role of the case worker in treatment,' *Family* 13,151-6, July 1932.

5 Fern Lowry, 'Objectives in social case work,' *Family* 18,263-8, December 1937.

6 Robinson, *A Changing Psychology in Social Case Work*, pp. 115-50.

7 Bertha Capen Reynolds, 'Between client and community,' *Smith College Studies in Social Work*, 5,98, September 1934.

8 Leah Feder, 'Early interviews as a basis for treatment plans,' *Family* 17,236, November 1936.

9 Erma C. Blethen, 'Case work service to a Florence Crittenton home,' *Family* 23,250-1, November 1942; Ruth F. Brenner, 'Case work service for unmarried mothers,' *Family* 22,211-19, November 1941; Sylvia Oshlag, 'Surrendering a child for adoption,' *Family* 26,135-42, June 1945; Leontine R. Young, 'The unmarried mother's decision about her baby,' *Journal of Social Casework* 28,27-31, January 1947; Frances H. Scherz, '"Taking sides" in the unmarried mother's conflict,' *Journal of Social Casework* 28,57-8, February 1947.

10 Donaldine Dudley, 'Case work treatment of cultural factors in adolescent problems,' *Family* 20,249, December 1939; Lillian L. Otis, 'Intake interview in a travelers aid society,' *Family* 22,50-1, April 1941; Martha E. Shackleford, 'Case work services with retarded clients,' *Family* 23,313-14, December 1942; Joan M. Smith, 'Psychological understanding in casework with the aged,' *Journal of Social Casework* 29,189-93, May 1948.

11 Gordon Hamilton, 'Case work responsibility in the unemployment relief agency,' *Family* 15,138, July 1934.

12 Crystal M. Potter and Lucille Nickel Austin, 'The use of the authoritative approach in social case work,' *Family* 19,19-24, March 1938; Gordon Hamilton, 'Basic concepts in social case work,' *Family* 18,150, July 1937; Lucille Nickel Austin, 'Some notes about case work in probation agencies,' *Family* 18,282-5, December 1937; David Dressler, 'Case work in parole,' *Family* 22,3-6, March 1941; David Dressler, 'Case work in an authoritarian agency',' *Family* 22,276-81, December 1941; Stephen H. Clink and Millard Prichard, 'Case work in a juvenile court,' *Family* 25,305-7, December 1944.

2   Self-determination: king or citizen in the realm of values?

Saul Bernstein

Probably some of the most poignant inner searching among social workers has been and is around self-determination, which may be regarded as a technique, a fact, a cultural assumption, or a value. Many and apparently diverse meanings are attached to this concept. There is the deeply rooted sense on the part of social workers that building on the feelings and wishes of those served is essentially sound. On the other hand, many situations arise in which other considerations seem paramount. Just how determining should self-determination be? 'Hard-to-reach' individuals, families, groups, and neighborhoods[1] throw up the question with force. They are not articulating requests for service. Under one concept of self-determination, we should leave them alone. The 'hard-core family' on public assistance should receive the regular allowance to which it is legally entitled and nothing more, according to this position. The gang of teenagers creating aggressive mayhem should likewise be left to go its self-chosen way. Further illustrations could be multiplied, but it is more important to move on to the somewhat philosophic question rooted in and around the great idea of self-determination.

It seems helpful to proceed—evolutionary fashion—from the simple to the complex. I shall start with a kind of one-celled notion and develop the theme into a complex organism of values.

Self-determination no. 1

The heart and extent of this concept is that we as social workers should help people to do what they want to do and not stimulate them to go beyond their wishes. Self-determination is the supreme value, and it maintains its top position in any hierarchy of values,

*Reprinted with the permission of the author and the National Association of Social Workers, from *Social Work*, vol. 5, no. 1 (January 1960), pp. 3-8

including those in which there are conflicts. For the worker the situation is pure and clear; help the people served to do what they want to do. There is little or no conflict between the values of the client and the worker. The latter's function is entirely devoted to providing the means and opportunities for the fulfillment of the desires of the client.

This position is clear and internally consistent as long as self-determination is maintained as the king value, with all others subservient to it. The working and meditating hours of the worker are relieved of the tearing-apart kinds of conflict which beset devotees of other concepts of self-determination. But 'Self-determination no. 1' is a simple soul who, if he ever existed, would not be helpfully related either to the practice of his profession or to the real world. There may be workers who sound as though they belong in this club, but usually one finds that questions bring forth many qualifications ('It depends,' and so forth), so that the simple and pure notion of self-determination is soon lost. Essentially, however, this concept is basic and should not perish. Rather, it needs a special kind of company and context.

Self-determination no. 2

Suppose we help a person do what he wants to do today, but tomorrow he wants the opposite. How do we know what he wants? By what he says? He may have been saying it for years without ever really acting on what he says. Ambivalence turns one straight path into at least two, going in different—sometimes opposite—directions. When a part of the client expresses a feeling and seems to reach a decision, the worker would be derelict if he moved quickly in this direction without devoting time, understanding, and skill to assessing whether this feeling and decision are in fact what the client wants, uncomplicated by other and even contrary wants.

Illustrations are common. A woman is so angry at her husband that she says she wants a divorce; as the situation unfolds, however, she shows much positive feeling and need for the husband, particularly if the worker is skillful in accepting her hostile feelings. A certain gang of girls made nasty remarks about a settlement house and everybody in it. They threw rocks at the windows, and unfortunately their aim was pretty good. Months later, after the worker had dealt with the girls and had come to know them well, she was convinced that the original hostile behavior was the method they used to ask for help from the agency, without being able to put their need into words. Behavior was their language.

'Self-determination no. 2,' then, recognizes ambivalence and nonverbal communication, and adds the dimensions of time and the worker's professional qualifications, so that the eventual decisions have increased stability, depth, and clarity resulting from some working through of conflicting feelings.

It is not always possible or even desirable to eliminate all conflict or ambivalence. Many situations have built-in and all-but-unresolvable conflicts. The client dealing with a chronically ill relative is doomed to mixed feelings. The unmarried mother is appropriately expected to be in conflict about the decision as to whether to keep or give up her baby. There is no satisfactory answer in the sense that it completely eliminates the appeal of the contrary decision or that no regrets will later be felt. People and life are not like that. But the contribution of the worker is around a new perspective on tense and mixed feelings. In assessing what the client wants and in helping him to achieve it, the aim is to take into full account the varieties of ambivalence and changes over time.

Self-determination no. 3

Reality in its multitudinous forms enters the self-determination picture. It can be biological, as in principles of health. It can be economic, as related to a balanced budget (even installment buying requires that the payments be met). It can be legal, as in obeying laws. There are other forms of reality, but the essential point is the stubborn quality of it, which sets up rules and expectations not controlled by our clients, but which must be met by them. These factors narrow substantially the range of reasonable choices open to the client—and to us all. A man may want his public assistance allowance trebled and may be able to make a good case for the increase, but he is not the one who should or can make this decision. The same line of reasoning goes for bad health practices, illegal behavior, spending well beyond one's income, and the like. A frequent problem faced by social workers is that many of those we serve have so weak a grasp on reality that they become enmeshed in its retaliations, and the client thereby loses the opportunity to express his self-determination in matters appropriate for it.

Reality has a fixed and final sound which can distort social work diagnosis and functions. The assumption is too often made that the client meets role expectations, that he 'adapts,' 'adjusts,' to his physical and cultural setting. The latter is presumed to be right, or rigid, something that does not lend itself to planned change. This is a strange position in a world full of dramatic and large-scale social, economic, and political change. C. Wright Mills in *The Sociological Imagination* makes the effective point that 'nowadays men often feel that their private lives are a series of traps.' These are large-scale societal changes which individuals do not understand or control. The writer pleads for 'sociological imagination,' which grasps the connection between the inner life of the individual and the larger framework of society.

This orientation does not give the client of a public assistance agency the right to decide on the amount of his allowance, but it does suggest that various social aspects of his situation might be examined and changed. Perhaps the agency should offer larger amounts, perhaps he can be helped to become self-supporting; perhaps there is a need for new economic institutions which will employ him. A crucial criterion for social change is whether it will increase the opportunities for appropriate self-determination for many people.

Returning to the original point about reality: the kind of exercise of self-determination that disregards reality is full of fantasy—it is unhealthy and self-defeating. A good part of the function of the worker may be to help the client distinguish what is fixed and stubborn from what is open to his decision. Skill in diagnosis inevitably involves the sorting out of what is relatively fixed from what is relatively changeable. Wise strategy of helping people to change is based on concentrating on what is most flexible. The client may still decide to flout reality (as all of us do at times), but then at least he will be better prepared for the consequences. It may well be that we can do our best work at the stage when the wallop of reality has been felt. There are great learning opportunities in such crises.

Self-determination no. 4

Almost always, other people are involved in the self-determination of the client. His sense of responsibility may encompass them in varying degrees. There are instances in which parents abandon their children, husbands desert their wives, the gang beats up an innocent victim just to express feelings. At the other extreme is the person who allows himself to be exploited by others so that he is not making for himself the kinds of decisions that are the right of every human being.

Self-determination is enmeshed in a complex network of social relationships which move the notion far from the simple level on which each client does what he wants to do, yields to his own impulses. Even Robinson Crusoe was not completely alone psychologically or culturally. The problem then is to find some principles that will offer guidelines out of this maze. One might be that the exercise of self-determination by one person should have minimum inconsistency with such exercise by others. This is a kind of equivalent to the golden rule and Kant's categorical imperative. It does not eliminate all conflicts—not necessarily a desirable goal—but it does provide a helpful framework and even rather specific guidance. As a homely illustration, it is not rare for a club of adolescent boys to plan an affair involving a girls' club without much consultation of the wishes of the latter. The group worker can easily make the suggestion to ask the girls about some idea that is being argued. A large area of potential contribution by social workers is embedded in this simple technique of consulting people who may be affected by a decision. How many times, in how many kinds of relationships, is this step omitted!

At the other extreme, with the person who is being exploited, the principle is rather different. The worker needs to diagnose carefully the areas in which legitimate self-determination is violated and then try to reinforce the client and influence the environment so that he may become able to enjoy the rights to which he is entitled.

With 'Self-determination no. 4' we are in the midst of a question that has burned hot throughout much of human history. Egoism versus altruism is a kind of statement of it—a misleading one, I believe. Altruism asks for a kind of selfishness which seems unrealistic and unsound. Some of the worst acts of egoism have been perpetrated under the guise of altruism. The sense of selfhood is too deep, strong, pervasive, and instinctive to build on its elimination. More hopeful is the approach which recognizes and respects the drive toward selfhood in all of us, striving to help people understand how each can achieve identity only as he respects the same drive in others.

Many therapists have been so intrigued by the methods and orientation of their professions that they have overlooked the social dimension of self-determination. Individual dynamics are so intricate and fascinating that there is the temptation to regard them as all of significant reality. Perhaps subtly, the therapist is beguiled into an acceptance of what the client says about his social setting as being all that is important for the therapist to understand about it. The culture that has impregnated the client may be lost, as may be the impact of the client on the people he intimately affects. In just these areas social work has paid a price—the weakening of the 'social' in its calling—for an otherwise fruitful dependence on psychiatry. It is a strange kind of ethic that elevates the desires of the client above those to whom he is socially related. The 'unseen audience' should not be victimized by therapy. Along with being an object of transference and other kinds of feelings, the therapist ought to be a kind of social conscience which helps the client relate his self-determination to all of those with whom he has relationships. To do anything else would contribute to social degeneration.

Self-determination no. 5

Here we come close to the center of the human enterprise—to what, one may hope, distinguishes us from animals and from blind followers of instinct. A useful handle, much discussed in social work and elsewhere, is the process of decision making. The infant when hungry 'decides' to cry. It is a simple, instinctive reaction. A mature decision, at the other pole, is guided by rationality and intelligence. The learning of the ability to make the latter kind of decision is regarded by some as more important than the benefits which may accrue from any specific act of decision. Learning how to approach problems rationally is thereby elevated to the position of one of the most prized skills.

A whole flood of implications flows from 'Self-determination no. 5.' One is the growing concern about the probable consequences for oneself and for others from any given decision or action. Another is the need to attain sufficient perspective so that unconscious distortions and urges are kept at a minimum. Still another is the generation of a more or less conscious method for dealing with problems. In addition, there is the more thoughtful examination of previously assumed values. The list could be elaborated.

The content of intelligent decision-making has been given considerable attention by John Dewey and many others. The current human relations movement, with its ideologies and activities, is devoted to this end. In grand terms, it is the application of the scientific method to human affairs.

The social work client may be ready in only modest and varying degrees to participate on these more rarified levels of human expression. Yet his self-determination takes on profundity only as he moves toward them. Each client needs our best diagnosis in terms of where he is and how far he can go, but the direction of change supported by the worker should be firmly derived from rationality. This may sound strange to those who strive so hard to understand all the perplexing irrationalities in people. But what is often overlooked is that the attempt to understand irrationality is essentially rational. Whatever concepts or constructs we may use to explain instinct-based behavior, they represent the struggles of intelligence to bring experience into some sort of order. The direction is clear.

The theme of freedom runs through this orchestration of the elements of self-determination. If one takes a pure and completely consistent deterministic position, self-determination is an illusion; it is simply acting in accord with controlling forces which may or may not be understood. In the Marxian context—i.e., the idea that history is economically determined, especially in terms of class—the behavior of many of us would have to be considered a current and potent example of determinism; although that point of view leaves open the choice to join with the class that will presumably be victorious.

Social work is based on the assumption that people are free to make significant choices and that they can be helped to make better ones. But the attempt to use freedom to make decisions that are contrary to reality or largely irrational is self-defeating. Confusion rather than creativity flows from the disregard of facts and reason. Only as one takes account of the relevant factors does true freedom operate in decision making. Yielding to unexamined impulses is more a surrender to instinctive drives than the expression of mature self-determination.

This is not to claim that we are predominantly rational. Social work has dealt too much with raw ids to make this error. The orientation is rather to the effect that the forces within and outside of us should be recognized and scrutinized with whatever rational capabilities we have. To help in this process is a major function of the social worker. Insofar as this help is successful, the worker is enabling the client to reach toward 'Self-determination no. 5'—a pretty high level of social functioning.

Self-determination no. 6

The subtitle of this paper, 'king or citizen in the realm of values,' raises the question of hierarchy or priority. It is hoped that what has been said makes clear that self-determination is *not* king, or a supreme value. The various qualifications and contexts are meant to show that the mere act or desire to act according to one's wishes is neither a final nor a complete basis for a professional point of view. Assuming this position, are we left in a kind of 'it depends' vagueness as to which values rise above others in specific situations and in general? I think not. Value problems cannot be reduced to the simplicity or specificity of administrative charts which show clearly who is above whom, but there are meaningful patterns and points of reference.

Most basically, the supreme social work value is human worth, an enormous idea, probably the greatest discovery in human history. Perhaps it suffers from too frequent mention in social work without sufficient elaboration of its rich meanings. It is based only moderately on what people are; much more on what they can be. It applies not only to those immediately before the social worker, but also to every human being on this earth (we may yet need an interplanetary concept). The specific content of the human worth idea evolves with history. It has many facets: legal and civil rights, standard of living, freedom to develop potentialities, intellectual and artistic interests, and others.

With this supreme value, self-determination then becomes modified. If what the client wants will result in the exploitation of others or the degradation of himself, the worker should try to help him change his desires.

The steps suggested in this paper are meant to be criteria for judgments about self-determination which will help to place it appropriately in a hierarchy of values in any given situation. It seems more useful to approach the hierarchy question in this way (human worth at the top and self-determination subject to a set of criteria) than to attempt a rigid blueprint or chart. All this leads to the definite position that self-determination is *not* the king value, is not supreme in the realm of values.

Conclusion

While self-determination is not supreme, it is supremely important. Only through the rich utilization of this concept can we fully honor the human-worth value. This is in line with the best in democratic traditions. As we study and diagnose each situation, our concern should be for maximizing the choices for the people we serve, subject to the framework suggested above. Even with young children, there are appropriate matters about which they should be helped to make decisions. In an even more extreme example, the man in prison has many conditions imposed on him, but he might be helped to make his own decisions about jobs in the prison, recreation, what to do after he is released, and other matters. The point is that the value system of social work requires this maximization of self-determination.

In addition to its values, the methods of social work themselves require great stress on self-determination. People can be and are manipulated, but constructive changes which take root inside the person, group, or community usually need to be based on participation and consent. The Supreme Court decision on desegregation attempts to manipulate the environment—to eliminate by force the practice of discrimination in schools. It does not pretend to change the feelings of the prejudiced. Some have concluded that therefore this historic decision is useless or harmful. I do not agree, and think that over the long pull the lessening of discriminatory practices can and does lessen prejudice. In the legal and perhaps other power-packed arenas, it is often necessary to override the self-determination of some people for the sake of human worth. The alternative would be to wait for complete agreement, an impossible political goal on most issues.

In social action, then, social work adapts its concept of self-determination to the realities of the process of political change; but the great bulk of social work practice has internal change as its goal. Here we find that imposing, telling, or giving orders do not work well. Only as the client is thoroughly involved and comes to accept on deepening levels the process of change can our methods be effective in relation to our goals. We may not be able to produce research-based proof (although there is some) for this position, but it is supported by so much practice experience on the part of so many of us that we fully accept and act on it.

There is a deeper and weightier support for self-determination: its existence and potency is a fact. Social workers and other professionals may enable, stimulate, impose, and even use force, but what the client feels, thinks, and values is ultimately his private affair and more within his control than that of the professional. The delinquent can be forcibly placed in a training school, but he cannot be forced to change his notions of the kind of life he wants to lead. For this the inner boy must be involved, must decide to re-examine himself and to change. This is a very important reason for emphasizing so much the significance of the relationship with the worker. Through it our boy learns to trust and have confidence in the worker so that he is ready to share some of his precious inward self with a view toward changing it. Only the boy himself can make this decision. Without his consent we can probably modify his outward behavior; with it there is the opportunity for changes in inward values, an essential and basic purpose of social work.

Notes

1 Social work has no general term for the people it serves. *Client, group,* and *community* are commonly used. *Clientele* is perhaps an approach to generalization. In the 'human relations field' there seems to be a growing use of the term *client system.* In this paper the term *client* will include individuals, families, groups and communities.

3

A critique of the principle of client self-determination*

Alan Keith-Lucas

The student of our culture writing, perhaps, in the year 2000 will be considerably puzzled by the use in social work of the term 'self-determination' in the two decades following World War II. He will find two major articles on the subject, by Biestek and Bernstein, one of which asserts that the principle is of a religious nature but needs to be limited severely, almost to the point at which the historian will wonder if the result can be called self-determination at all, and one that describes ascending levels of desirable self-determination but reduces the principle from 'king' to 'citizen' in the realm of social work values.[1] The historian will find the principle hailed as a 'fundamental freedom'[2] but will note that it appears most often in articles on social work practice in the form 'I believe in it, but . . .' He may wonder about its place in a vocabulary that increasingly includes such words as 'intervention,' 'psychological authority,' 'responsibility' and 'social control.'

If he is something of a semanticist, as all historians of ideas should be, he may come to one of two conclusions. He may assert that the words have no exact meaning at all, that they represent the sort of principle one is either 'for' or 'against,' as one is for or against democracy, free enterprise, liberalism, or the 'American way.' Alternatively he will suspect that the so-called principle is by no means unitary, that it is a sort of verbal umbrella covering quite different and even contradictory concepts or ideas that exist in different categories of thought. He may even find reason to suggest that some of these concepts are quite misleadingly named, adding to the confusion, and he will almost surely conclude that different writers have something quite different in mind when they make use of the term. This is nearly always what happens when a principle is given a name. The name becomes more important than the idea

*Reprinted with the permission of the author and the National Association of Social Workers, from *Social Work*, vol. 8, no. 3 (July 1963), pp. 66-71.

itself. As a name it begins to have an independent existence to which all sorts of connotations are added long after the original concept for which it was created has been modified or forgotten.

Disentangling the components

The historian then may try to disentangle the components of this principle, to see what these concepts are and to what extent there is still belief in them, and, if possible, to give them names of their own. He will, if he is wise, begin with Mary Richmond, noting that although she does not use the term she does enunciate a principle that could be called that of *client participation* in the solution of problems.[3] He may recognize that although there are, and have been, differences of opinion about the participation of certain groups of individuals—e.g., very young children—this is a more or less constant principle, limited only by one's belief in its practicality.

He will find the term 'self-determination' beginning to be used in the late 1930s. He may be pardoned if at first he wonders why, for, at least whenever the concept of a right is attached to the term, what is being discussed by many workers is better described as a principle of *non-interference except in essentials.* Hollis, who perhaps summed up most accurately the essentials of this principle, although she does call it 'self-determination,' makes clear that the client's right to make his own decisions exists 'until it is well demonstrated that the exercise of this right would be highly detrimental to himself or to others.[4]

Now this is not a principle of self-determination at all. It does not start from any assumption that the client is really in control or that he has any inalienable right. The final decision as to what he may or may not make decision on lies with the social worker acting in the name of the community or of the profession, who may decide that a particular decision is too vital for the client to be allowed to make. This is, of course, what gave rise to the paradox whereby social workers represented themselves as 'granting' this right. Rights can be granted only by someone in control of the situation who accepts his right to be so. Quite obviously, also, the social work concept of what constitutes essential causes for intervention can, and has been, modified. For this to have happened in no way violates the principle that has been named, which is in fact not a principle about a client's rights but a statement about the way social workers behave.

It would have been much simpler and a great deal more realistic if this had been recognized in the beginning. When, for instance, a social worker writes that the practices she finds helpful in work with neglecting parents require 'a realistic redefinition of the "right of self-determination" as applied to the parent'[5] she is forced to be somewhat defensive. There is an implicit suggestion that the worker is tinkering with an important matter, that somehow she is against something everyone should believe in. How much simpler it would be to say that this kind of situation requires social work intervention at a rather earlier point than is perhaps necessary in other kinds of work. And when a social worker lists 'professional emphasis on the client's right to self-determination within the limits of reality' as one of the safeguards thrown around a client's 'vulnerability'[6] would it not be more realistic to state that the safeguard intended here is the profession's ethical undertaking not to interfere in all those small matters of taste, opinion, and day-to-day living that make one client different from another and give him a sense of being an individual? Why have recourse to a 'principle' that has to be modified with words which to a great extent prevent it from being a principle at all? Perhaps if this principle had been given a more realistic name the profession might have arrived at clearer answers to some important questions, such as by what right and to what extent a social worker should intervene in a client's life. These questions rarely are faced squarely; they are taken care of (as in both Biestek's and Bernstein's articles) by general statements that social workers are 'representatives of the community,' 'allied with social, moral, and legal good,' or simply that in some situations the social worker should 'try to help' the client change his mind [see p. 40 above].[7] Any of these statements may be true, but surely they, rather than the ethical bases for man's—any man's, not just a client's—right to decide things for himself, are what needs debating.

Why, then, was this principle, which is quite straightforward, useful, and commendable, although of course somewhat relative and dependent on the current culture and social work's self-image, erected into a high-sounding absolute that has caused confusion ever since? It is here suggested that there were present, at the time social workers began to adopt this kind of code, a treatment theory, a political belief (curiously enough arising from almost diametrically opposite philosophical roots), and an inescapable fact, all of which had something to do with man's choices about himself, and all of which tended, at that time, to run in the same direction and to suggest that there might be something of an absolute principle here.

Self-determination in fact was not merely an ideological belief. Through its use as Hollis asserted, the multiple objectives of casework were most likely to be achieved.[8] This concept is, of course, related to the earlier writings of Freud, and has its counterpart in theories of permissive child rearing. Psychologists and psychiatrists today have largely rejected it. It is the reason Witte can write of self-determination as having become, all too often, the basis for inaction in cases of parental neglect of children, or another writer believes that the principle 'if carried to its logical conclusion' would end in family suicide.[9] It is what Biestek calls 'license' and Bernstein 'Self-determination no. 1,' which is '. . . a simple soul who, if he ever existed, would not be helpfully related either to the practice of his profession or to the real world' [see p. 34 above].[10]

Social work's liberating role

But the concept of self-determination did exist. It existed not because social workers, teachers, and others were naïve or unskilled in psychological knowledge, but because they shared with the early Freud (or rather, they adopted his theories because they found in them something that appeared to support their political and social attitudes) a concept of psychology as a liberating force. They wished to free the id in its struggle with society. They were allied with the individual against many aspects of the culture, and they considered the individual a better judge of his own interests than law, morality, or that culture itself. For that reason they quite shamelessly protected many of their clients from the social and legal consequences of their actions. Politically they leaned far to the left, as can be seen in papers such as *Social Work Today* and the contemporary writings of Bertha Reynolds. It is hard for us today to remember how much social workers in the 1930s felt themselves outside the culture and, indeed, opposed to it.

This feeling was, of course, strengthened by the fact that social work clients, or at least those in need of financial help, were often denied rights enjoyed by the populace as a whole. In 1940 fifteen states still denied paupers the right to vote. In this respect there was actually, if only for a while, a principle of client self-determination with emphasis on the word 'client'—the principle that a client's right to make his own decisions should not be different from anyone else's. This, however, is a specialized use of the term and not what most people believe client self-determination to mean. There may also have been, under this liberating principle, some tendency to want to make social work clients' rights wider than other people's, since these were for the most part the only rights about which social workers could do anything.

Today 'reality' has been defined, more or less, as adaptation to the culture. No wonder then that this liberating principle is looked upon as unrealistic. It is not so much that social work comprises more knowledge about people or that it has achieved a greater degree of realism, although something of both may be true. It is rather that its orientation has changed. Social work is trying to produce a different type of character, hence the switch from trying to strengthen the id to psychologies that support the ego and the superego. It can and is, of course, argued that there has been an actual change in the *needs* of clients, that today many more people suffer from character disorders than from repressions, but it is also true that 'need' is a highly relative term inseparable from the concept of what is desirable behavior. One also tends to find the problems that one looks for.

This concept is again, then, not a statement about self-determination that needs to be modified, but a statement about what social work is and does. The original concept may be termed social work's *liberating role,* recognizing that it is both pragmatic and ideological. It may be argued that whatever one's feelings about or the objective reasons for the shift in social work's alignment with contemporary culture this shift is more or less a fact. The liberating concept, therefore, makes little sense to social work today. It could be discarded quite comfortably, if such were desired, without doing damage to any inalienable right and without modification of social workers' ethical commitment to interfere only in essentials.

Contractual limitation

Social work would still have to deal, however, with another concept that took shelter under the same umbrella. This concept did not argue, as did the liberating theory, that man would be better if he were left in control of his own life. It argued, instead, that certain decisions were irrevocably his, however poorly he made them and however much other people wanted or felt it was their responsibility to make them for him. Since the client's right to request or refuse service was viewed as absolute the client- worker relationship was seen as a contract between a person asking for help and an agency, or a worker, offering it. For that reason the principle will be called that of *contractual limitation on service*. Politically its mainspring was a Lockeian liberalism and a belief in the rule of law, which is why it found its ultimate prophet in Delafield Smith. Its most exact formulation was in the area of public assistance where, in Grace Marcus's words:[11]

> In administering assistance as a right, the agency is bound not to use the individual's economic helplessness for purposes that have not generally been declared and defined even though these purposes are presumably inspired by interest in the individual's welfare or the welfare of his dependents.

It was not, however, confined to the public welfare field but was practiced in agencies of all kinds.

To understand the essential nature of this concept we could examine our political system. No one actually believes that either voters or legislators always make the 'right' decision. In fact, some of the decisions made are clearly disastrous, irrational, or immoral, which has led many social scientists, especially of the schools of Lasswell and Kaplan, to maintain that such decisions ought to be left to appropriate experts. Yet both the Constitution and popular opinion insist on a fallible and clumsy procedure of election and so-called debate. However foolish people are, however gullible or corrupt, they are not prepared to leave matters to a self-appointed élite. To the governed is reserved some external touchstone, some formal machinery ouside the immediate control of those with authority, on which the weak can take their stand.

The principle of contractual limitation is a principle of this kind, and should, in fact, be more understandable since social workers have recognized more clearly the force of psychological authority. Wisely or unwisely it limits the social worker's sphere and leaves the decision whether a man is to be helped against his will or in areas for which he has not requested help to the law, which is itself provided with a similar limitation known as 'due process.' Social workers are not content, in fact, to leave the client's right to make his own decisions entirely to their self-limiting principle—interference only when essential—recognizing this to be a relative rather than a fixed concept.

This concept, too, has been rejected by most social workers today. Its last great bastion fell in the 1956 amendments to the public assistance titles of the Social Security Act. Miss Marcus's statement reads almost like treason to one familiar with the new formulations of social work responsibility. But before the principle is forgotten it might be well to recognize some of what it did or did not say. It was not, for instance, a psychological theory—it was rather an anti-psychological one—and it was very far from what it has often been accused of being, a doctrine of irresponsibility. It did not promise freedom from authority or freedom from the social and legal consequences of one's acts. Service could always be refused or limited on the client's initiative, but sometimes, as in the case of probation or protective services, only at the cost of certain consequences. In some cases the concept was able, in fact, to free the client from the illusion that he could do what he liked, as, for instance, when the contract involved responsibilities as well as rights, as in the case of placed children, when breach of the contract would mean either the return of the child or court action for its protection.

A fact, not a right

With the possible exception of the insistence that the rights of a social work client should be the same as those of any other person, at law and in the community, our mythical historian would not as yet have come upon anything that could properly be called a principle of client self-determination. Yet such a principle does, and did, exist. It is not a right; it is a fact. Certain kinds of decision cannot be made by anyone other than the person about whom they are made.

Writers in the early days of social work's at that time 'new' psychological orientation ascribed this to psychic determinism. As Bertha Reynolds said:[12]

> It is no longer a question of whether it is *wrong* to try to make our fellow beings think and feel as we want them to. In the long run it is simply silly. The vital needs of their being will in the end determine what they shall feel and how they shall act.

This, if it really meant what it appeared to say, should have made any principle about the client's *right* to self-determination unnecessary, but actually Miss Reynolds was not discussing the multifarious little decisions of everyday life but a kind of major decision, a commitment of the whole being to certain values or courses of action, which has since then been explored and clarified by Anita Faatz in *Nature of Choice in the Casework Process.*[13] Grace Marcus was at the time a lone voice protesting against the absorption of this fact into social work's apparent principle of the 'right to self-determination':[14]

> How difficult it is for us to accept this harsh truth is revealed by our distortion of it into the facile concept of 'self-determination,' whereby we can relapse once more into a comforting dependence on free will and, by talking of self determination as a 'right,' flatter ouselves that a fact which is often intolerably painful to the individual and to society is still within our power to concede or refuse as a social benefit.

Today social workers are less certain that these choices are predetermined. They simply know that the choices exist. They know that there is a kind of choice—to take help or not to take it, to get well or to remain ill, to grow or to regress—that will affect the use a client will make of their services, but which they cannot make for him. Some do not like the word 'choice' and would prefer to believe that this is simply a part of the personality they have not as yet learned to manipulate. All, no doubt, would agree that there are certain elements of relationship and process that tend to produce or make possible constructive choice of this nature, but which do not always do so. And all know that this kind of choice has very little to do with personal freedom to make even quite important decisions about one's life. It can be made by a man in prison as readily as by a business executive; in fact, since it is inevitable, it will be made by both. In neither case will it be of necessity constructive choice.

There is apt to be confusion, however, resulting from still another way in which the term self-determination has been used. Self-determination is sometimes spoken of as one of the goals of social work. Bernstein says that 'the value system of social work requires this maximization of self-determination.'[15] [see p. 41 above.] But here 'determination' has been given a special value content, not entirely divorced from its secondary meaning in daily speech as a synonym for 'grit' or 'guts.' It does not simply mean that man *will*, and still less that he ought to be allowed to, decide what he will do. It means that he *should* become capable, without constant help or supervision, of making constructive decisions, or at least decisions that do not leave him dependent on others for the necessities of life. To entangle this with the so-called 'right' of self-determination is again to muddy the waters. For, quite frequently, if not always, the attainment of this kind of constructive ability requires a period of surrender to the helping skills of another. Social workers may of course disagree about the nature and extent of this needful dependency, and especially about the dangers, political or psychological, of such a dependency imposed, as it were, by the will of the helping person, as in so-called 'parenting' cases. Indeed, they do disagree, but some such process is inevitable in any helping situation and is only made more difficult to identify and to discuss if it is either denied or asserted as if it were a contradiction or modification of a universal principle about clients' rights.

Summary

There are, therefore, two more or less relative principles in social work concerning a worker's relationship with his clients—client participation and non-interference except in essentials. Because of social work's cultural alignments, which are comparatively new, there is no longer belief in a mission to liberate the id, except perhaps in a few instances. Social workers have apparently rejected, or are in the process of rejecting, a theory that was once developed restricting their operations to matters that could be the subject of contract. They recognize in their clients certain more or less unpredictable and immovable abilities to use or not to use their services, and they have, as part of their goal, development of their clients' capacities to make certain constructive decisions about their own affairs.

Each of these principles, however, can be discussed, debated, rejected, or modified, and should in fact be so, without radically affecting each other and without doing damage to any traditional, high-sounding, and indeed elusive principle of client self-determination.

Notes

1 Felix P. Biestek,'The principle of client self-determination,' *Social Casework*, vol. 32, no. 9 (November 1951), pp. 369-75; and Saul Bernstein, 'Self-determination: king or citizen in the realm of values?', *Social Work*, vol. 5, no. 1 (January 1960), pp. 3-8 [reprinted above, pp. 33-42].

2 Swithun Bowers, 'Social work and human problems,' *Social Casework*, vol. 35, no. 5 (May 1954), p.189.

3 Miss Richmond's actual phrase was 'the fullest possible participation of the client in all plans.' *What is Social Case Work?* Russell Sage Foundation, New York, 1922, p. 256.

4 Florence Hollis, *Social Case Work in Practice: Six Case Studies*, New York: Family Welfare Association of America, 1939, p. 5.

5 Lorena Scherer, 'Protective casework service,' *Children,* vol. 3, no. 1 (January-February 1956), p. 31.

6 Elliot Studt, 'Worker-Client authority relationships in social work,' *Social Work,* vol. 4, no. 1 (January 1959), p. 23.

7 For the first two statements, see Felix P. Biestek, 'Religion and social casework,' in *Social Welfare Forum 1956,* Columbia University Press, New York, 1956, p. 92. For the third concept, see Bernstein, *op. cit.,* pp. 7-8 [see p. 40 above].

8 Hollis, *op. cit.,* p. 5

9 Ernest Witte, 'Who speaks now for the child on public assistance?' *Child Welfare,* vol. 33, no. 3 (March 1954), pp. 9 and 12; and Lionel C. Lane, '"Aggressive" approach in preventive casework with children's problems,' *Social Casework,* vol. 33, no. 2 (February 1952), p. 66.

10 Bernstein, *op. cit.,* p. r [see p. 34 above].

11 Grace Marcus, *The Nature of Service in Public Assistance Administration,* Public Assistance Report No. 10, U.S. Government Printing Office, Washington, D.C., 1946, p.29.

12 *Re-Thinking Social Case Work,* Social Service Digest, San Diego, Calif., 1938, p. 15.

13 University of North Carolina Press, Chapel Hill, N.C., 1953.

14 'The status of social case work today,' in Fern Lowry (ed.), *Readings in Social Casework 1920-1938,* New York: Columbia University Press, 1939, p. 130. The article originally appeared in *Proceedings of the National Conference of Social Work, 1935,* University of Chicago Press, 1935.

15 Bernstein, *op. cit.,* p. 8 [see p. 41 above].

4   The right to fail *

David Soyer

The right of self-determination is a most precious casework axiom;
yet the self-chosen goals of clients often seem unrealistic, and
caseworkers must always stand for reality. This author maintains
that the principle of self-determination is frequently violated in the
name of good diagnosis and representing reality. Social workers
often discourage rather than enable, and sometimes we belie our
strong basic faith in the worth and ability of human beings by
grinding down the aspirations of our clients. While this paper is
directed to caseworkers, the same points might be raised with
vocational counselors, psychologists, and others in the helping
professions.

The dangers are more acute, or at least more obvious, in some
agencies than in others. This is true for two reasons. First, there are
those agencies that have some actual control over their clients. A boy
in institutional placement simply cannot apply to a special high
school unless his social worker arranges for him to do so. Similarly,
a person with a disability may get nowhere without the backing of a
state or voluntary agency. In the writer's experience, workers in such
agencies are constantly being faced with clients who have 'unrealistic
goals,' and these workers are in a much more powerful position to
affect their clients' aspirations than are their colleagues in a family
agency who work with a 'freer' population. (Not to imply that the
latter workers are more virtuous; they may discourage their clients in
more subtle ways.)

Second, certain agencies serve individuals whose aspirations,
although healthy for our culture, may be completely impossible of
fulfillment because of the individual's physical or environmental
circumstances. This is true of persons with disabilities, minority
group members, ex-prisoners, and so on. Sometimes the impossi-

*Reprinted with the permission of the author and the National Association of Social
Workers, from *Social Work,* vol. 8, no. 3 (July 1963), pp. 72-8.

bility results from factors intrinsic to the individual and the chosen goal (for instance, a blind person cannot be a baseball star); often it is prejudice or ignorance in the community.

For both these reasons, workers in an agency such as The Jewish Guild for the Blind must be acutely attuned not only to the aspirations of their clients but even more so to their own reactions to these strivings.

The Guild is a multifunctional, nonsectarian, specialized agency. Among agencies for the blind, it was a pioneer in introducing professional casework, group work, and vocational counseling.[1]

The writer has seen a number of clients with multiple physical and personality disabilities in whom the validity of their strivings was one of the few 'normal' things about them. The case of Mr A is an example.

Mr. A, age 28, came to the Guild after having been to several other agencies for the handicapped. He is a serious visaged, balding young man, fat around the middle (due to the Lawrence-Beidl Moon syndrome), with a peculiarly stooped and stiff-legged gait. His speech is halting and tentative because of his starting a sentence, stopping before completing the thought, going back, jumping to a new idea, and so on. He says 'wabbit' for 'rabbit.' His general appearance and manner are such that once when he sought a furnished room, the landlady opened the door and shrieked, 'Get out of here, you creep!' Mr. A sees hand movements in one eye and has 10/200 vision with best correction in the other. He travels with a cane. Psychological tests reveal normal intelligence.

Mr. A is hostile, at times feeling persecuted. His pattern is to ask the worker for help, be unable to accept the help in the way the worker can give it, and then turn on the worker, complaining that nobody wants to help him anyway and that all these agencies and workers are a 'waste of the public's money.' He has wanted to be a mechanic or a TV repairman, which, considering the marginal work he does in the Guild sheltered shop, seems unrealistic. It is felt that Mr. A's character structure is primitive, with many anal and oral traits and a great deal of conflict about dependency. Denial, projection, and displacement are seen as major defense mechanisms. The displacement seems to grow from an intense rage and a feeling of frustration at least partially caused by his limited opportunities. It is felt that Mr. A needs his defenses, despite their rigidity. A real look at himself might be intolerable.

Despite all this, Mr. A would like to get somewhere. The idea of spending the next forty years in a sheltered workshop earning minimal wages is as painful to him as it would be to any young man. His aspirations and desire to be productive are among his few strengths.

Self-determination conflicts with 'representing reality'

The principle of self-determination is basic to casework. Hamilton states:[2]

According to professional ethics he [the worker] must learn to accept others as distinct personalities, with their own right of self-realization and self-determination.

. . . how much harder to see that each individual must make his own solution, not in the sense that he is master of his fate and captain of his soul in a reckless defiance of external reality, but because his goals and life objectives are unique for him.

That a client has a right to be himself, to make his own decisions, to use his own abilities and resources, and to work out his own problems in an extension of the deeply rooted casework belief in self-help.

Periman refers to:[3]
. . . the democratic tenet that each individual has the right to self-determination: within the limits of reality each man has the right to be master of his soul and of his fate.

Wright, a psychologist, uses the expression 'the Principle of Comanagement,' which seems to have elements of the same meaning.[4] Starr writes:[5]

The blind and visually handicapped individual has as much right as the sighted person to self-determination, to affirm his need for social services, to state whether he wants to be visited in his home and to terminate his relationship with the social service department with a resulting closing of his case; with a decision, that is, to be or not to be a client.

This is stressed because blind people traditionally were denied this right in some agencies, and they still are. Chevigny blasts this practice, although there has been much improvement since he first wrote about it.[6]

Even in the definitions of self-determination, the word 'reality' appears. Caseworkers must always represent reality to their clients, and the literature stresses the importance of realistic goals, with the assessment of what is realistic being based on sound diagnosis. Barker refers to:[7]

> . . . the problem of getting the disabled to give up impossible hopes; under the pressure of very central needs disabled persons are prone to cling to unrealistic behavior aspirations long after these have become impossible. . . . The disabled person must know what he is up against. This involves knowing the areas in which opportunities lie as well as those from which he is excluded . . . (but) an attitude of resignation and acceptance of meagre goals . . . should be avoided at all means. For almost every disabled person there are richly satisfying goal hierarchies which he can pursue and within which he can achieve great and lasting satisfactions.

Wright sees as the main theme of her book the fact that '. . . acceptance of a disability requires basic changes in values so that new and *reachable* goals become meaningful.'[8] Lowry writes:[9]

> It is important to differentiate between individuals in terms of expectation; in other words to gear the level of expectation to the individual's capacity to function.

How are these two sound principles—the right of self-determination and the representing of reality—brought to bear by the caseworker upon the client's aspirations? The client might mention a striving that seems farfetched. The worker's response is usually muffled in the cliché 'Worker raised question regarding this, in terms of . . .' What this often means is that the worker raised every conceivable objection in an effort to discourage the client.

Suppose the client is a youngster in an institution who wants to go to a high school specializing in art and for which there is an entrance examination. The conscientious worker will do a careful study, have psychological tests done, and perhaps refer the boy to a vocational counselor. Depending on what the study shows, the client may gently be told that there are many fields allied to art, such as sign painting, that he might consider; or it might be suggested that he is really college material and that he can always pursue art as a hobby.

The impossibility of earning a living as a fine artist would be stressed. Should the youngster persist against the worker's persuasiveness, the worker then might arrange for him to take the examination. However, other workers would reason that the client would be deeply hurt by the probable failure and would not make the arrangement. In such a case, reality and self-determination have met head-on, and the former has won.

The writer has known a number of professional fine artists who probably never had counseling of any kind. Several never finished high school. They may have been college material, but their interests were so one-sided, even obsessive, that art school was all they would or could consider. They even risked failure and the chance of not earning a living. Might not a caseworker or vocational counselor have questioned their lofty aspirations? They would have made sad sign painters or unhappy hobbyists.

Within our client populations, there are those who for all their lives have been deprived yet overprotected. They include many disabled and institutionalized individuals, and perhaps others too. They have forever borne with a host of caseworkers, counselors, advisers, and other predigesters of the facts of life. Certainly, one of their deprivations is that they have never had the adventure of putting to the test of reality their adolescent 'dreams of glory' without first having soberly looked at the pros and cons with a social worker.

Challenge to aspirations

Blind people, especially, seem to be subjected to an intense challenge of their aspirations. Often more than one agency is involved in the process. By the time a vocational or educational goal is considered feasible, the person may consider himself so committed, and feel as if he has already had so much invested in him, that he dare not fail. He may also have had stressed to him that as a blind person he is serving as a trail-blazer or an example and he had better make a good showing, much the way Jackie Robinson was asked to serve as an example when he became the first Negro in organized baseball. Even the blind individual whose aspirations (albeit tested, challenged, and modified by caseworkers and counselors) are being supported by the agencies has lost some freedoms, including the freedoms to explore goals in a relaxed and informal way and to fail and learn through the failure.

Before looking at two reasons for backing the client's aspirations, despite apparent divergences from the realistic, two cases will be presented.

Mr. B is in his early twenties. He is soft-looking, paunchy, has a receding chin, balding head, and noticeably small hands and feet. His mouth tends to twist to the side, and he moves his arms awkwardly. His vision is 10/200 in both eyes with best correction. The disability is caused by an hereditary, progressive condition. He was born with extra fingers and toes that were removed at age two and there is a history of endocrine imbalance. Mr. B self-travels with a cane. He was referred to the Guild by another agency which found his behavior impossible to contain within its rehabilitation program. At the Guild, he was seen in regular casework interviews and was placed in a sheltered workshop. His parents, with whom he lives, were also seen by the caseworker.

Mr. B is unbelievably provocative. He quickly antagonizes coworkers, shop supervisors, and even professional workers. His vile language, teasing, putting of hot cigarette ashes into the hand of a blind deaf mute, his scuffling with coworkers, his complaint that he is being cheated out of pay by shop personnel —all contribute to his being universally disliked. With the caseworker, he constantly demands appointments which he fails to keep, only to insist on seeing the worker when the worker is busy. Mr. B tells jokes, but when the worker laughs, he sharply reprimands the worker, petulantly demanding that he be taken seriously at all times. His behavior is stereotyped, having remained consistent through changes in worker and counselor.

Even more provocative than this hostility is Mr. B's inappropriate and aggressive sexual behavior. This ranges from the bizarre attempt to 'make out' with an 80-year-old woman to his frequently 'accidentally' touching women in embarrassing places and his telephoning obscene remarks to young girls. He frequently speaks of being madly in love, but when the situation is examined it turns out that he is pursuing some middle-aged woman who is known to be sexually promiscuous but who is nevertheless rejecting Mr. B's every advance.

Mr. B is seen by the Guild psychiatrist as suffering 'a mixed form of schizophrenia.' The client was referred for treatment with a private psychiatrist who sees him as bordering on schizophrenia but as basically a character disorder of the passive aggressive type. Mr. B's sexual identification is called 'chaotic.' The caseworker also sees oral-dependent and oral-aggressive traits. Not only does Mr. B seem to have low self-esteem, but he seems skillful at re-creating in the people around him the hostility and derogation that he feels toward himself. The worker also sees a thin thread of normal aspiration that leads the worker to think at least some of Mr. B's hostility and bitterness grow out of understandable feelings of profound frustration with his life situation. These feelings are displaced upon individuals and the agency. Interviews with the father, an aggressive salesman, take the form of debates, with the father rationalizing away the son's problems and the worker being put in the position of attacking him with the son's behavior.

After two years in the Guild shop, Mr. B and his father began talking about getting newsstand training for Mr. B. The father put much pressure upon the state agency to sponsor this training. Both father and son saw this as a way out, a chance for eventual independence for Mr. B (it is definitely a higher goal than continued sheltered workshop employment). When the state agency turned to the Guild for its recommendation, the caseworker and vocational counselor conferred and agreed that Mr. B should be given the chance. Once he was accepted for training (at another agency), he seemed far more relaxed. Of course, the psychotherapy, his experiences at the Guild, maturation, and so on, probably also contributed to this relaxation. When last heard from, Mr. B was doing far better than might have been expected.

It is to be noted that the caseworker and the vocational counselor had real control over Mr B's possibilities for training. If they had said Mr B did not seem ready, he might not have been accepted. This worker also confesses that his first impulse was also to 'raise question' in the time-honored way with the client about the feasibility of this plan 'in terms of the client's difficulty in relating to people.' It was only when he shifted his 'terms of' to the client's 'right to fail' that he fully supported the plan for training.

Miss C weighs 50 pounds. She is 21 years old. Her tininess and drawn and aged appearance are due to rheumatoid arthritis. She has had no puberty. Her vision began to fail in early child-hood, and she was totally blind by age 16. Being too light for a dog and afraid of using a cane, Miss C does not self-travel. She is a high school graduate and has been to a number of agencies and rehabilitation centers. Throughout the reports from other agencies is a running theme of Miss C's wanting to go to college (her goal: social work), of this being considered an unrealistic goal for the present, and of her 'accepting' the need to postpone this plan to take up transcription typing as a possible career. Several such rehabilitation plans were started, but each time Miss C became ill and had to stop.

She is highly verbal and articulate, writing poetry that is a moody cross between Emily Dickinson and popular songs.

Miss C came to the Guild at a time of desperation. She was living with her parents and several healthy, attractive, younger sisters. The relationship between Mrs. C and Miss C was characterized by violent screaming, name-calling, fights over food, and, finally, mutual vomiting in the bathroom. Miss C feared for her sanity, while Mrs. C felt that only institutional placement would help.

First, Miss C was placed in a boarding home. Intensive casework was offered, and Miss C was registered in the Guild group work program. A multidiscipline conference was held, and it was decided, with full support of the Medical Director, to plan as rich a program as possible.

An earlier psychiatric diagnosis was of 'anxiety reaction, chronic, moderate.' The caseworker sees Miss C as the product of a family dominated by Mrs. C's orality. At the same time, since earliest childhood, her illness brought her into contact with many other parental figures, from whom she felt much warmth and with whom she identified. With this, her self-image was that of a child on the receiving end of the care and attention she learned to expect from these parent substitutes. She seems to have great ambivalence about dependency, wanting to grow up, but feeling safety in the child-invalid status.

As Miss C felt the caseworker's acceptance of her as an adult and his acceptance of the validity of her own aspirations, a tremendous spurt of movement was seen. She began again to discuss going to college and, as a trial of her capacities, took two summer courses. The caseworker made every effort to abet this plan. For the first time in her life, Miss C felt she was playing a part in her own planning. She made most of the arrangements for registration entirely on her own, although the

Guild supplied guides and readers. She is now taking two additional courses and has enjoyed school tremendously.

The gains have been great. Miss C shows much greater tolerance for frustration, has been in increasingly good spirits, and has had her characteristic pessimism tempered. She has reached a more mature understanding of her relationships, including that with her mother, and is truly beginning to think of herself as an adult. She speaks of having faith in herself that she never had before. At this point, Miss C is requesting cane travel instruction and is thinking of applying for full-time college attendance.

The client's aspirations

There are two reasons for supporting the self-determined aspirations of the client, even when they may seem farfetched. The first reason is simple: the client might be right, the worker wrong. This might have been so in Mr B's case if the caseworker and the vocational counselor had not been ready to consider the possibility that Mr B might succeed. The diagnostic tools are just not so exact that a worker can always judge a person's capacity. This is supported by Wright. Although she refers to vocational counselors, her point is also true for caseworkers. She writes:[10]

> . . . the fact that our fund of knowledge is often not sufficiently exact to enable the counselor to know which course of action is best for the client. On these grounds alone it would seem desirable to allow for the views and intentions of the client.
>
> Isn't a judgment of employability at best an estimate of probability and isn't an unwarranted wisdom assumed on the part of even the most expert vocational counselor when he feels able to say with assurance that a particular individual will be unable to put his training to productive use?

The second reason for backing the client's aspirations is that only through life itself can the client really try, test, and temper his abilities, his fantasies, and his goals. No amount of talking about 'heads' and 'walls' or testing the comparative strengths of heads and walls will have as real an impact on the client as his banging his actual head against a real wall. This is how all people grow, how they gain a more mature view of themselves and the world. They succeed and fail and through success and failure they learn. In the case of

Miss C, the goals may be unrealistic and adolescent fantasy. However, only through real life experience will she know whether she can reach them, and only through such experience will she modify and adjust this fantasy. If she is counseled out of trying, the aspirations may only go underground, and she will be left not only with her supposedly unrealistic fantasy but also with a bitter feeling that she was talked out of something and might have succeeded had she been allowed to try. For this particular client group, the need for real experience is most important, particularly since they have often experienced a large amount of casework and counseling and have often been sheltered from much of life.

There is ample theoretical support for this point. Wright states:[11]

Considerable learning often takes place in coping with frustration. The person learns about the sources of frustration, what he can and cannot do, the nature of the physical environment and its human inhabitants, all of which are important differentiations of his reality.

One of the general consequences of such learning is that he adjusts his goals (usually referred to in this context as the level of aspiration) to his experiences of success and failure. With success, his aspirations usually rise; with failure they decline. To be sure, this balancing mechanism of the level of aspiration may be counteracted by other factors . . . but it is certainly not typical for a person to continue to concentrate on unattainable goals.

LeShan, writing about changing trends in psychoanalytically oriented psycho-therapy, states;[12]

The new viewpoint is that the patient can learn by doing and must learn to use his abilities by using them effectively and that he cannot attain his potentialities by just talking about them; he must activate them by use.

This does not negate the role of the caseworker or the counselor. Rather than prejudging the validity of the client's aspirations, the worker first attempts to help the client identify his strivings; then he works toward enabling the client to reach toward his goal; he helps the client to understand and integrate the experiences he is having in pursuit of the goal; and, finally, he may help the client to formulate and identify new or modified (upward or downward) aspirations. In the case of Miss C, this has led, so far, to a much more profound level of casework treatment than would have been possible if the worker had not respected the client's right to choose goals for herself.

Attitudes of workers

Why do caseworkers sometimes dampen rather than fire the aspirations of their clients? Since this could be the topic of another paper, three possible reasons will be presented only briefly.

1. In spite of his professional orientation and self-awareness, the worker may be infected unconciously with some of the general attitudes toward the disabled (and other disadvantaged client groups) that, behind clucks of pity, tend to derogate the disabled individual and prejudge him as totally incompetent. The literature contains many discussions of such attitudes.[13] It is doubtful that among competent professional workers these attitudes exist in their gross forms. However, they may linger in subtle ways. For instance, one might expect professional social workers to be among the first to try to break through the employment barrier for persons with disabilities. Yet how many voluntary, non-specialized agencies have hired blind social workers or transcription typists?

2. Workers may want to save their clients from the pain of failure. Every sensitive parent has experienced the torture of watching his young child battle with some comparatively easy task. But because we respect his need to learn and because we may be pushed away by a determined 'Me do!' we often allow him to continue struggling, despite the impulse to protect him from frustration. Perhaps this same protective feeling prevents us from heeding the client's version of 'Me do!' This is a kind of countertransference that calls for increased self-awareness.

3. Perhaps social work attracts cautious, risk-avoiding people. There is evidence of this in the way in which we treat our own workers, often preventing them, through close and overly extensive supervision, from fully developing and taking responsibility for their own ideas and methods. Our stress on 'planfulness' and carefully assessing positives and negatives before taking a step may also reflect a basic conservatism.

Conclusions

This is a call for more daring on the part of caseworkers—including a greater alliance with the aspirations of clients, even when these seem beyond the reach of the client and contain the risk of failure. The right of self-determination includes the right to fail and it is the life experience itself with its success, failure, and in between that is what really enables the client to evaluate himself and, in the end, to set his goals realistically. The caseworker can help with the evaluation and integration of this experience. While discussion has been based on the client group of a specialized agency and rather extreme examples have been presented, it is believed that the points raised are pertinent to much of social work.

When some of these ideas were discussed with Miss C, she quoted to the worker these familiar lines from 'Andrea del Sarto' of Browning:

> . . . *Ah, but a man's reach should exceed his grasp,*
> *Or what's a Heaven for?*

Notes

1 For discussion of the role of casework in agencies specializing in work with blind persons, see Elizabeth M. Maloney, 'The special contribution of the social caseworker in an agency for the blind,' *New Outlook for the Blind*, vol. 46, no. 9 (November 1952); Maloney, 'Social casework approach to the visually handicapped client,' *New Outlook for the Blind*, vol. 50, no. 4 (April 1956); and Florence C. Starr, 'The role of the social service department in an agency for the blind,' *Jewish Social Service Quarterly*, vol. 29, no. 2 (Winter 1952).

2 Gordon Hamilton, *Theory and Practice of Social Case Work*, 2nd ed., revised; Columbia University Press, New York, 1951, pp. 40, 41 and 44.

3 Helen Harris Perlman, *Social Casework: A Problem-Solving Process*, University of Chicago Press, 1957, p. 60.

4 Beatrice A. Wright, *Physical Disability—A Psychological Approach*, Harper & Brothers, New York, 1960, p. 345.

5 Starr, *op. cit.*, p. 222.

6 Hector Chevigny, *My Eyes have a Cold Nose*, Yale University Press, New Haven, 1946, pp. 101ff.

7 Roger G. Barker, 'The social psychology of physical disability,' *Journal of Social Issues*, vol. 4, no. 4 (Fall 1948), p. 37.

8 Wright, *op. cit.*, p. 338.

9 Fern Lowry, 'Basic assumptions underlying casework with blind persons,' in Samuel Finestone (ed.), *Social Casework and Blindness*, American Foundation for the Blind, New York, 1960, pp. 16-17.

10 Wright, *op. cit.*, pp. 347, 348.

11 *Ibid.*, p. 92.

12 Lawrence L. LeShan, 'Changing trends in psychoanalytically oriented psychotherapy,' *Mental Hygiene*, vol. 46, no. 3 (July 1962), p. 459.

13 For discussion of these attitudes, see Sydell Braverman, 'The psychological roots of attitudes toward the blind,' *New Outlook for the Blind*, vol. 45, no. 6 (June 1951); Chevigny, *op. cit.* (attitudes are described and discussed thoughout the book); Thomas D. Cutsforth, 'Personality crippling through physical disability,' *Journal of Social Issues*, vol. 4, no. 4 (Fall 1958); Irving Lukoff, 'A sociological appraisal of blindness,' in Finestone, *op. cit.*; and Wright, *op. cit.*, especially ch. 2.

5   Self-determination: reality or illusion? *

Helen Harris Perlman

If I were forced to answer at once the question posed by my title, instead of being given the privilege of meandering toward it, if you demanded of me, 'Tell in ten words or less what your answer is,' I would have to say, 'I believe self-determination is nine-tenths illusion, one-tenth reality.' And I would have to add, 'But I believe self-determination is one of the "grand illusions" basic to human development and human dignity and human freedom.' Therefore I am committed to supporting and enhancing that illusion and also to making the most, the very most, of the exercise of that one-tenth of it that is real, present, and possible in our lives. That is what this paper is about.

I

Somehow, despite the fact that the concept of self-determination is old in the value system of professional social work and that it has been competently and convincingly analyzed and argued in our literature, it recurrently calls for re-examination. It seems to hold within it some conflicts and paradoxes that demand that we lift it out now and again from the matrix of our value system and view it afresh in the light of changing emphases and directions. We are at such a time now. Not only in social work, but in scientific and humanistic circles too, there is today an impelling interest in questions of 'determinism' and freedom of the individual. We are all—social workers, clients, everyone— caught in the rising tide of a prefabricated, preplanned, preorganized, predetermined social order. We are members of a society so socialized, rationalized,

*This article was prepared for presentation at the Great Lakes Regional Institute of the National Association of Social Workers, held in Chicago, Illinois, on June 23, 1965. Reprinted with the permission of the author and the University of Chicago Press, from *Social Service Review*, vol. 39, no. 4, 1965, pp. 410-21.

organized, bureaucratized, specialized and mechanized that there is less and less room for individual freedoms and choices. If students of our present-day life read it correctly, the problem of the individual's 'other-directedness,' which is to say of his responsivity to external cues and signals rather than to taking counsel with himself, and the problem of identity diffusion, which is to say of having no secure sense of self except as it is reflected back by others—these problems are endemic among us. Both are problems of some loss of selfhood. And the sense of selfhood, of humanness, of self-worth depends heavily upon the sense of self as cause. 'I *am* because I *will*' is the essence of self-determination: 'I am because I will to choose, to decide, to be responsible for, a cause of, the consequences that follow on my actions.'

The opposing and engulfing trend in present-day life seems to make man increasingly less master of his fate. Social workers are both victims and perpetrators of this phenomenon of the planned and regularized society of this latter half of the twentieth century. Our present-day vocabulary is full of new words and phrases that bespeak new controlling trends and intents: 'intervention,' 'reaching the hard-to-reach,' 'social workers as agents of change—of social control,' clients of 'client-systems' as 'targets of change,' 'strategies of prevention'—and so on. Faced with what we hold to be 'good' or 'bad' in these trends, and with the implacable dilemmas that they present for human wellbeing, we struggle to hold some margin for self-affirmation by the individual. Self-determination names this margin.

It is of interest that the concept of self-determination apparently developed in social work in another decade of radical social change—in the 1930s. Before then the idea of client participation in the process of problem-solving was iterated and reiterated as both a means and an end in casework. I have not been able to discover when that subtle turn of the screw occurred that shifted 'participation' with helper to 'self-determination,' but the newer idea was espoused by social workers with emotional intensity. Its emotional freightage is understandable when one looks at the political, economic, and psychological pressures of those times. In his critique of the principle of self-determination[1] Alan Keith-Lucas points to its relation to the liberating force of Freudian psychology. Imperative in this psychological theory was the idea that man's powers and drives needed to be freed of the inhibitions and prohibitions that shackled them. Thus casework took to the techniques of the passivity and neutrality that were characteristic of the psychoanalytic model, sometimes to points of absurdity, to be sure, but always in the hope of fostering the client's exercise of self-determination. Paralleling psychiatry was the progressive-education movement, whose interpreters and misinterpreters of John Dewey retreated from classroom controls and curricula into permissiveness that sometimes yielded creativity in children and sometimes yielded chaos. Group work for a time took on this model.

But it was more than psychological theory that pushed social workers to make 'self-determination' a professional password. The decade of the 1930s was a decade of the rise of totalitarian governments. The reaction among social workers, as among most citizens of this country, was the passionate affirmation and reassertion of democracy and of the rights of each individual man to be his own man. Accompanying the political holocausts in Italy, Spain, and Germany was the economic holocaust in this country. What we social workers saw for the first time was that people who were or could have been our friends or relatives, who were like ourselves in background, social status, education, mores—such people in large numbers were suddenly subject to circumstances that, despite our lip-service to the contrary, we had reserved for people who were not like us. Among these circumstances were the coercions and insults and strictures that accompanied having to take relief or look for jobs or deal with creditors. Each of us thought, 'There but for the grace of God go I,' and each of us quaked and rebelled inwardly against the evidence that loss of economic self-dependence can mean loss of self-esteem and self-identity. So we underlined and reiterated 'the client's right to self-determination' as the basic safeguard to his integrity.

Today the threats to selfhood are of a different sort—more insidious, perhaps, because they arise from social conditions and provisions that are both good and bad, provisions that eradicate one complex of social problems even as they give birth to another. These threats have been analyzed by social and political critics, often with brilliance and persuasiveness, but no powerful solutions to them have been proposed. So it seems fitting that social workers, among others who stand for humanness, should strive to hold and in some small ways to expand the narrow margin of self-determination, because it is chiefly in the exercise of his will that man knows himself and feels himself responsible for his choices and his fate.

'All theory is against the freedom of the will; all experience for it.'

So said the perspicacious Dr Samuel Johnson. Now, two hundred years later, this statement still holds true. 'All theory is against the freedom of the will,' and all scientific and empiric fact is too. The infant organism enters the world with a constitutional set and built-in behaviors that are common to the species. It is subject from the moment breath enters the lungs to stimuli and intrusions that press in upon it physically, psychologically, socially. Each act, thought, feeling becomes linked with some experience that has preceded it, each shaped and colored by firm patterns of the culture in which the infant grows, by the patterns of the personalities with which he is in continuous transaction, and, later, by the habitual patterns which structure his own personality and behavior. Not only are physical characteristics and innate capacities predetermined, but the individual's personality, temperament, and bent are, according to recent careful longitudinal studies, fairly well set before the child has reached what can be considered to be the age of rational choice.

Yet there remains one fact to which the most rigorous of physical sciences attests: in living organisms no two cells are exactly alike; among human beings no two persons are exactly alike; and, therefore, because of the uniqueness of each man, the prediction of what he can and will do and be is not possible in any but the most general way. In other words, while each man is the product of his inheritance and his personal history, he also carries within him some part or process that breaks from the mold. It is this individuality that social workers reach for. It is this unpredictability based on each man's uniqueness, combined with the belief that as long as he is alive he is in the making, that makes room for the experience and promotion of self-determination. Dr Johnson was right: as living is consciously experienced, we feel ourselves—or perhaps one should say the fortunate among us experience ouselves—as choosers, as deciders, as persons free to will.

We wake up in the morning trailing dreams about yesterday's or all our yesterdays' problems behind our half-open eyes. We wake up not to our inner time clock, but to a clock set by a system other than our personal one. Somewhere along the way we made the choice of meeting this necessity. We get out of bed and consider what we will wear. We choose narrowly, between work-proper suits or work-proper dresses. These choices are very limited ones, because for the most part they have been made in advance by a powerful fashion and garment industry, bolstered by custom, which places role, age, and climate norms on what is or is not proper to wear. We breakfast. Will you have toast or muffins, egg or cereal, coffee black or with cream? You are not asking yourself if you will have toast or a marsh-mallow sundae, coffee or a gin sling, because your choices have been narrowed and limted for you by breakfast customs, by medical opinion, by parental dicta established or rebelled against long ago. But you treasure the privilege of making these small choices, limited though they are. Breakfast finished, you go to work. It is, one hopes, work you have chosen to do. How much freedom went into that choice? How far was it predetermined by conditions and people and happenstance to which you were unwittingly subject?

Yet there was some small spark or thrust in you that pushed you to want what you 'chose' to do. This motive (which was itself predetermined), combined with the sense of free choice among several alternatives, is what differentiates the slave from the free man, the victim from the empowered man. If you feel that what you work at, what you do, was preordained, whether by some inexorable fate or by powers outside yourself, you will react in one of two ways. You will accept your fate with resignation and with the low level of physical and psychic energy and investment that accompanies resigned acceptance. Or, in rebellion, you will burn out those energies that might be invested in work and love. (One does not need to look far to see this proved. It is those sectors of the population whose self-determination, either as small reality or grand illusion, has been missing which are characterized by apathy and resignation or by blind impulsive revolt.) If, on the other hand, you feel that the choice of what you undertook to work at was your own choice and that, furthermore, the daily tasks involved are not so predetermined that they make you an automaton, a switch-flipper, but, rather, they allow you to exercise judgment and choice—then you feel responsible and invested in your tasks. You are 'your own man.'

What you choose to do, you take on as your own. Its accompanying responsibilities and rewards are acknowledged and shouldered. Even if there are frustrations involved (as must almost always happen, because there are few perfect choices in real life), even if there are disappointments or unanticipated difficulties, they are more palatable, more digestible if they are part of one's own (and owned) choice than if they were imposed from outside the self. One of the things we must learn and face about self-determination—and this is learning that desirably begins in infancy and is part of personality maturation—is that choice always involves some compromise, some renunciation. And it always involves, too, the possibility of its being a poor choice, of yielding an unhappy outcome. We take these imperfections and these chances, either by abandoning the self in a blind and helpless way to chance or fate or to dependency upon others, or by girding up our loins and taking the responsibility both for rational choices and for their consequences.

It is the thesis of this paper that self-determination, even though it may be more illusory than real, is the very essence of mature humanness; that man's exercise of choice rather than his coercion by his own blind impulses or the power of others is what builds in him his sense of effectiveness, of identity and selfhood, and of responsibility. This is why I believe that whatever fraction of self-determination is given us should be exploited and exercised to its fullest, for ourselves and for anyone in whose lives we intervene.

In considering the social worker and the client in relation to self-determination, I have to make certain choices that contain renunciations and compromises. These choices are predetermined in part by limits of space and capacity, but in part they are 'free' choices set by my judgment of what is more rather than less pertinent. I shall not touch on self-determination as it occurs in the social work methods of group work and community organization. The questions of whether the concept is equally applicable across all the social work methods or whether it is usable chiefly when the client can be designated as a 'self' are worth more attention than they have had. Moreover, I shall not deal with the aspects of self-determination that have already been cogently set forth in our literature—aspects of its difference from license and impulse gratification, its inseparability from the rights of others, its dependence upon capacity for social responsibility, and so forth.[2] I shall confine myself to what the exercise of self-determination for an individual person consists of, how it fits within the framework of ego psychology, and how the social caseworker may promote and enhance it in his client.

II

Those persons who come into adulthood with a sense of self-respect, with a sense of being more at one with their fellow men than against them, more master of themselves and their problems than defeated, who can, in brief, be called 'mature' and 'adaptive'—these are persons who have had a life-experience more benign than noxious. Not everything has gone well for them. An examination of their life-histories (and we need to study many more life-histories of well-adjusted persons if we are ever going to make psychodynamic theory more than a theory of pathology) will show trauma and disapointments, mothers who fell far short of the ideal, and fathers who failed here and there. But, I would postulate, they are persons who have had a fairly continuous experience of feeling themselves to be actual or potential 'cause,' of being choosers and doers in contrast to being dependent upon the choices and actions of persons more powerful than they. They have had a fairly continuous and expanding experience from childhood of exercising their powers of decision and responsibility, and of having rewarding rather than hurtful consequences result from their self-determined acts.

In the development of a child the will—which is to say the assertion of drives to actualize the self—makes itself known almost at birth.[3] At birth these drives to assert self-needs and wants begin to be shaped and directed by the forces and persons with whom the infant is in continuous and expanding interaction. Every life-stage of the developing child holds innumerable daily transactions between him and others in which self-determination is allowed, promoted, exercised or is prohibited, restricted, blocked. There are probably some life-stages in which the assertion of the self and the developing sense of mastery are crucial. But even in the innocence of infancy the push to self-assertion can be seen. Anyone who has watched babies, even before they talk and walk, has observed the thrust and push in them to make things happen, to be the cause of consequences, to feel themselves as doers. To push toys off the high-chair tray and to find that grownups must duck and bob to pick them up is the occasion for gurgles of pleasure. Turning the face away from the proffered spoonful of mush and then the sudden grabbing of a fistful of the stuff and pushing it into the mouth—this is sheer triumph. These and like acts hold the pleasure and triumph of self-assertion.

Probably the most dramatic struggle for self-determination comes in the phase of childhood that Freud called 'anal' and Erikson has described as the period when either a sense of autonomy is achieved or the child incorporates a sense of shame and doubt. In this phase the child's decision to conform to the parental will, his choices, so to speak, as to whether he will yield to training or not, and, beyond this, his coming to know both his strengths, through the exercise of all his body muscles, and his limits, through his encounter with immovable persons and objects—these experiences build into him the primitive but basic sense of self-determination which is: 'I can determine—choose—whether I will hold on or give out, whether I will stay or go, whether I will yield or rebel. That power is in me. I choose to renounce some pleasures because I want the rewards, the alternate pleasurable consequences that renunciation will bring me.' This is the essence of the first vital self-determination experience of the very little child. Its happy outcome depends, of course, on the combination of parental limiting and loving. Its unhappy outcome, the result of too heavy or too harsh parental domination, is seen in the child who gives up his sense of autonomy, who doubts his powers, or who, in blind revolt, becomes not self-determining at all but the victim of his own driving rage.

In the oedipal phase—or again to use the Eriksonian formulation —in the phase in which initiative or guilt is the crucial outcome, the child's experience is decisive for whether he will develop the sense that he has a selfhood of his own, separate from his parents, and that certain rights and responsibilities commensurate with his age go with this unfolding sense of self. I do not think this sense rises out of parents' permissively giving the child free choice and placing him in what is often the confusing situation of deciding whether he wants or does not want something, the nature and outcome of which he cannot even visualize. Rather it comes from parental feeding of the child's insatiable hunger to know who he is now, and where he came from, and what he is going to grow up to do and to be, and from helping him know and take pleasure in his predetermined identity. As part of this, his sense of responsibility grows as he takes into himself the qualities of those he loves and feels at one with, qualities which include the 'shoulds' and the 'oughts' and the 'shall nots' that begin to form the internal system of guides to what is 'right' and what is 'responsible.'

When the child enters school his world expands and the arena for self-made decisions widens too. Simultaneously the social require- ments to do and to desist from doing proliferate. He is likely to choose to go to school rather than malinger when his teacher and parents and schoolmates offer him more gratification for this choice than frustration. He is likely to choose to study rather than dawdle if he finds that in his own head is the power to make sense out of those squiggles called numbers and letters. He is likely to choose to expand his horizons by moving from home into clubs and outside play if he is not coerced in one direction or another by inner fear or outer force. And he is likely to develop further his feeling of 'I am,' 'I will,' 'I decide' if his activities and small hour-by-hour decisions yield results that are more rather than less gratifying. Then he achieves that resolution of the conflict of latency that Erikson called 'industry versus inferiority.'

Perhaps adolescence, especially in its middle and late years, presents the most unsettling and fearsome tasks of choice and decision. Decisions about what to be and what to become, choice of school, of occupation, of sexual behavior, and of sexual partner—all these and other choices are thrust upon the adolescent, plus many opportunities, plus overwhelming uncertainties, shared by parents, about what consequences may ensue. Sometimes I have thought that for the middle- and upper-class adolescent today there are both too many choices and too many possible alternatives in their world of abundance and parental permissiveness, and also too little notion of what these choices will yield in this time of moral and technological revolution. Self-determination or free choice becomes too complex and confusing when limits and boundaries are too loosely defined. Thus, we may account for the role diffusions and personal confusions pervasive among adolescents today. As for the lower-class adolescent, the world in its gaudy and glamorous representations lies open to his perceptions, exciting his wanting—but already there is for him a gaping disparity between what he will choose to have or to do and what he realistically can have or do. For him, perhaps, the problem is not role diffusion so much as role constriction; his world snaps shut too soon.

What I am trying to suggest by this whisk through child development is that by the time adulthood is reached each of us has had potent and personality-shaping experiences that determine how capable we are of grasping and using the freedoms and responsibilities of self-determination. Such tracing through of the development or the dwarfing of the will to choose and the capacity to choose freely and realistically deserves more detailed attention. The child-parent, child-other, child-self, child-thing relationships that make up a child's world can lead to his coming to feel himself either a 'doer' or a receiver of others' doing, a cause or a victim of circumstances, to experience himself as one who sees a connection between his acts and consequences or as one who defends himself against such insights, as one who has a sense of mastery or as one who feels chronically angry or depressed that he is mastered.

III

Unhappily, the clients of social workers are often persons who have not had the life-experience of continuity and support in finding and knowing themselves and in having freedoms to choose. They have been denied these freedoms They have been smothered by others, pushed into dependency upon the powers of others; their realistic opportunities to choose among alternatives have been puny and constricted; their early assertions of self or experiments with self-chosen actions have resulted in consequences of failure or punishment, either from powerful people or from overpowering circumstances. The chronically poor, the chronically sick, the chronically outcast have rarely been self-determining. They have experienced themselves as victims and pawns, helpless except as momentary impulse or anger empowers them. Choice and self-determination have not been proffered them. So the sense of autonomy, of identity, of self as center of self-government and social responsibility—these basic images and concepts of selfhood are not often part of their personal psychology. The 'right' to self-determination seems all but incredible to them, and indeed it is all but non-existent, so narrow is the margin of their possible choices. Thus we know people as clients who have abdicated their right to choice; these are the apathetic, dependent personalities. We know clients who cling stubbornly to pseudo-autonomy by saying 'No!' to people and to life; it is their only way of asserting selfhood. We know clients whose impulsive 'acting-out'—which is to say their unrational drive to gratify needs—is in no sense free choice but only blind drive. Our concern must be that so many of these adults are parents of growing children whose perceptions of the world and of their being and becoming in it will be shaped and colored by their parents' interpretations and behavior.

So, for every person the social worker encounters and tries to influence, and especially for those persons who are faceless, there ought to be a conscious effort to foster, to exercise, and to enhance the choosing of actions and facing of outcomes. This exercise of self-determination may take place in any social work setting, in any single interview, and also repeatedly in the course of any case. It may be exercised in as simple and single a decision as whether or not to go to the dentist, or in as complex decisions as whether to go back to one's family or to live alone; whether to work or to follow the doctor's orders for rest; whether to try to learn to walk again or to remain in the wheelchair; whether to suffer the anger and hurt of parent-child conflicts or to suffer the guilt and hurt of self-examination toward self-change. Life-experiences for each of us are made up mostly of small decisions and only a few large ones. It is the repeated exercise of choice in these small day-to-day problems, based upon reasoned considerations of consequences and upon realistic recognition that there are few perfect solutions in life, and that, therefore, compromise and tolerance for some frustration are inherent in choice—it is this repeated exercise that builds what, in professional shorthand, we call 'ego strength.'

The personality operations and affects involved in self-determination are in complete congruence with the ego's functions and affects. The process, in rough outline, is like this:

The problem-to-be-solved or the question-to-be-answered must be recognized, felt by the person who faces it. Beyond awareness of it he must perceive it, see it, realistically. Perception is the primary function of the ego, basic to all functions that follow on it. Perception, to be clear and realistic, must be free of distortions created by excess need or stress and must take in both the external situation and the person's own inner responses to it.

Social workers encounter their clients in the throes of stress and crisis. In addition, their clients often do not have the knowledge by which to understand either the situation they face or their particular reaction to it. So our first job is to help the person perceive, to get the facts of, and to take knowledgeable measure of the problem in which he is involved. Simultaneously, weaving in and out of this perception of the problem, our client must be aided to see himself as reactor to and interactor with the problem, that is, as one whose feelings and responses both color the problem and affect it in ways that make it peculiarly *his* problem. The social worker's mutual and supportive exploration with his client of the nature of the problem, big or little, and the relation between it and the person's emotional involvement is the first step in enhancing the ego's perceptive functions. It is also the first step in the process of self-determination.

In the automatic operations of the ego, perception is followed or sometimes accompanied by a rallying of the mechanisms of protection or adaptation or coping. All of these may be called up at once, or in alternating sequence, or singly. For any problem that requires reasoned choice and decision the substitute for automatic process is conscious consideration. There must be lifted to the mind's eye the question of what kinds of action and reaction are possible, appropriate, useful in dealing with the problem. Between self-determination and automatic or impulsive action lies a major difference between the strong ego and the weak. The weak ego is subject to impulses or to stereotyped behavior. The adequate ego of the self-determining person has the staying power that enables the person to delay decision and action while he considers alternate modes of action, alternate possibilities, and his feelings and his capacities in relation to these possibilities.

Thus, the social worker who would help his client develop the delaying capacities that mark the difference between the primitive and the mature pleasure principle helps him to know about and to think about the possible ways in which this question or problem can be tackled. These possible ways lie in the person himself, the ways he can behave (defend himself, adapt himself to the situation, or cope with it by changing it as well as his relation to it), and they lie also in resources within and outside the social agency. Often these possible means must be introduced by the social worker. Almost always the client's thinking over, reflecting, considering the ways of acting and reacting must be stimulated, nursed, supportively coaxed along by the social worker by thought-provoking questions, tentative suggestions, supportive or provocative comments, and always the repeated underpinning of warm recognition of how hard, how tough a business it is to think something out instead of waving a wand or taking a chance.

Another major function of the ego is the anticipation of outcomes or consequences, based upon accrued and remembered past experience and/or upon new knowledge supplied by others. The strong ego carries this anticipatory function that shapes decisions. Without it the person's actions are chiefly trial and error. The anticipation of outcomes or of the possible consequences of one's choice is basic, too, to the exercise of self-determination. Free choice involves not simply deciding what one will do or have done but considering what the possible results of choice may be. In anticipating the effects or consequences of choices, the individual does two things. First, he faces up to the fact that the chooser is in part responsible for what comes after; and, second, he recognizes that he is choosing, not between an evil and a good, not between a poor and a perfect solution, but, almost always, between better or worse, between more good and less bad, between the lesser of two imperfect outcomes. To recognize this, to chew it over, to digest it, and to 'stomach it' comfortably—this is part of what we mean by ego integration. It involves the acceptance not of what I would wish for but of what I can realistically hope for, and the accompanying sense of responsibility that *I* shape my hopes and my behavior for change in the situation and/or in myself.

To enable a person to visualize and then appraise the possible consequences of his choice; to help him substitute realistic hope for childish wish; to bring him to the point at which he knows himself to be the chooser (though often a reluctant one); to help him to express, know, and handle all the new emotions that are roused by having to extend himself further to cope with difficulties ahead—to do all this takes all the technical and nurturant skills the social worker has. From this tasting, chewing, and digestion process the executive functions of the ego move out to carry into action, by overt or internal coping, the determination that has been arrived at.

It is the exercise of these functions of perception, suspended action, consideration, judgment, choice, and decision that builds into and then begins to constitute ego strength. This exercise was long ago recognized and posited as the necessary condition for the achievement of human freedom. Over one hundred years ago John Stuart Mill wrote his 'Essay on Liberty,' which set forth those ideas of man's freedom that have seeded all subsequent thought about self-determination. Arguing for the development of free men, Mill said: 'The human faculties of perception, judgment, discriminative feeling, mental activity . . . are exercised only in making choices.' He added: 'The mental and moral, like the muscular powers, are improved only by being used.' It is these powers and faculties that we group together in that elastic and versatile function of the personality we call 'the ego,' used and exercised in choice and self-determination.

One further aspect of the ego must be touched upon in this all-too-superficial review of its functions, because it bears so immediately upon self-determination. Our understanding of the ego is still very impressionistic, still very much in the unfolding. In the past two decades or so, in the shift from id psychology to ego psychology there have been some careful observations and studies that have underpinned new propositions about the nature of the ego. These propositions and their partial verifications hold promise and direction for social work. Briefly, the expanded concept of the ego is that it is far more than a messenger and mediator between inner needs and outer demands, more than defender against and neutralizer of the archaic and anarchic drives in our dark depths. It is proposed that potential ego functions come into being when the human comes into being, at birth; that the drives of the ego are autonomous, independent energies; that these drives are motored not only by conflict and frustration but by an inborn push to expand the experience of the self, the boundaries of perception, and to gain pleasure in the use of innate powers of body and mind. The ego is motivated by an 'instinct to mastery.' This 'instinct to mastery' has been observed in young animals, babies, and young children who reach out aggressively and pleasurably to explore their small worlds at points, not of hunger and stress, but when their basic needs have been satisfied and they are in a state of 'needlessness' or balance. It has been postulated, thus, that a major drive of the ego is for 'effectance,' which is to say for finding one's self to be the cause of an effect; and that, when that effect is gratifying, is felt to be 'good,' there rises in the person—child or adult—the sense of competence. To these postulates of Hartmann, Hendrick, Erikson, and White one may add the supporting conclusion that Murphy draws from her studies of young children: that 'I do' precedes and is basic to the sense of 'I am,'[4] that the expending sense of self follows the experience of using muscle and mind.

Look at emergent ego psychology just this far, and the relation between these ideas of the inborn push for self-actualization and the exercise of self-determination becomes apparent. The implications within any therapeutic or educative endeavor for fostering repeated practice in making responsible choices also seems clear. True, there are many things we do because we must by the currently imposed or long-ago introjected decrees of others. But our self-esteem and sense of responsibility are based upon our awareness of ourselves as cause, as mover, as chooser. Ego psychology now gives psychodynamic support to our long-held humanist philosophic stance.

If we reject self-determination as a viable means and end, if we deny its inherence in every daily transaction between ourselves and those we profess to help, then what do we choose as a workable psychology and philosophy in its place? What alternatives are there? These, in brief: A dehumanized view of man as animal or machine; a view of choice and responsibility as the right of some governing few—the Fascist concept, or, at its opposite pole, a state of anarchy; a view of social workers as robots manipulating other robots to the predetermined whims or plans of power-holders; a view, in short, that is intolerable to entertain.

I have come far beyond the time when I thought that if I believed in Tinker-bell he would become real. But if there is some margin of reality in a grand illusion, in an illusion that enhances the image of man, I choose to support and affirm it, to push at the boundaries of that margin to make it wider and more real. We push at that margin with every small transaction between ourselves and a client when we say to him: 'What do you see as the difficulty—big or little? What do you want? What are the possible ways you can get what you want, or its reasonable facsimile? What is likely to happen one way or the other? What is bad about it? And how does that make you feel? What is good about it? Whom will it hurt or help? So, then, what is your decision, your choice? Can you stomach— or will you let me help you to stomach—the disappointments or frustrations that imperfect solutions must hold?'

Self-determination, then, is the expression of our innate drive to experience the self as cause, as master of one's self. Its practical everyday exercise builds into man's maturation process because it requires the recognition of the actual, the consideration of the possible, and, in the light of these sometime sorry prospects, the adaptation involved in decision and choice. Self-determination is based upon a realistic view of freedom. Freedom, in essence, is the inner capacity and outer opportunity to make reasoned choices among possible, socially acceptable alternatives. True, each man's exercise of self-determination is predetermined and limited by his nature and nurture, by past and present people and circumstances, and by his society's prevailing commitments to humanistic ideals. Yet within all these uniquely individual boundaries and within a larger society such as ours which forges chains even as it speaks for liberty, within these paradoxes we must help man to find in himself some wish and power to be captain of his soul and master of his fate. We may be able to do so only in small ways. But as we support his wish and exercise his latent powers to consider and to choose, to bear compromises and to gain small pleasure from responsibly chosen outcomes—as we do this we build into each man's sense of himself as a person and affirm his worth as a human being. This one-part reality in the stubborn human illusion about self-determination is palpable and vital, ready for its potentials to be plumbed and realized.

Notes

1 A. Keith-Lucas, 'A critique of the principle of client self-determination,' *Social Work*, vol. 8 (July 1963), pp. 66-71 [reprinted above, pp. 43-52].

2 The most relevant of these discussions, in order of their publication chronology, are: Helen Harris Perlman, 'The caseworker's use of collateral information,' in *Social Welfare Forum*, 1951, pp. 190-205; Anita J. Faatz, *Nature of Choice in the Casework Process*, University of North Carolina Press, Chapel Hill, 1953; Herbert Aptekar, *The Dynamics of Casework and Counseling*, Houghton Mifflin Co., Boston, Mass., 1955; Felix P. Biestek, S.J., *The Casework Relationship*, Loyola University Press, Chicago, 1957, pp. 100-19; Helen Harris Perlman, *Social Casework: A Problem-Solving Process*, University of Chicago Press, 1957, esp. pp. 60, 124, 132, 135; Saul Bernstein, 'Self-determination: king or citizen in the realm of values?' *Social Work*, vol. 5 (January 1960), pp. 3-8 [reprinted above, pp. 33-42]; and Keith-Lucas, *op. cit.*

3 The concept 'will' has in the past—and perhaps still in the present—held charged and negative connotations for many social workers, because it is central to Rankian psychology. I call attention here to its recent emergence in the writings of neo-Freudians. See in particular Erik Erikson, *Insight and Responsibility*, Norton & Co., New York, 1964, in which, among a number of references to 'will' as an 'ego disposition,' he defines it (p. 119) as 'the unbroken determination to exercise free choice as well as self-restraint.'

4 Ives Hendrick, 'The discussion of the "Instinct to master,"' *Psychoanalytic Quarterly*, vol. 12, no. 4 (1943), pp. 561-5, and 'Work and the pleasure principle,' *ibid.*, no. 3 (1943), pp. 311-29; Erikson, *Childhood and Society*, Norton & Co., New York, 1950; Hans Hartmann, *Ego Psychology and the Problem of Adaptation*, International Universities Press, New York, 1958; Erik Erikson, 'Identity and the life cycle,' *Psychological Issues*, International Universities Press, New York, 1959, vol. 1, no. 1; Lois Barclay Murphy, *The Widening World of Childhood*, Basic Books, New York, 1962; and Robert W. White, 'Ego and reality in psychoanalytic theory,' *Psychological Issues*, International Universities Press, New York, 1963, vol. 3, no. 3.

6   Self-determination re-examined *

Colin Whittington

The principle of client self-determination has been accorded a special place in nearly every consideration of the values underlying social casework practice. Various writers in their attempt to give the concept practical application have chosen alternative terminology, namely, client self-direction, and client self-responsibility, yet the subject remains controversial. Why should this be? The reason seems to lie in the fact that the gulf between the theoretical definitions and their application in practice is often wide, and rife with inconsistencies. My aim is to show that the concept has so many limitations that a serious re-examination of its position in professional social work ideology is essential.

Biestek defines the principle of client self-determination as 'the practical recognition of the right and need of clients to freedom in making their own choices and decisions in the casework process' [see p.19 above].[1] One activity which he considers to be at variance with the principle is that of manipulation, by which he means the manoeuvering of the client 'to choose or decide modes of action in accordance with the caseworker's judgement in such a way that the client is unaware of the process; or if he is aware of it, he feels "moved about" against his will' [see p. 22 above].[2]

Florence Hollis, to whose work on casework theory I shall make special reference, prefers the term 'self-direction' which, she says, denotes not the absolute independence implied by self-determination but rather 'the capacity to guide oneself through the maze of interactions that make up the pattern of life. This is the capacity that the worker seeks to enable the client to increase.' Hollis qualifies, as do most other writers, that self-determination is a

*This article is an abridged version of the extended essay submitted for the Certificate in Social Work. Reprinted with modifications from the *British Journal of Social Work*, vol. 1, no. 3, pp. 293-303, by permission of the author and the editor.

relative, not an absolute value: 'If the client is endangering others or himself, it must be superseded by another, namely, the worker's responsibility to prevent suffering.'[3] The basis of her view is in keeping with that of other writers and is concerned with the client's right to make his own choices. Except in extreme situations this right to self-direction should not be interfered with by the caseworker.[4]

This emphasis on self-determination—implying the converse of a purely deterministic position—has long been a basic tenet of social work philosophy, and though it has been adopted by the British social work profession its development has been most notable in the American social work scene, as has most casework theory.

Hollis sees casework historically as representing a turning away from *laissez-faire* doctrines. 'From its inception it has stressed the value of the individual and for the past thirty years, at least, has been quite outspoken about the right of each man to live in his own unique way, provided he does not infringe upon the rights of others. This emphasis on the innate worth of the individual is an extremely important, fundamental characteristic of casework.' From it, says Hollis, grows an essential feature of the caseworker's attitude towards his client: the belief in self-determination.[5]

Just as casework, in Hollis's view, embodies a rejection of certain nineteenth-century doctrines, it might be suggested that self-determination constitutes, in part, a rejection of previous attitudes or methods in social work itself. In fact, in 'Ego-Orientated Casework', she comments that, although distortions lie in the popular image of the early caseworker as an interfering, authoritarian do-gooder imposing her own rigid, moralistic, upper-middle class ways of life on the client, the image has its elements of truth.[6] What, though, effected the swing from the more directive techniques of the early worker towards the relatively permissive methods which are valued today? Consideration of the influence of psychoanalysis on casework proves illuminating here, since the work of Freud and his followers has provided a dominant frame of reference for casework.

Beginning with Freud's substitution of free association for hypnosis, the prevailing trend in writings on psychotherapy has emphasized the desirability of therapists using more indirect methods of influences. Treatment goals are expressed in terms of the patient being helped towards greater self-actualization, spontaneity, maturity, creativity and so on. The therapist facilitates the patient's 'movements' by empathizing with him, accepting him, collaborating with him, respecting him, and being permissive. Persuasion and advice are to be kept to a minimum since they impede the patient's growth towards emotional maturity.[7]

This trend from directive techniques in psychotherapy and the parallel one in casework may spring partly from democratic values which place a higher worth on self-directed, spontaneous behaviour than on that obviously cause by outside influence. For psychotherapy the swing also derived in part from experience that many 'cures' achieved through directive methods proved transitory.[8] This example was followed by caseworkers and the principle of client self-determination, developing out of democratic values and clinical experience, took form, both as an ideal and as a therapeutic technique. The importance of recognizing these two aspects of the principle will be seen later. I shall now consider its application in practice

Many caseworkers have, in the past, been so intrigued by the methods and orientation of their profession that they have over-looked the social dimensions of social work. Individual dynamics are so intricate that there was the temptation to regard them as all of significant reality.[9] It required a sociological view of social work to point this out.

It is a now familiar notion that social work can be seen sociologically as one of the methods used by society to secure conformity to its expectations by individuals and groups. This control may be coercive or persuasive, or a combination of both depending on the statutory powers of the agency.[10] Probation agencies and social workers functioning within child care legislation spring most readily to mind here because of the legally authorized powers they carry.

The powers which social workers have over clients and the limitations on self-determination in cases of delinquency, truancy, neglect or cruelty are obvious. If the child or parents do not change, serious sanctions may follow. But, as an article in *New Society* by Handler[11] showed, the former child care officer's coercive potential is not limited to such cases.

The 1963 Children and Young Persons Act for example, gave children's departments the authority to pay rent arrears or make other arrangements with housing authorities to prevent evictions. For some families who are behind with payment of an electricity or gas bill, the local authority social worker may be the only person who can prevent the service being cut off; either by his negotiating with the utility board for them to delay any action, or by his helping towards the bill.

Handler found in his study of three London boroughs that these powers were indeed used to coerce change. 'Officers have let electricity remain off for considerable periods (but only in the summer) in order to induce more co-operative efforts . . .' in budgeting. 'There are', he writes 'cases where departments have let families get evicted and rehoused in welfare accommodation to induce them to view their situations more "realistically"; all part of a therapy plan.'

Certainly such actions arose in some instances from agency policy of avoiding paying bills outright or immediately, and from concern about paying out money for potentially recurring items. Nevertheless, we must acknowledge from Handler's findings significant limitations to client self-determination in these areas of practice which derive, ironically, from a section of an Act hailed as sanctioning the provision of a casework service.

Turning to our second example it is my impression that probation officers have been amongst the most self-questioning of the social work profession in appraising their role in relation to client self-determination. This, of course, has been due largely to the fact that the elements of enforcement in many of their relationships with clients is undeniable. In recent years, writers have tended to concentrate more on the positive features of the enforced relationship, than on searching for aspects of that relationship which could be labelled as examples of client self-determination. Even so, the desire to find a rationale for their work, and one that is closely aligned to the methods and theories of other caseworkers must have been intensified by writers like Eshelby who comments that the probation officer's attempts to discipline his clients 'may put him outside the fold of caseworkers'.[12]

The much-needed rationale—and a highly respectable one in terms of psychoanalytically orientated casework—is to be found in theories which teach that the delinquent's offence represents an unconscious search for someone who will become a respected and controlling authority because he has been deprived of this in his family relationships. Clare Winnicott puts forward this concept and reinforces the likelihood of its acceptance by exhorting the probation officer not to miss the point of the 'symptom' (the offence), for if he does 'the client either gives up hope or commits another offence to ensure the re-instatement of legal machinery'.[13]

This view seems to remove the probation caseworker from his dilemma of reconciling the enforced relationship with self-determination, since it suggests that the client is demanding his self-determination be significantly restricted. However, a wide variety of individuals find themselves on probation and other theories of delinquency suggest different, but equally convincing, causative factors. It is likely, therefore, that a number of probationers are in their situation for other than unconscious needs, at least of the kind Winnicott suggests. The aim with these, and it may be said with all probationers, is at the least to prevent them coming back into conflict with the law. This is the agency's function; to control behaviour.

This is not to suggest social workers take over complete control of client's lives. The point is rather that significant areas of decision and choice are interfered with. In the areas of social work described so far, self-determination is restricted by the agency's or the worker's view of certain of the client's choices as 'unrealistic'. If he does not accept this then coercive force may be needed. This also applies to the statutory function of the Mental Welfare Officer, though a medical opinion will necessarily be involved with reference to what is 'realistic'. The limitations on client self-determination in compulsory admissions to hospital are self-evident.

'The function of using coercive force to compel submission to authority' Biestek tell us in his chapter on self-determination, 'is avoided by caseworkers and delegated to licensed public servants' [see p. 28 above].[14] This must inevitably pose problems for the three areas of social work mentioned so far, since in each the worker is both a caseworker and a licensed public servant with legal coercive powers. That other social workers, even without statutory powers, potentially exert strong influence on their clients will be seen later.

There are probably instances in most agencies where the setting or structure exerts limits on client's self-determination. In social work in the psychiatric hospital for example it is my impression that the worker's non-directive role may be negatively affected by his minority position in the institutional structure. Working alongside doctors and nurses who tend, because of their training and the expectations of patients, to have a more authority-based role, the worker who 'goes at the client's pace', and attempts to extend to the client the opportunity for self-determination may come to be termed, detrimentally, as 'permissive' or 'soft', by the other staff. His difference in approach to clients/patients may make both sides feel that the worker is out of step with the team and begin to alienate him from them.

In most instances the medical staff have the ultimate authority in the staff hierarchy and the social worker is dependent on them for referrals. In order to perform his function then, he may have to get back in step with the team, and this may involve his taking on a more directive role. Additionally, the patient's length of stay may not be influenced so much by the amount of time the worker feels is necessary to deal non-directively with the patient's and relatives' problems, as by the doctors' assessment of the patient's condition balanced against the demand for beds. Thus, pressure of time and uncertainty of length of stay may, in an obvious or subtle way, diminish the worker's tendency and opportunity to offer self-determination.

This latter situation may also arise in the general hospital where the medical staff's concern with the physiological often leaves them little room for awareness of emotional and social needs. Furthermore Beatrice Wright makes the point in reference to rehabilitation that 'involving the client in a comanagement role takes more time than having the specialist accumulate the data and present the prescription. One can retort that time is saved in the end, but the immediate pressures in the light of severe personnel shortage and staggering numbers of clients in need make expedient the authoritarian role of the expert.'[15]

This observation, though running in direct contrast to the ideals of casework theory (e.g. Perlman writes 'the casework process . . . includes . . . always . . . the fullest involvement and participation of the person himself')[16] would probably reflect, in varying degrees, the situation of not only many doctors and hospital social workers but that of workers in statutory agencies all over the country. They, unlike the private psychiatric clinics and private agencies of America in which much of casework theory originated, are frequently in no position to gear caseloads to the number of workers available.

The limitations on client self-determination which result from agency function, the worker's power over clients, the setting of the agency and the realities of time, pressure and high caseloads have been mentioned; and it has been shown that limitations are not exclusive to legally specific coercive functions. It is necessary now to look more closely at the relationship between worker and client, and the application from theory to practice therein.

A question which is fundamental to casework practice and to the principle of client self-determination is: is there not an inconsistency in believing so firmly in the client's right to self-determination on the one hand, and having in one's mind on the other hand treatment goals towards which one is trying to move him, although he may not himself even know what these goals are?

Florence Hollis[17] faces this question and begins to answer it by giving a case example which illustrates the formulation of treatment goals of which the client is unaware. She tells us of a wife who comes to an agency complaining about her husband. Listening to her the worker begins to form the opinion that a large part of the conflict in the marriage is the result of the wife's responses which have their foundation in her childhood relationship with her mother. Hollis discusses potential treatment goals and amongst other things emphasizes that the movement to these goals will be dependent on the client's 'willingness to seek understanding'. The case example then continues by showing how later, throughout a skilful treatment process, the client was 'helped' to an 'understanding' and modification of her responses (the treatment goals), so that a substantial change in their whole relationship' (which at the outset of treatment contained sufficient conflict to bring the case to the agency) 'took place'.

Thus far the question regarding the incompatibility of the 'undeclared goals' and self-determination has not been answered, but what Hollis has shown is that treatment goals of which the client is not aware can be justified if, within the caseworker's value system, the client has benefited by the achievement of these goals. That many readers will have just such a value system may in itself dull their critical evaluation of the sincere but, I think, unconvincing argument which follows.

Hollis writes, 'a dual responsibiltiy is involved for the worker. [i]* He must offer the highest level of assistance which he is equipped to give and which he believes the client may be able to use, and he must exercise his highest skill in overcoming the client's resistance to using this degree of help, but at the same time he must refrain from coercive methods and [ii] must at all times be willing to offer help of a more limited type if this is what the client ultimately wants and can use.'

Leaving aside discussion of 'coercive methods'—they are not relevant to the particular question which Hollis seeks to answer—it is part (ii) which contains the significant concessions to client self-

*[i] and [ii] do not appear in the original text and have been added here for clarity.

determination. But what does closer examination reveal? First, that the implications of (ii) are always borne in mind by the worker does not alter the fact that in the example given, and in many other cases, it was not necessary to implement them. What actually happened was that the worker skilfully directed the client towards the goals he had formulated.

Secondly, since the worker decided on the treatment goals according to his assessment of the help the client 'may be able to use', it seems that the only way she (the client) could, thereafter, affect these goals would be either to display—in the worker's assessment—less capacity to achieve and use understanding than that which is required for the achievement of the goals; or to show resistance greater than the worker has skill to overcome. If we remember that the client is unaware of the goals the worker has for her, and is therefore not aware of her influence on them, we can hardly say that, in this context, she is exercising self-determination.

Thirdly, *who* decides when the 'client's resistance' is no longer seen as something which the worker must 'overcome', and becomes merely an indication that she (the client) cannot use the 'degree of help' being offered?—the client? And where does the worker delineate between 'what the client ultimately wants', and what she 'can use . . .'? Surely, if the worker 'believes' that the client can ultimately use what is being offered, he is likely to see her wanting help of 'a more limited type' as 'resistance' which he 'must exercise his highest skill in overcoming . . .'!

Where then is the compatibility between the 'undeclared goals' and the belief in the client's right to self-determination? Hollis, as I said earlier, shows that treatment goals of which the client is not aware can be justified if, within the worker's value system, the client has benefited (or has the opportunity to benefit) by the achievement of these goals. But we should not confuse justification with compatibility.

The reason Hollis, such an eminent writer, has been inspired to such theoretical exercises seems to lie in the problem of reconciling client self-determination, the democratic ideal, with certain therapeutic methods. The problem becomes even more complicated when one attempts to to reconcile client self-determination, as a democratic ideal, with certain aspects of client self-determination, as a therapeutic technique. For instance, as a therapeutic technique it promotes the desirability for the client to be an active participant in the treatment process. One of the reasons for encouraging such an attitude is that it forestalls or combats the client's tendency to become dependent on the worker. It also has other possible and therapeutically desirable results which may heighten the worker's influence in at least two ways. The more the client's active participation can be obtained, the more he commits himself to the 'movement' which the worker is trying to induce. Furthermore, the client has greater difficulty in mobilising his resistance against a collaborative than a directive worker.

It can hardly be maintained that these effects are not desired by the worker, or even that they can be avoided in so-called non-directive therapy. However, they heighten the worker's influence; and a person's freedom to choose in a relationship with another must be interfered with by the other's influence on him. It seems, then, that client self-determination not only conflicts with certain basic casework methods, but also that two basic aspects of the principle can come into direct conflict. But there are still further limitations to the principle as the following observations will show.

Peter Leonard[18] comments that work on psychological reinforcement 'provides a good deal of evidence that the social worker reinforces by verbal or non-verbal communication ("grunting techniques") certain kinds of disclosures in an interview and inhibits others. This inhibition and reinforcement of behavioural responses' he writes, 'is clearly a subtle form of control'. Similarly, the work of Hildum and Brown on the influence of the comments of 'Mm-hmm' and of 'good' on the responses of interviewees found them powerfully reinforcing.[19] This reinforcement is aided by the perceived authority of the worker, and contrary to the view that was once held, it has been noted in recent years that all social workers use authority in some way or another.[20]

Further evidence of the directiveness of non-directive therapy is referred to in a paper by Jerome Frank.[21] He writes of a content analysis of a case, 'Herbert Bryan'. In this case, statements in categories disapproved by the therapist fell from 45 per cent of the total number of statements in the second hour to 5 per cent in the eighth. Statements in approved categories rose from 1 per cent in the second hour to 45 per cent in the seventh.

As Frank points out, the case of Herbert Bryan has particular interest because it was offered as an example of non-directive therapy. The therapist presumably believed that he was not influencing the patient's productions, yet different rates were able to classify his intervention as implicitly approving or disapproving with a high degree of reliability. Apparently a therapist can strongly affect his client's productions without being aware he is doing so.

One might conclude, then, that the evolvement of a principle which may have eliminated the crudely directive approach of the 'early caseworker' has not excluded reinforcement which may influence the client's productions in the direction expected or desired by the worker.

Underlying the client's susceptibility to the worker's influence must often be his motivation to win the worker's approval. One of the most likely sources of this motivation would appear to be the client's expectation that the worker will relieve his distress. Thus Hollis writes: 'The ideal therapeutic situation is one in which the client is anxious enough to want help and to keep coming for it . . .'.[22] The caseworker, therefore, though he may profess commitment to client self-determination, non-directiveness and the client's freedom to choose, finds his therapeutic aims greatly aided by the client's susceptibility to his influence and subtle directiveness.

As caseworkers we aim to accept the client, do not react sharply to his attempts to reject us, rarely overtly direct his actions and choices, understand and empathise with him, communicate our perception of his worth, and attempt to convey that we are not judging him. In short we attempt to offer him a relationship of a type he may rarely encounter, and one in which he feels the focus of concern and attention is on him. Our aim is to make the relationship, and therefore ourselves, important to the client—even though we may successfully convey that we are professionals, representatives of an agency—for the relationship is basic to all casework treatment. The more successful we are the more susceptible to our influence the client is likely to become, and therefore the more effective our communication, verbal and non-verbal, reinforcing and inhibiting, will also become. Hollis observes that the client makes the goals we have for him his own 'only to the extent that he is willing to accord us a place of influence in his life'.[23] The professional caseworker attempts not to leave this to chance. He does not adopt a 'take it or leave it' attitude. Embodied in his approach, in his attitude to the client, in the relationship he offers is the aim to increase the client's willingness to accord him a place of influence in his life.

These views may be distasteful to some caseworkers for they cast doubt on the concept of the democratic ideal, on our ability to extend to the client the right to freedom in making his own choices and decisions in the casework process. They run in direct contrast to

Hollis's view that 'except for procedures of intervention' (e.g. removing a child from cruel or highly neglectful parents, or compulsorily admitting a psychotic client to hospital) 'we do not influence the client without his assent'.[24] How does the client give his assent to being influenced—by his request for help? That would be assent to being helped. Surely it is the worker who, attempting to reconcile the democratic ideal of client self-determination with the realities of some casework methods and techniques, and the dynamics of the casework relationship, manages by a legerdemain chain of logic, to convince himself that a client is actually assenting to these things when in fact he (the client) may not be in possession of the necessary information from which to make a choice. Being helped in the casework process necessarily and unavoidably means being influenced and, as Halmos comments: 'Unless we mean therapy to be therapeutic and, therefore, determining and directing in important ways, we can hardly expect to be helpful'.[25]

It is sometimes argued that the limitations to client self-determination in practice result only from factors like agency function or limited finances which are outside the worker's immediate control. However, even if caseworkers were not given the statutory function and powers of controlling behaviour and inducing clients to make different choices; were allowed limitless financial and material resources for their work; were not subject to the pressures of working in a minority position alongside others from different disciplines, and could be freed of the problems of time, pressure, and high caseloads, the principle would not be without severe restrictions. The elimination of all these aspects, foreseeably impossible, would not rule out the limitations inherent in the treatment relationship itself.

To increase the client's capacity to evaluate choices may be a goal of treatment, and participation may be a technique used to this end, but to maintain that treatment is carried out without directiveness because the latter's skilled and subtle nature has made it less easy to observe, requires nothing short of self-deception. Whilst we continue to profess belief, sincere as it may be, in the practicability of a principle which, remaining unmodified, is irreconcilable with so many fundamentals of casework therapy and the realities of most casework practice it would seem difficult for us to justify our claims to self-scrutiny. If this situation persists, it is my opinion that we will be unable to reach a realistic appraisal of our role and aims in relation to our clients and society.

Notes

1 F. P. Biestek. *The Casework Relationship*, Allen & Unwin, London, 1961, ch. 6, p. 103.

2 *Ibid.*, p. 107.

3 F. Hollis, *Casework: A Psychosocial Therapy*, Random House, New York, 1964, ch. 5, p. 95.

4 F. Hollis, Principles and assumptions underlying casework practice', *Social Work* (London) 1955, 12, pp. 41-5.

5 F. Hollis, *Casework: A Psychosocial Therapy*, Random House, New York, 1964, p. 12.

6 F. Hollis, *Ego-Orientated Casework* (ed. H. Parad), F.S.A.A., 1963, ch.1.

7 Jerome Frank, 'The Dynamics of the Psychotherapeutic Relationship', in J. Scheff (ed.), *Mental Illness and Social Processes*, Harper & Row, New York, 1967, pt. 3, pp. 168-206.

8 *Ibid.*

9 S. Bernstein, 'Self-determination: king or citizen in the realm of values?', *Social Work* (U.S.A.), vol. 5, no. 11 (January 1960), [reprinted above, pp. 33-42].

10 P. Leonard, 'Social control and class vaues in social work practice', *Social Work* (U.K.), vol. 22, no. 4, October 1965.

11 J. F. Handler, 'The coercive children's officer', *New Society*, 3 October 1968, pp. 485-7.

12 S. R. Eshelby, 'The probation officer as a caseworker', *Brit. J. Psychiatric Social Work*, vol. 6, no. 3, 1962.

13 C. Winnicott, 'Casework and agency function', *Case Conference*, vol. 8, no. 7, 1962, pp. 178-84.

14 F. P. Biestek, *op. cit.*, p. 114.

15 B. A. Wright, *Physical Disability—A Psychological Approach*, Harper & Row, New York, 1960, p. 363.

16 H. H. Perlman, *Social Casework: A Problem-Solving Process*, University of Chicago Press, 1957, p. 60.

17 F. Hollis, 'Principles and assumptions underlying casework practice', *Social Work* (London), 1955, 12, pp. 41-5.

18 P. Leonard, *op. cit.*

19 Study by D. C. Hildum and R. W. Brown (1956) referred to in P. Halmos, *Faith of the Counsellors*, Constable, London, 1965, ch. 3, p. 91.

20 For discussion of social workers and authority see: E. Studt, 'Worker-client authority relationships in social work', in E. Younghusband (ed.), *New Developments in Casework*, Allen & Unwin, London, 1966, ch. 12; and Robert Foren and Royston Bailey, *Authority in Social Casework*, Pergamon Press, Oxford, 1968.

21 J. Frank, *op. cit.*, p. 187.

22 F. Hollis, *Casework: A Psychosocial Therapy*, Random House, New York, 1964, p. 209.

23 *Ibid.*, p. 95.

24 *Ibid.*

25 P. Halmos, *op. cit.*, p. 92.

7 Determinism and the principle of client self-determination

R. F. Stalley

I The apparent conflict between determinism and self-determination

A number of writers on the theory of social casework have felt that there is a conflict between the principle of client self-determination and the determinism which seems to be required by a scientific attitude towards man. Thus, in discussing the implications for casework practice of the assumption that human behaviour is governed by psychological or social laws, Florence Hollis writes:[1]

> The first question to be raised about these scientific principles is often the philosophical one of whether the assumption of lawfulness in behaviour and of cause and effect relationships in behaviour does not mean that casework has become completely deterministic. How can this be reconciled with the principle of self-determination?

I wish to consider this problem in the light of recent philosophical discussions of determinism. In particular there are two main questions which I wish to ask: first, 'Is the principle of client self-determination really incompatible with determinism?'; and second, 'If the principle is not compatible with determinsm, can it be reconciled with any form of indeterminism which a reasonable man could adopt in the light of present knowledge?'

In discussing these topics the first need is to define 'determinism' and this is surprisingly difficult. According to one version determinism is the doctrine that all events, including human actions, are governed by causal laws, but before we can accept this version we need to know more about what is meant when it is said that an event is governed by causal laws. Appeal is often made here to the notion of predictability. To say that an event was governed by causal laws is to say that it was in principle predictable by means of those laws. Thus determinism becomes the doctrine that all events, including all human actions, are in principle predictable. In other words, any event including any human action could in theory have been predicted by an intelligence which had a sufficient knowledge of the laws of the universe together with a sufficient knowledge of the previous states of the universe to enable him to use those laws to make predictions. Something like this is what is generally understood by philosophers as the doctrine of determinism, but we have to recognise that even this version contains a number of difficulties. Indeed some philosophers have felt that the difficulties in understanding what is meant by determinism are so great that we cannot at present usefully discuss whether the doctrine is true or false because we do not know exactly what it is. However I shall ignore these difficulties and assume that the formulation which I have just quoted is clear enough for our present purposes.[2]

It is important to remember that there are different kinds of sciences with different kinds of laws. For example psychologists may claim to describe laws which govern human behaviour. So one thing which a person who said that human actions were determined might mean is that, if we had a sufficient knowledge of the laws of psychology together with a sufficient knowledge of an individual's personality, we would be able to predict with certainty what he would do in any given situation. A doctrine of this kind is often known as *psychological determinism*. But it may also be claimed that human beings are a kind of physical object and are ultimately composed of atomic particles. The science which is concerned with the behaviour of such particles is physics. So another kind of determinism would consist in saying that if we had a sufficient knowledge of the laws of physics together with a sufficient knowledge of the physical state of an individual's body and nervous system we would be able to predict exactly what he would do in any given situation. This doctrine is called *physical determinism*. It is clear that it is quite possible to accept both forms of determinism at the same time. Indeed many psychologists hold that human actions are determined in accordance with psychological laws and believe that psychological laws are ultimately reducible to physical laws, so their belief in psychological determinism rests on a belief in physical determinism. On the other hand it is quite possible to accept one of these forms of determinsim without accepting the other. In particular many philosophers accept physical determinism but reject psychological determinism. They believe that the laws of psychology could never be made precise enough to admit exact predictions of human action but that the laws of physics could in theory permit such predictions.

The reason why it has often been felt that the acceptance of the principle of client self-determination cannot be reconciled with a belief in determinism is that determinism appears to imply that human acts cannot be free. According to the doctrine of determinism everything we do is determined by what has happened previously and so all our actions could ultimately be traced back to features of our environment or heredity. Thus it might be said that if determinism is true all our acts are brought about by events over which we have no control. This might seem to imply that none of our acts is genuinely free. But the principle of client self-determination rests on the assumption that at least some human acts are free, for it requires the caseworker to respect the client's freedom to choose his own course of action and this would be nonsense if the client could have no such freedom. Thus if the acceptance of a doctrine of determinism led us to abandon our belief in human freedom it would appear that we would also have to abandon the principle of client self-determination. But this would not be the only consequence of the loss of our belief in human freedom. Many of the attitudes which we adopt in everyday life also depend on the assumption that human beings can be free. In particular we do not normally hold people morally or legally responsible for their actions unless we believe that they acted freely. Thus if we came to believe that human beings are never free we would have to abandon all our notions of moral and legal responsibility. So there is a difficulty about reconciling ordinary ideas of human responsibility with determinism which is very similar to the difficulty of reconciling the principle of client self-determination with determinism. Professional philosophers have not said very much about the problem of self-determination and determinism, but they have said a great deal about the problem of moral responsibility and determinism. It may therefore be helpful to consider some of the solutions which have been offered to this latter problem in order to see whether any of the ideas involved in them may be applied to the principle of client self-determination.

Determinism and moral responsibility[3]

Many philosophers have tried to show that a belief in determinism can be reconciled with the acceptance of ordinary notions of moral responsibility. One way in which they have tried to do this is by insisting that for an action to be free, in the sense in which freedom is required for moral responsibility, it does not have to be uncaused or unpredictable. According to these philosophers, when we say that an action is free we normally mean that the agent was not subject to certain kinds of constraint, usually external constraints. Thus the sort of thing we mean when we say that somebody acted freely is that he was not acting as a result of physical coercion by another person, that he was not acting under a threat, or that he was not suffering from some psychological compulsion. This list is not complete but it should give some idea of the sort of consideration which would normally lead us to say that someone had not acted freely. It should also be clear that if we say that a person was not subject to constraints of this kind, we are not thereby committed to saying that his action was uncaused or undetermined. My act of drinking coffee rather than tea this morning was free in the sense that no one physically compelled me to drink coffee, no one threatened me with dire consequences if I failed to drink it and so on, but this does not necessarily mean that it was not caused by features of my environment or heredity or that it could not have been predicted by a being with sufficient knowledge of the state of my nervous system. So it may well be said that there is a sense in which my act was certainly free and yet at the same time my act may have been determined.

A similar point has sometimes been put in a slightly different way. For someone to be held morally responsible for his act, he must, it is said, have been free in the sense that he could have done otherwise. But 'he could have done otherwise' does not mean that his action was not causally determined. It means that he could have done otherwise if he had chosen. In saying that someone could have done otherwise if he had chosen we are not implying that he could have chosen otherwise. His choice may itself be causally determined, and if the choice was determined the action must also have been determined. Thus in saying that a person's act was free in the sense required for moral responsibility we are not suggesting that it was not causally determined but that it was one of those actions which would be regarded as stemming from his choice. Since we normally regard an action as having been chosen unless the agent was subject to some kind of constraint this doctrine is in practice very similar to the one I have just described.

It is possible in this sort of way to show that there is a sense of 'free' in which a human action can be both free and determined, but it still has to be shown that this gives us what is required in order to preserve ordinary concepts of moral responsibility. To hold a person responsible for something which he has done is to say that it would be inappropriate to praise, blame, punish or reward him for it. If all actions are ultimately caused by circumstances which the agent cannot control, why should we be prepared to hold people responsible for those acts which we regard as unconstrained but not for those which we call constrained? Both kinds of act are equally the product of forces beyond our own control. The usual way in which this question has been answered is by saying that the point of praising or rewarding someone is to encourage him and other people to do the same sort of thing in future and that the point of blaming him or punishing him is to discourage him and other people from doing the same sort of thing in future. It can then be claimed that the reason why we do not hold a person responsible for acts done under constraint is that such acts are not of a kind which could be influenced by the promise of praise or reward and the threat of blame or punishment. If, for example, I am physically compelled to act no prospects of praise or blame, reward or punishment will influence what I do. Such measures would be inappropriate in these circumstances because they would be pointless, and that is why those who act in these circumstances are not regarded as responsible for their actions. Thus, it is claimed, a concept of moral reponsibility is compatible with determinism.

Many competent philosophers have felt that this is sufficient to show that a belief in universal causal determinism would not requ ire the abandonment of ordinary concepts of moral responsibility. However it is not clear that the problem has been solved because it is not obvious that the concept of moral responsiblity which has been shown to be compatible with determinism is the same concept as the one which is generally accepted in our society. In particular it is customary nowadays to allow that a person's responsibility may be diminished by factors such as a particularly difficult environment in early life or provocation. We may, for example, regard a person who has been deprived of affection in early life as being somehow less responsible for his crimes than someone who has had a normal upbringing. It would be natural to suppose that the reason why we do this is that we know that a bad environment can cause crime and that we make a distinction between the two cases because we believe that in the one case there is a causal explanation of the crime whereas in the other case there is none. This would clearly be absurd if we believed that all acts were determined, for the acts of those who are brought up in good environments would be just as much causally determined as the acts of those who are brought up in bad environments. It is true that we know more about the ways in which bad environments cause crimes than we do about the ways in which good environments cause crimes but this gives us no good reason for making a distinction between the two cases. Neither can we justify the distinction by saying that punishment would not be effective in the case of the person with the bad early environment, for it seems fairly clear that punishment can be effective in these circumstances. Indeed it might well be argued that more severe punishments are needed in order to outweigh the effects of the bad environment and this would produce a view of responsibility which is the precise opposite of that held by a sophisticated modern moralist. Thus although it may well be true that *a* concept of moral responsibility is compatible with determinism, it is by no means clear that this is the same concept as that which is generally held today. This does not, of course, prove that determinism is false, it may well be that the concepts of moral responsibility in question are muddled.

An attempt to reconcile determinism and self-determination

It is clear that one could put forward an argument to show that the principle of client self-determination was compatible with determinism which would be analogous in many ways to the argument which I have just set out purporting to show that moral responsibility is compatible with determinism. One could begin by conceding that the principle requires the caseworker to respect the client's freedom and that this would be nonsense if human beings could not be free, but one could go on to argue that when we say that the client is free we do not mean that his actions are not causually determined, but merely that he is not subject to constraints. So when we say that the caseworker should respect the client's freedom we mean merely that he should not try to affect the client's behaviour in coercive or quasi-coercive ways, or in other words he should try to avoid imposing constraints upon the client. Clearly this in no sense implies that the client's behaviour is or could be undetermined, for an act can be free in the sense of 'unconstrained' even though it is fully determined. There is, thus, a sense in which even a caseworker who believes that all human actions are totally determined by environmental factors, can still treat his client as a free being. He does this so long as he refrains from influencing the client's behaviour in a controlling or constraining manner.

At this point the question might be raised, 'Why should the caseworker refrain from exercising control over his client?' 'After all', it might be argued, 'if determinism is true the client's behaviour is going to be determined by causes outside his control whatever happens. If the caseworker does not exercise control then the client's decision will probably be determined by chance features of his environment. The caseworker is simply another object in the client's environment, but he differs from other objects in the environment in that he understands the client's problems and is trying to help him. Very often the caseworker will have a very good idea of what is best for the client. Surely then it it better that the client's behaviour should be determined by the controlling influence of the caseworker than by some quite accidental combination of circumstances in his environment.' In this way it might be argued that the principle of client self-determination has no rational basis. It requires that one particular kind of environmental circumstance, namely the controlling influence of the caseworker, should not be allowed to determine the client's action and in doing so leaves the way open for the client's action to be determined by other kinds of environmental cause. What is more, the kind of environmental influence which is ruled out is one that might be expected to have a good effect on the client's behaviour. Thus in a deterministic universe the principle of client self-determination may appear to be simply unreasonable.

It is possible to think of a number of answers to this kind of argument. Even in a deterministic universe there may still be reasons why the caseworker should refrain from exercising a controlling influence over his clients. To begin with it is clear that if the client believes that decisions about his life have been taken out of his hands he may well have feelings of resentment or hostility about it. These feelings may aggravate his problems and they will certainly damage his relationship with the caseworker. Thus it may well be wise to adhere to the principle of client self-determination in order to avoid creating such feelings. Putting the matter more crudely we could say that, even if the client's actions are in fact causally determined, he nevertheless likes to feel that he is free and the caseworker does well to take account of these feelings. Again one of the aims of casework is precisely to equip the client to live without the aid of the caseworker. He has to be helped to manage on his own. But if the caseworker takes the client's decisions for him this is unlikely to happen. So another reason for adhering to the principle of client self-determination is that if the caseworker takes too much responsiblity upon himself he will be making the client more dependent upon him rather than equipping him for living on his own. Lastly we should be wary of the assumption that the caseworker necessarily knows best. The client may be aware of features of his situation which he is unable or unwilling to tell the caseworker about, and it is even conceivable that he may be more intelligent than the caseworker. One cannot therefore assume that a decision taken by the caseworker will necessarily be better than one taken by the client. We could sum up these points by saying that the casework process will in general be more effective if the worker refrains from exercising a controlling influence over his clients. If we assume that the aim of casework is to make the client a happier and better adjusted human being then we can say that these goals are more likely to be achieved by treating him as self determining than by attempting to control his behaviour.

Difficulties in the attempted reconciliation

These arguments show, I think, that it is possible to produce some sort of an answer to those who say that the principle of client self-determination is incompatible with a doctrine of determinism. We can do this by arguing: (a) that the principle does not require that human acts be free in the sense of undetermined but merely requires caseworkers to treat their clients as free agents in the sense of not exercising control over them; and (b) that there are good practical reasons why, even in a deterministic universe, caseworkers should not attempt to control their client's behaviour. In this way it is clear that a principle of client self-determination can be reconciled with determinism, but it is by no means clear that this is precisely the same principle as that which is advocated by leading casework theorists. In particular there seem to me to be two important points which indicate that it is really a very different principle.

1. The interpretation we have just given to the principle makes it encourage caseworkers to treat their clients as self-determining because this is seen as a means to the more effective pursuit of other casework goals. The caseworker should in general refrain from exercising a controlling influence over his client's behaviour because as a matter of fact this normally hinders rather than helps the achievement of the aims of casework. In other words self-determination, according to this interpretation, is valued purely as a means

and not as an end in itself. But it is clear that many of the leading casework theorists see self-determination as being valuable as an end and not simply as a means. Self-determination is seen as a right of the client which must be respected unless there are overwhelming reasons against doing so. For example Felix Biestek writes: 'The principle of client self-determination is the practical recognition of the right and need of clients to freedom in making their own choices and decisions in the casework process' [see p. 19 above].[4] It is not, it appears, simply a technique which caseworkers have found useful. Again some writers obviously see the principle as in some way determining the goals of casework. One of the aims of the caseworker is precisely to increase the client's capacity for self-direction and the principle of client self-determination is seen as a recognition of this aim. So Biestek goes on to insist that caseworkers have a duty 'to stimulate and help to activate that potential for self-direction by helping the client to see and use the available and appropriate resources of the community and of his own personality' [see p. 19 above].[5] Thus it appears that self-determination is not valued simply because it makes casework effective. Rather casework is judged to be effective to the degree that it promotes self-determination.

The same sort of attitude is found in the writings of other casework theorists. Thus, in *Casework: A Psychosocial Therapy,*[6] Florence Hollis makes it clear that she sees the principle of client self-determination as a 'primary value' of casework. 'What we really mean by this concept', she writes, 'is that self direction, the right to make his own choices, is a highly valued attribute of the individual. The more he can make his own decisions and direct his own life the better, and the less the caseworker tries to take over these responsibilities the better.' By this she does not mean that self-direction overrides all other considerations. She allows that 'in extreme situations, where there is a danger of real harm to others or to the client himself, or where the client is incapable of carrying this responsibility, the caseworker must take over and make decisions for him. But he does so only where the necessity for such action is clear',[7] This does not of course mean that self-direction is not ultimately valued for its own sake. Indeed it indicates the very opposite, for if self-direction were not valued for its own sake it would not be only in extreme cases that it could be set aside. If self-direction was valued simply as a means to other casework goals it could be set aside whenever the caseworker considered that those goals were likely to be achieved without it. So for Hollis the principle of client self-determination sets out one of the ends of casework and she expects that the methods of casework will be related to that end.

Similary Harris Perlman describes the main point of her paper 'Self-determination: reality or illusion?'[8] in the following terms [see p. 70 above]:

> It is the thesis of this paper that self-determination, even though it may be more illusory than real, is the very essence of mature humanness; that man's exercise of choice rather than his coercion by his own blind impulses or the power of others is what builds in him his sense of effectiveness, of identity and selfhood, and of responsibility.

None of these authors draws a very clear distinction between saying, on the one hand, that client self-determination is valued as a means to other casework goals and, on the other hand, that it is valued as good in itself. Nevertheless their general position is fairly clear. They value the principle partly because it is a means of achieving beneficial results such as the reduction of the client's fears and timidities, but chiefly because self-direction is something which is valued for its own sake. The development of the client's capacity to make his own decisions, the encouragement of what Hollis calls 'the growth that comes from within' is itself a fundamental aim of casework. Indeed both Hollis and Perlman seem to be committing themselves to a view very similar to that known in some philosophical circles as the doctrine of respect for persons, a doctrine which states that the idea of the individual person as of supreme worth is of fundamental importance to our morality, and claims that what is valuable about persons is precisely their capacity for self-determination. Thus I do not think that either of these authors could be happy with the sort of account of the principle of client self-determination which I offered to the determinist, for that account treated self-determination purely as a means to an independent end.

2. I argued that one could say that a human act was self-determined and also determined by environmental or genetic factors, if by 'self-determined' one meant 'unconstrained'. But when the writers we have been discussing talk of self-determination they are not referring simply to freedom from constraint. A human being can be free from everything which would normally be regarded as a constraint and yet not be self-determining. For example, all of the writers I have discussed would agree that a caseworker would be infringing his client's self-determination if he attempted to exercise

any strong form of persuasion upon his client. But we do not normally regard even strong persuasion as a form of constraint. Again Perlman illustrates the ways in which our capacities for self-direction are limited by describing what we do when we get up in the morning and take our breakfast. 'You are not asking yourself', she writes, 'if you will have toast or a marshmallow sundae, coffee or a gin sling because your choices have been narrowed and limited for you by breakfast customs, by medical opinion, by parental dicta established or rebelled against long ago' [see p. 69 above]. Thus the customs of our community, medical opinions and parental dicta from long ago are seen as limiting our self-determination, but these could not normally be regarded as constraints, so if we persist in operating with the narrow sense of freedom as 'absence of constraint' which is available to the determinist, we cannot regard these as restrictions on freedom. What then is it which distinguishes automatic actions such as our taking coffee rather than a gin sling for breakfast from actions which are genuinely self-determined? The obvious answer, indeed the only answer which I can see, is that the former kind of action is determined purely by environmental or genetic factors while the latter is not. But this answer is obviously not open to a determinist for he is committed to the view that all actions are ultimately determined by environmental or genetic factors. Thus, so far as I can see, a determinist cannot accept that any human action is self-determined in the sense in which the writers I have been discussing use that phrase. It would follow that a determinist could not accept the principle of client self-determination in the form in which these writers understand it.

If these arguments are correct then the acceptance of a thorough-going doctrine of determinism would certainly require some modifications in the theory of social casework as it is expounded by the authors I have been discussing. At the very least there would, first of all, be a need to think out afresh what is meant by saying that a client's act is self-determined or self-directed and to indicate a sense in which an act could be both self-determined and also determined by environmental forces. When this had been done, it would be necessary to show what it was about self-determined acts which made them valuable. Casework theorists would either have to replace their present conception of self-determination with something like the conception I offered to the determinist or they would have to devise some other more satisfactory alternative. Thus it appears that we must agree with Hollis and with Perlman when they argue that casework, as they understand it, presupposes a degree of indeterminism. How much difference the adoption of a determinist position would make to the practice of casework, as distinct from the theory, is difficult to assess, particularly for an outsider who is compelled to rely on other people's descriptions of casework rather than his own experience. But if casework practice conforms at all to the accounts of it in the textbooks, then one would suspect that it ought to make some difference. If caseworkers did see the principle of client self-determination simply as indicating a practice which generally assists the achievement of other goals, then one would expect them to be prepared to set aside the principle, not just in extreme cases, but whenever it seemed on balance likely that they could help their clients by doing so. But the main effect of the acceptance of a doctrine of determinism with all its implications would probably be to turn the attention of social workers away from casework with individuals to other kinds of social action. If human behaviour is determined by man's environment, then any problems which individuals encounter must ultimately stem from environmental causes, and the most reasonable way of trying to solve these problems would be to change the environment by effecting social improvements. No doubt there would always be some need for casework with individuals but this would only be a second line of defence. Social improvement would be the most important thing to aim at. If, on the other hand, human behaviour is not determined by the environment there will still be some problems, however much the environment is improved, and only work with the individual could help to solve these. Moreover if it is the element of self-determination (as opposed to environmental determination) which gives an individual his unique value, then casework is particularly important because it addresses itself to what is most valuable in human beings. Social improvement cannot by itself bring about the goal of helping the client to be a more fully self-directing person. Clearly this controversy between those who believe that social workers should concentrate on improving social conditions and those who prefer to concentrate on individual casework is one of the most important issues in social work today. Some sort of indeterminist doctrine seems to be presupposed by much of what one might call the 'ideology' of casework as it is propounded by writers such as Hollis and Perlman. The adoption of a thorough-going determinism would thus require changes in casework theory and, one suspects, marked shifts of emphasis in casework practice.

II The problem of reconciling self-determination with indeterminism

If I am right in arguing that the acceptance of a doctrine of determinism would require changes in the conception of the principle of client self-determination which is embodied in the writings of the authors I have been discussing, the question arises, 'Can we save this conception of the principle by adopting an indeterminist view?' or, to put the matter another way, 'Can this conception of the principle be reconciled with the view that human actions are *not* predictable in accordance with causal laws?'

Philosophers of a determinist bent have claimed that if human acts are not causally determined they must be purely random, and they have argued that this view is untenable for two main reasons. (a) To say that an act is random would appear to be the same as to say that it occurred by chance, but the view that human acts are purely chance occurrences would seem to be even more damaging to ordinary conceptions of responsiblity than is the view that they are causally determined. On such a view it is difficult to see how we could regard an individual's acts as arising out of his character and personality. There would then be no sense in praising or blaming him, in rewarding or punishing him. We would have to regard all human acts in the same way as we do those which we now call accidents. (b) It is argued that we are in fact aware of regularities in human behaviour and can often predict what people will do, particularly if we are familiar with their characters. Sometimes, indeed, human actions may be as predictable as any physical event. As Hume puts it:[9]

> A prisoner, who has neither money nor interest, discovers the impossibility of his escape, as well when he considers the obstinacy of the gaoler, as the walls and bars, with which he is surrounded; and, in all attempts for his freedom, chooses rather to work upon the stone and iron of the one, than upon the inflexible nature of the other.

Thus ordinary experience appears to show that human actions are, at least in some measure, predictable and that they cannot therefore be random.

Both of these arguments can be adapted to the problem with which we are concerned and may well seem to show that the idea that human acts are random is even more damaging to orthodox casework theory than is the idea that they are causally determined.

(a) The principle of client self-determination presupposes that a distinction can be drawn between on the one hand, those acts which are genuinely the client's own acts, and, on the other hand, occurrences which are not genuinely the client's own acts. But if all human behaviour is purely random it is difficult to see why anything should be regarded as the client's own act. They are all like accidents which merely happen to him. To put the point in another way, if the client's behaviour is purely random, how can we make sense of the notion of its being self-*determined*? This idea requires some sort of conception of the behaviour as arising from the client's character or personality and this is incompatible with the notion that human acts are random. The principle also presupposes that self-determined acts are somehow to be valued more highly than those which are in every respect determined by environmental factors, but is difficult to see why we should set such a high value on this class of purely chance occurrences. So if 'self-determined' implies 'random' there seems to be no reason why we should prefer self-determined to environmentally determined behaviour. (b) It is a basic assumption of the social work profession that it is possible to have knowledge of general patterns of human behaviour and that a social worker can use this knowledge in helping his clients, but there clearly could be no such knowledge if human acts were random. Indeed the problem may be even more pressing than this would suggest. It is now generally accepted that a knowledge of the laws of psychology and sociology should be part of the professional equipment of social workers, but it may well seem that if we accept that human behaviour is governed by such laws we are committed to determinism. Thus it may seem that if a social worker embraces some form of indeterminism in order to defend his belief in the principle of client self-determination, he must abandon his commitment to a scientific approach to human behaviour. This difficulty is obviously felt quite forcibly by both Hollis and Perlman. For example, in discussing whether the use made of social and psychological laws means that casework has become completely deterministic and whether this is compatible with the principle of client self-determination, Hollis writes:[10]

> The casework position, I would think, would not be that of absolutism in either direction. We certainly do not take the libertarian stand that each action of man is completely free and unaffected by his previous character, life history, or current

experience. On the other hand, neither do we believe that all choice, all behaviour is the determined, necessary and inflexible result of previously exisiting physical or environmental causes.

Thus Hollis believes that her view of casework presupposes a position somewhere in between a complete determinism and a complete indeterminism. What I now want to do is to consider whether it is possible to indicate a doctrine of this kind which would meet the difficulties I have described and which could be accepted by a reasonable man in the light of present knowledge.

Some forms of indeterminism and the difficulties they present

The answer to the problem of free-will and determinism which is most likely to occur to the ordinary man is that there is in human beings a non-physical 'self', which causes or gives rise to human actions but is not itself subject to causation. This self would be an immaterial entity, distinct from the body but somehow dwelling within the body and activating it. Clearly this kind of view would give us all the self-determination we need. In treating the client as self-determining the caseworker would be respecting the activity of the client's self. He would be endeavouring to free the client's behaviour from determination by bodily or environmental factors and to leave it open for behaviour to be determined as far as possible by the self. It might even be claimed that the principle of client self-determination presupposes such a view of the self as an independent entity capable of determining action but not itself determined. But doctrines which claim that there is an immaterial self inhabiting our bodies have notoriously been the subject of much philosophical criticism. There are general difficulties in understanding what it means to say that there are non-physical entities of this kind and there are also particular difficulties in seeing how the self could cause occurrences in the physical world without being itself subject to physical causation. But the difficulty which is most relevant to the present discussion arises out of the point that human actions are, to at least some extent, governed by causal laws. Psychological and social laws do sometimes appear to explain human behaviour, and, perhaps even more importantly, our character and our actions are affected by physical factors such as brain damage or changes in the chemical balance of the body. One cannot therefore contend that human actions are purely the product of a self which is in no way subject to causation because, if this were correct, human actions would be subject to no causal influences apart from the activity of the self, and this is clearly not the case. If we want to solve the problem with which we are confronted we have to show that human behaviour can be subject in some degree to causal laws without being totally determined.

It may be important here to consider more closely exactly what we mean when we say that human actions are governed by scientific laws or are predictable by means of such laws. Clearly one thing which one might mean by this is that every individual human action could in principle be predicted by a being which had a sufficient knowledge of the state of the universe at some time previous to the occasion of action together with an understanding of the laws of the relevant science. We have seen that if human actions are governed in this sense by scientific laws, then there are considerable difficulties for the principle of client self-determination as it has been understood by some leading writers on casework. However, if we consider sciences such as psychology or sociology it is not clear that they have laws which govern human action in this sense, for in their present state at least, the sciences do not normally enable us to predict exactly how a given individual will behave. In a textbook of psychology, for example, one characteristically finds many statements about how people generally behave or how they normally behave. Correlations may be established between certain types of personality, or certain types of environment and certain types of behaviour. There may also be quite precise claims about the percentage of people who have been found to behave in one way rather than another. This sort of information is useful and important but it does not enable us to make precise predictions about what a given individual will do in a given situation. At best all it can enable us to do is to predict the proportion of a group of people who will behave in a given way or to predict the probability that a given individual will behave in that way. It does not license exact predictions about individual cases. Thus, for the most part, the laws of the social sciences in their present state appear to be statistical or probabilistic in nature. Many social scientists would regard this as a defect which they hope to remedy in due course as their knowledge advances. They would agree that at the moment they can only offer us generalisations of a statistical kind but they would attribute this to the infancy of their sciences. They would hope that as they learn more they will come ever closer to a situation in which they can predict the behaviour of individual human beings with the same kind of certainty with which a space scientist can predict the path of a satellite. However there is no reason why this should be the case. It is quite conceivable that the laws of the social sciences will always be of a statistical kind and that this is not due simply to the defective state of present knowledge. It may be that, so long as we stay at the level of the social sciences, it will never be possible to lay down exact laws governing human behaviour. If this is the case then a social worker can clearly accept the discoveries of psychology and sociology without committing himself to the view that human actions are totally predictable. To put it another way, if the laws of the social sciences are only statistical generalisations then they leave room for a substantial degree of indeterminacy in the behaviour of individual human beings. However this does not, in itself, get us very far, for there remains the possibility that human actions are predictable in accordance with the laws of natural sciences. So even if the laws of the social sciences leave room for a degree of indeterminacy in human actions, it does not follow from this that human acts are not fully determined.

Some philosophers who are opposed to determinism have hoped to find support for their views in the branch of physics known as quantum mechanics. The situation, as I understand it, is as follows. It is possible to establish an experimental system in which there occur events which cannot at present be predicted. These are usually individual events in the 'microscopic' world of sub-atomic particles, although it is possible to arrange a mechanism so that these sub-atomic events trigger off events in the 'macroscopic' world of our everyday experience. According to the orthodox interpretation of these phenomena, the impossibility of predicting the events in question does not arise out of any failure of present knowledge which might one day be remedied. It is part of the theory that the events in question are unpredictable in principle. But, although one cannot normally predict the results of an experiment on an individual particle, it is possible to predict with almost complete certainty the statistical result of repeating the same experiment a very large number of times. Thus although one cannot predict whether an individual event will occur or not, one can predict the probability of its occurring. One could sum this up by saying that if orthodox quantum theory is correct there are some events within the universe which are not determined. Clearly this does not, in itself, show that determinism as applied to human actions is false. In order to do this one would have to show that the human nervous system contains some mechanism which could convert indeterminacies at the sub-atomic level into indeterminacies at the level of human action. It has not been established that there is such a mechanism, though some attempts have been made to suggest ways in which it might operate. Nevertheless quantum theory has had a very considerable impact on discussions of determinism and human action, for it removes or at least weakens one of the main props of the determinist's position. Previously it seemed that a belief in universal causal determination was an essential presupposition of science or indeed of any attempt to reach a rational understanding of the universe. So anyone who suggested that human acts were not determined seemed to be rejecting a scientific attitude towards man and to be insisting rather arbitrarily that human beings must somehow stand outside the natural order of things. If, on the other hand, we admit that there are some events in the universe which are unpredictable in principle, then the picture changes. It becomes clear that a belief in universal causal determinism is not an essential prerequisite for a rational understanding of the universe and that one can concede that some human actions may be undetermined without being totally obscurantist or arbitrarily exempting human actions from the natural order of events. The point is not that human acts have been proved to be undetermined but that the presupposition in favour of determinism has been weakened. It is, I think, possible at the present time for a reasonable man to adopt the view that at least some human acts are not fully determined, although the probabilities of their occuring may be predictable. Thus it is possible for an indeterminist to answer the objection that a belief in determinism is required by a scientific attitude towards man. However we are still left with the difficulty of showing how acts which are undetermined can be said to be the agent's own acts and to arise out of his own character and personality in a way in which mere accidents do not.

Some writers have suggested that if there is a degree of indeterminacy in the physical universe this would leave room for the intervention of a non-physical self. So one might argue that the brain is a physical system and as such is governed by physical laws. This no doubt means that the majority of brain events are predictable, but if there is some indeterminacy in the system, then there will be occasions when it will be unpredictable which of two or more brain events will occur. So, for example, there might be occasions when it is unpredictable whether there will occur within me the brain event corresponding to a decision to tell the truth or the brain event

corresponding to a decision to tell a lie. On such occasions my 'self'
could intervene to 'push' the brain mechanism in one direction or
another. Thus the decision is determined by the 'self'. A view of this
kind would no doubt leave plenty of room for the principle of client
self-determination, for it enables us to make quite a clear distinction
between acts which are self-determined and acts which are not.
Nevertheless when we examine such a view more closely it does not
appear very attractive. The 'self' postulated in this theory is not the
soul or the mind as these terms have traditionally been understood.
Those thinkers who have believed that human beings do have an
immaterial soul or mind have usually regarded it as the only source
of our decisions and choices and also of our thoughts, our desires
our hopes and so on, but the 'self' postulated by the theory we are
now discussing is merely something which sometimes intervenes in a
purely physical chain of causes leading to a human decision. Otherwise it leads a wholly mysterious existence. So this view lacks the
undoubted attractions of the view which regards the 'self' or the soul
as the only source of all our decisions. Moreover it is difficult to
understand how a non-physical self could affect the physical system
of the brain. In order to state the theory one has to use metaphorical
language and talk as though the self could push an atomic particle,
but this sort of talk is literally absurd, for clearly a non-physical self
could not push anything and atomic particles are not the sort of
thing which can be pushed. But there is no way in which this sort of
metaphorical talk can be given any 'cash value', so the mechanism by
which the self intervenes remains wholly mysterious. Again if the
indeterminacy in the physical system of the brain which leaves room
for the self's intervention was an indeterminacy of the kind postulated by quantum theory, it would seem that the activity of the self
would be liable to upset the probability distributions on which that
theory is based. Thus although this kind of view would solve some
problems, the difficulties in it appear overwhelming.

A tentative solution

Could we justify a belief in human *self*-determination without postu-
lating the intervention of some non-physical entity? In a recent essay
Professor David Wiggins offers an interesting suggestion about how
we might do this. [11] He claims that in order to reach a reasonable
view of human action it is not necessary to suppose that actions are
predictable in accordance with rigorous scientific laws; it is sufficient

if we can fit them into meaningful sequences. We do not need to postulate the intervention of something non-physical.[12]

> What we must find instead are patterns which are coherent and intelligible within the low level terms of practical deliberation, even though they are not amenable to the kind of generalisation which is the stuff of rigorous theory. On this conception the agent is conceived as an essentially straightforward enmattered or embodied thing. His possible peculiarity as a natural thing among things in nature is that his biography unfolds not only non-deterministically but also intelligibly; non-deterministically in that personality and character are never something complete, and need not be the deterministic origin of action; intelligibly in that each new action or episode constitutes a comprehensible phase in the unfolding of the character, a further specification of what the man has by now become.

Wiggins's suggestion here is sketched out in a very vague way but I think it does offer a possibility of solving the problems with which we have been concerned and I want to explore more fully how this might be done and, in particular, how an analysis of practical deliberation might help us.

Deliberation is the process of thinking by which we make up our minds how to act. The most influential account of this process is still the one given by Aristotle. He held that we begin the process of deliberation with the wish to achieve some objective, we then investigate whether there is a means by which we can bring about this objective, and if we find a means which is within our power we adopt it. According to this account the course of action which we adopt would seem to be determined by the wish which we have to achieve the objective and the beliefs which we have about how this objective could be brought about. But we cannot choose what to wish for or what to believe, so it would seem that according to this account our actions are ultimately determined by factors over which we have no control. Thus, although Aristotle himself does not draw this conclusion, his account of deliberation appears to imply a form of psychological determinism.

The Aristotelian account of deliberation would no doubt fit many of the decisions of everyday life. Often we wish for an objective, see a way of achieving it, and so act without any further hesitation. But the decisions which give us most trouble (and these would include most of the decisions with which a social worker is called upon to help his clients) are not like this. Normally when we find a decision difficult this is because there is not one clear objective which we wish for. Sometimes we have conflicting wishes. There may be two or more courses of action open to us, we realise that we cannot adopt both and yet we find both in some way attractive, so we have a difficult choice to make. Again we may find it difficult to decide because we are obliged to adopt one or other of two or more courses of action all of which seem unattractive to us. Or the difficulty could arise because we have to make a choice but have no particular inclination one way or another. The examples which Biestek uses in discussing the principle of client self-determination illustrate this point rather well [see pp. 23-4 above]. One of the cases he describes is that of a Mrs Allen who, after a period in hospital, required nursing care either in her own home or in a nursing home. Both courses had attractions and disadvantages. If she stayed at home she would be close to her children while if she went to the nursing home she would be better looked after. Clearly this situation presented itself as a problem because Mrs Allen wanted to be close to her children and also wanted the best nursing care but these wants could not both be fulfilled. Another of Biestek's examples is the case of a Miss Clark, an unmarried mother who had to decide whether to keep her child herself, to allow her married sister to adopt it, or to release it to an agency for adoption. Her problem seems to have been that she desired to keep her child and also desired to avoid the disapproval and hostility of the community in which she lived and it was impossible to satisfy both these desires. Some people faced with problems of this kind might simply do nothing and let circumstances drift until there is only one course available. Others might choose one course rather than another quite impulsively. But the rational thing to do is to consider carefully all the consequences of each course of action and to weigh up their respective advantages and disadvantages. One of the functions of a social worker is to encourage and assist this process of deliberation. Sometimes when one has considered the implications of each course of action which is available it becomes clear which is the best one to adopt. So, according to Biestek, it became obvious to Miss Clark that releasing her child for adoption was the most realistic choice. But this does not always happen. Sometimes even when one has considered carefully the implication of all possible courses it may still not be clear which is best. Nevertheless one still has to opt for one course rather than another. Judging from Biestek's account this may be what happened in the Allen case. In any case we are all familiar enough with situations where we are torn between two courses of action and have to jump one way or another.

This account of deliberation differs from the Aristotelian account in that it does leave room for an element of indeterminacy. When a person experiences conflicting desires it may be unpredictable which he will choose to satisfy. Even we ourselves in retrospect may find it difficult to say what made us go one way rather than another. So it is plausible to say that on such occasions our desires and beliefs do not fully determine which way we act. It would have been possible to have precisely the same desires and beliefs and yet to act differently. To put the matter another way, even if our behaviour always does arise out of our desires and beliefs, it does not follow that our decisions about which of two conflicting desires to act upon are pre-determined. In this way we can make sense of the notion that our behaviour arises out of our character without treating our characters as the deterministic origin of our actions.

Some philosophers would resist this conclusion by suggesting that in conflict situations we always act upon whichever of our desires is strongest. The trouble with this is that there is no independent way of checking which of a person's two desires is strongest at the moment of decision except by seeing by which way he acts. So to say that a person always acts in accordance with his strongest desire is simply to say that he always acts in accordance with the desire in accordance with which he acts. This obviously tells us nothing. Thus once we are aware of the importance of cases where we have conflicting desires, no form of psychological determinism is likely to be very attractive. Of course it remains possible that when, in a conflict situation, we finally act one way or another, our decision is the result of some event of which we are unaware and which is physically determined. So the account of deliberation which I have suggested would be compatible with some form of physical determinism. But it is also compatible with the view that our decisions on such occasions are not determined. Thus this view of deliberation is incompatible with psychological determinism but it is compatible both with some forms of physical determinism and with some forms of physical indeterminism.

This account of practical deliberation may enable us to see how a human act could be regarded as arising from the self, without being totally determined. It is the agent's own action in so far as it arises from his own wishes and his own desires, but this does not necessarily mean that his wishes and desires determine his action, for it is possible that the same set of wishes and desires could have given rise to a quite different course of action. Furthermore our wishes and desires need not themselves be determined by our environment or heredity. Our present character is in part at least the product of a whole series of choices which we have made in the past. If those choices were not determined so also our characters would not be determined. Even if the range of choices open on any one occasion was limited, there could still be a vast number of different ways in which a personality could develop over a lifetime, and it could well be quite unpredictable which way any given individual would develop.

I do not think it is possible to prove that this account of human freedom is true. Nevertheless I think it is an account to which in the present state of knowledge a reasonable man could give his assent, and I think it would give writers such as Hollis and Perlman all they need in order to defend their conception of the principle of client self-determination. The function of the caseworker is not to direct the client but to assist his deliberation. This helps to ensure that the client acts on his own reflective desires rather than on impulse or in response to external pressures, but this need not necessarily mean that one kind of environmental determinant is being substituted for another, for to say that someone acts on his desires is not necessarily to say that his desires determined his action and in any case his desires may not be determined purely by environmental or genetic factors. In this way one can defend the assumption that human action can be more or less self-directed in the sense of more or less free from external determination, and one can understand what is meant by 'the growth which comes from within'. This belief in human self-determination is not necessarily incompatible with accepting the discoveries of the social sciences, for if the laws of these sciences are statistical in nature they do not require that every individual act be totally determined.

Conclusions

There are four chief points which I think should emerge from this discussion:

1   There is a problem about the relationship between determinism and the principle of client self-determination. The problem arises because the principle apparently requires that human acts can be

free in a sense which implies that they are not determined by outside causes.

2 A form of the principle may be compatible with determinism but this is not apparently the form in which the principle is propounded by leading casework theorists.

3 There are also difficulties in reconciling the principle with an indeterminist doctrine, but it may be possible to describe a form of indeterminism which could accommodate the principle as it is usually understood.

4 In any case the problems which determinism raises for the principle of client self-determination are closely analogous to the problems it raises up for ordinary notions of moral responsibility. If the principle of client self-determination had to be abandoned because of problems connected with determinism it is likely that we would also have to alter many of the basic moral assumptions of our society.

Notes

1 Florence Hollis, 'Principles and assumptions underlying casework practice', a lecture given at a United Nations seminar for the advanced study of social work; printed as an appendix in Jean Heywood, *An Introduction to Teaching Casework Skills,* Routledge & Kegan Paul, London, 1964.

2 A general discussion of what determinism is and the problems it presents can be found in most textbooks of moral philosophy, for example, R. B. Brandt, *Ethical Theory,* Prentice-Hall, Englewood Cliffs, N.J., 1959, ch. 20; and Stanley I. Benn and R. S. Peters, *Social Principles and the Democratic State,* Allen & Unwin, London, 1959, ch. 9. There are further discussions in D. F. Pears (ed.), *The Freedom of the Will,* Macmillan, London, 1963, and S. Hook (ed.), *Determinism and Freedom in the Age of Modern Science,* New York University Press, 1957.

3 For attempts to reconcile determinism with moral responsibility see A. J. Ayer, *Philosophical Essays,* Macmillan, London, 1954, ch. 12; P. H. Nowell Smith, 'Freewill and moral responsibility', *Mind,* 57, 1948; and J. J. C. Smart, 'Freewill praise and blame', *Mind,* 70, 1961. For criticisms of these attempts see C. A. Campbell, 'Is freewill a pseudo-problem?', *Mind,* 60, 1951, reprinted in the same author's *In Defence of Free Will,* Allen & Unwin, London, 1967; and Paul Edwards, 'Hard and soft determinism', in Hook, *op. cit.*

4 F. P. Biestek, *The Casework Relationship,* Allen & Unwin, London, 1961, p. 103
5 *Ibid.*
6 Florence Hollis, *Casework: A Psychosocial Therapy,* Random House, New York, 1964, p. 13.
7 *Ibid.*
8 Helen Harris Perlman, 'Self-determination: reality or illusion', *Social Service Review,* vol. 39, no. 4, 1965 [reprinted above, pp. 65-80].
9 David Hume, *An Enquiry Concerning Human Understanding,* ed. L. A. Selby-Bigge, Oxford, 1902, section 7, p. 90.
10 Florence Hollis, 'Principles and assumptions underlying casework practice', in Jean Heywood, *An Introduction to Teaching Casework Skills,* Routledge & Kegan Paul, London, 1964, p. 163.

11 David Wiggins, 'Towards a reasonable libertarianism', in *Essays on Freedom of Action,*Ted Honderich (ed.), Routledge & Kegan Paul, London, 1973.
12 *Ibid.,* p. 52.
13 Biestek, *op. cit.,* pp. 107-9.

8   Against the persuasive definition of 'self-determination'

F. E. McDermott

Although revered as one of the most fundamental of social work values, the principle of client self-determination has always been something of a problem in social work theory. With its apparent stress on the right of the client to go his own, possibly wilful way, it has seemed a threat to the fine balance which it is thought social workers should maintain between permissiveness and control. Consequently, much of the literature on the subject is devoted to the question of containing the principle within its proper limits; to domesticating it, as it were, within the existing corpus of social work values. One of the ways in which this has been done is by the identification of self-determination not simply with the making of one's own choices and decisions, but with the making of these in conformity with the law, morality, and the norms of 'constructive decision making'. Only actions that flow from choices and decisions of this kind, it is argued, are truly free or self-determined.

Something approaching this view of self-determination is to be found, for instance, in F. P. Biestek's well-known analysis of the principle of client self-determination, published originally as an article,[1] but incorporated later in a modified form in his book *The Casework Relationship*[2] (see pp. 17-32 above). Much of his analysis is concerned with the drawing of what seem to me unduly restrictive limits to the client's right of self-determination; but this is not the issue I wish to discuss here. What interests me is a subsidiary argument involving the sort of conceptual indentification of self-determination with, and only with, acceptable and constructive behaviour, referred to in my opening paragraph, which seems to be very much in favour in social work thought.

From Biestek's definition of the principle of client self-determination as 'the practical recognition of the right and need of clients to freedom in making their own choices and decisions in the casework process' (p. 19 above), one might infer that self-determination consists simply in the making of one's own choices and decisions free from external constraint. On reading further, however, it transpires that this would be a mistake: 'A person's freedom to choose and decide', we are told, 'is not synonymous with license . . . . Human freedom is a means, not a goal in itself; it is a means for attaining the legitimate proximate and ultimate goals in life' (p. 24 above). In other words, since self-determination is being construed in terms of the freedom to choose and decide, and the latter in terms of the pursuit of legitimate goals; the exercise of self-determination would on this interpretation appear to consist in the making of one's own choices and decisions in the pursuit of legitimate goals. And if this is what it is to be self-determining, then the principle of client self-determination would presumably require of the social worker that he should not hinder his client but, indeed, help him in his efforts to obtain these, and only these, goals; goals which, according to Biestek's original article, include 'the perfection of his own personality and the perfection of his relationship to other men and to God'.[3]

Given that the ultimate aims of social work are usually seen as the client's personal development and the improvement of his social relationships, it is not altogether surprising that an interpretation of the principle of client self-determination which, apart from its reference to God, fits in so very conveniently with them, should appeal to the profession. Nevertheless it is, I believe, a fundamentally misleading interpretation. It is a product of what the American philosopher C. L. Stevenson called 'persuasive definition'; and like all persuasive definitions it tends to confuse rather than clarify the issues in which it is involved.

The purpose of this paper is to try to substantiate this contention. Its aim, as the title suggests, is negative, and the arguments adduced not particularly original. The only justification for publishing them is that they do not as yet appear to have made sufficient impact upon social work theory.

Persuasive definition

In his book, *Ethics and Language*,[4] Stevenson defined 'persuasive definition' as follows:[5]

In any 'persuasive definition' the term defined is a familiar one, whose meaning is both descriptive and strongly emotive. The purport of the definition is to alter the descriptive meaning of the term, usually by giving it greater precision within the boundaries of its customary vagueness; but the definition does not make any substantial change in the term's emotive meaning. And the definition is used, consciously or unconsciously, in an effort to secure, by this interplay between emotive and descriptive meaning, a redirection of people's attitudes.

To illustrate what this means, let us consider the definition of the word 'democracy'. To say of a government that it is democratic is normally, Stevenson would argue, not merely to describe it, i.e. not merely to convey such information as, for instance, that it was elected by a majority of the citizens, but also to express one's approval of it, to influence the attitudes of others towards it, etc. In other words, besides having descriptive meaning, the word 'democracy' and its cognates also have emotive meaning: the power to express, evoke and influence attitudes.

Given its strong emotive meaning or force, it is obviously of considerable advantage to any protagonist in political controversy to be able to claim that the government, or the policy of the government he is defending is democratic, since this will tend to dispose at least the uncommitted favourably towards it. But his right to make this claim will depend, in part, on the descriptive meaning of 'democracy'; that is to say, on whether the criteria for its application correspond with the characteristics of the government or the policy he is defending. If its descriptive meaning were precise there would be little scope for dispute about who could and who could not lay claim to the word. In fact, however, its descriptive meaning is notoriously imprecise; and it is this imprecision that has enabled 'democracy' to become, in Bernard Crick's words, 'perhaps the most promiscuous word in the world of public affairs'.[6] With so much competition for her favours, attempts are bound to be made to secure exclusive rights to her; and it is in the implementation of these jealous designs that the process of persuasive definition plays its devious role.

To define 'democracy' persuasively is to try to limit the descriptive component of its meaning by definition to characteristics one favours, thereby annexing its emotive force to those characteristics alone, and excluding from its influence other less welcome characteristics with which, nevertheless, the word may customarily have been associated. Thus, given that 'democracy' is customarily associated with, amongst other things, the notion of government by the people as well as the notion of government by elected representatives; a persuasive definition of the word might consist in defining 'true' democracy as the determination of all important legislative decisions by the votes of the entire adult population. This would direct the laudatory force of the word towards government by referenda, and, by implication, cast a shadow over representative government as the corruption of a noble ideal. There are, of course, other more direct and rational ways of commending one's cause to others; but they place upon one the burden of explaining, possibly in the face of hostile criticism, exactly what it is that renders it superior to its alternatives. By contrast, to succeed in gaining the widespread acceptance of a congenial definition of a word like 'democracy', is, through the emotive 'fall out' of the word, to be well on the way to securing the same results in a relatively painless manner.

The trouble with arguments conducted in this fashion, i.e. arguments based on rival persuasive definitions, is not only that they are chronically unsettleable, since, given their chosen definitions each side has an impregnable position; but also that they tend to divert attention from the real issues involved. It may give one or other of the protagonists a polemical advantage to have the political system he advocates characterised as democratic; but this is not what renders the system desirable in the first place. Ultimately, what is important, is not what the system is called, but the desirability of the ends it is intended to promote, its chances of success, and considerations of this kind relating to alternative systems. It is these questions that need to be debated rather than the question which of alternative definitions gives the 'true' meaning of the word 'democracy'.

Of course, political disagreements, as Stevenson argues, are not just disagreements in belief, but also disagreements in attitude. It matters just as much how people feel about the facts as what the facts are. A large part of political discourse, therefore, is inevitably persuasive. We can, however, try to ensure that the rhetoric of political debate does not altogether obscure the relevant facts, or the full implications of the decisions being debated. It is against these dangers that an appreciation of the logical properties of political and evaluative terms in general, and of the uses to which they lend themselves, is a useful prophylactic.

Before going on to examine the relevance of the concept of persuasive definition to the interpretation of self-determination in social work theory, I should explain that the general theory within which Stevenson expounded his views on persuasive definition, the emotivist theory of ethics, has been largely superseded by subsequent developments in analytic philosophy. It is not that what Stevenson and others had to say about the emotive function and effect of certain words has been shown to be false, but rather that the descriptive/emotive distinction is now seen as an inadequate basis on which to analyse the meaning of all evaluative words. Linguistic meaning, it is argued, is a matter of the rules and conventions governing the use of a word rather than of the psychological effects it tends to have. It is these rules that give to words the relative stability and constancy of their meaning even though their effects on one's emotions are extremely variable and unpredictable. A word can, of course, have as part of its meaning the function of expressing favourable attitudes or of commending, but this can be regarded as part of its meaning only in so far as its having that function is one of the established conventions of the language to which it belongs. It will, no doubt, because of its meaning, be capable of being used to produce an indefinite variety of effects upon others, but it is a mistake to construe its tendency to produce these effects as part of its meaning.[7]

These criticisms of Stevenson's general theory of meaning do not, however, detract from his insights into the role of definition in evaluative discourse. Whether the emotive force of a word is regarded as part of its meaning or not, whether it is construed in psychological terms, or in terms of the rules and conventions governing a particular language, there is no denying that some words have it. Nor, I think, can it be disputed that words which have such a function or force are liable to what Stevenson called 'persuasive' definitions. And this is all that need be granted for the purpose of this paper.

The persuasive definition of 'self-determination'

Turning now to the world 'self-determination', it is easy to see that owing to the traditional status of the principle of client self-determination in social work, 'self-determination' acquired just the sort of emotive or commendatory force among social workers as would render it liable to persuasive definition. It became, in the words of Helen Harris Perlman, 'a professional password' (p. 67 above). A social worker would not have been speaking the same language as his colleagues if he did not appreciate the extent to which in saying of a decision or policy that it promoted client self-determination, he was thereby expressing his approval of it and commending it to others. Being in favour of client self-determination, just as being in favour of the good life, was for him hardly a matter for choice. What he could do, though, was to try to determine what was going to count as self-determination in social work. And this is just what much of the literature on client self-determination has been about: attempts by theoreticians of varying moral, political and religious persuasions, to ensure that the commendatory force of the expression 'client self-determination' should not commit them or their colleagues to supporting policies or decisions that they found unacceptable.

This is illustrated by the passage in Biestek (pp. 24-5 above) from which I have already quoted. Having earlier defined the principle of client self-determination in terms of the client's right to freedom in making his own choices and decisions, he amplifies this definition:

> The principle of client self-determination can become a meaningless cliché, however, if the client's right is not balanced realistically with the limitations to that right. A person's freedom to choose and decide is not synonymous with license. The rights of one individual are circumscribed by the rights of other individuals in society. The right of the individual is accompanied by the duty to respect the right of others. Human freedom is a means, not a goal in itself; it is a means for attaining the legitmate proximate and ulitmate goals in life. It cannot, therefore, sanction self-injury or injury to others.

Now the fact that the client's right has to be weighed against the rights of others is not in question. What is, is the nature of the right that has to be so weighed. Is it the client's right to go his own way, or his right to go in ways that others find constructive, moral, socially acceptable, etc.? It is the answer to this question implicit in Biestek's argument that smacks of persuasive definition.

The way in which this is achieved is illustrative of the ambiguities on which persuasive definitions thrive. Consider the difference between being free to do x, and doing x freely. To say that one is free to do x is, in one sense of this expression, to make a normative claim to the effect that one is not morally or legally prohibited from doing it. It follows, therefore, that if one is free to do x, it cannot be an act of licence; for an act of licence is by definition one against which there is some moral or legal prohibition. On the other hand, to say that one does x freely is to make a descriptive statement to the effect that one does it without being compelled to. This is perfectly compatible with x's being an act of licence.

Now of these two concepts of freedom, it is clearly the latter, i.e., doing x freely, that most closely resembles what we mean by the word 'self-determination'. This is shown by the fact that to demand the right of self-determination is not to demand the right to be free to do what one wants, i.e., the right not to have any moral or legal obligations; but to demand the right to act freely without compulsion by others. But the use of the generic term 'freedom' to elucidate what is meant by the principle of client self-determination tends to blur the distinction between these two concepts, with the result that self-determination's connection with the descriptive concept of doing x freely is transferred to the normative concept of being free to do x. And because being free to do x is not compatible with x's being an act of licence, self-determination also comes to be contrasted with acts of licence. Add to this the emotive effect of branding certain freely-committed acts as acts of licence, and one is well on the way to associating the word 'self-determination' with only such acts as are morally and socially acceptable.

Similarly, in an article entitled 'Self-determination: king or citizen in the realm of values?', Saul Bernstein argues as follows (p. 39 above):

> Social work is based on the assumption that people are free to make significant choices and that they can be helped to make better ones. But the attempt to use freedom to make decisions that are contrary to reality or largely irrational is self-defeating. Confusion rather than creativity flows from the disregard of facts and reason. Only as one takes account of the relevant factors does true freedom operate in decision making. Yielding to unexamined impulses is more a surrender to instinctive drives than the expression of mature self-determination.

Here, once again, 'true' freedom is contrasted with its alleged counterfeit. It is not any choice a client might make that is to count as an exercise of self-determination, but only 'significant' choices i.e. choices that are realistic, rational, constructive, etc. By this means the laudatory force of the expression 'client self-determination' is deflected from the rather disturbing idea of a client's doing what he wants to, on to the altogether more congenial notion of his doing what is prudent, rational, moral, and in every way praiseworthy. In fact, by the time Bernstein has finished with the expression, it is made to represent what he describes with understandable satisfaction as 'a pretty high level of social functioning'.

Finally, to quote from what is perhaps the most eloquent and impassioned defence of client self-determination in social work literature (see H.H. Perlman, p. 79 above):

> Self-determination, then, is the expression of our innate drive to experience the self as cause, as master of one's self. Its practical everyday exercise builds into man's maturation process because it requires the recognition of the actual, the consideration of the possible, and, in the light of these sometime sorry prospects, the adaptation involved in decision and choice. Self-determination is based upon a realistic view of freedom. Freedom, in essence, is the inner capacity and outer opportunity to make reasoned choices among possible, socially acceptable alternatives.

With most of this passage I have no quarrel. It is a constant theme in social work literature that clients need self-determination to mature, to develop the capacity to face reality, to gain confidence, etc.; and this, quite rightly, forms one of the grounds for the justification of the principle of client self-determination. But it is, surely, a rather curious view of the capacity to choose in terms of which the concept of self-determination is being defined. Taken literally, the statement that self-determination is based upon 'the inner capacity . . . to make reasoned choices among possible, socially acceptable alternatives' seems to imply that there is a special capacity for making choices among socially acceptable alternatives, which is different from the capacity simply to choose, whether from acceptable, unacceptable or mixed alternatives. So radical is the difference that to exercise the former is to be self-determining, whereas to exercise the latter by, for instance, choosing to tell the truth rather than lie in court, is, because of the mixed alternatives involved, to lack self-determination. This is so implausible that we must assume that the passage was meant to be understood differently. Perhaps the capacity in question is simply the capacity to make socially acceptable choices, rather than the capacity to make choices among socially acceptable alternatives. Self-determination, however, can hardly consist in the mere having of a capacity. It must involve its actually being exercised. So, presumably, self-determination according to this interpretation consists in making socially acceptable choices. In other words, a self-determined life is a virtuous one.

Now why is it that Perlman and so many other social work theorists make this close identification between self-determination and virtue? At least part of the answer, I suggest, lies in the influence on their views of the emotive or commendatory force that the world 'self-determination' has acquired in social work theory. For this creates an understandable reluctance to apply the word to courses of action which, even if chosen freely by the client, ought, because of their harmful consequences, to be discouraged. Rather than swim against the emotive currents set up by the word, however, and insist that self-determination is sometimes disastrous and unacceptable, they have chosen a process of re-definition, purporting to give its 'real', 'true' or 'essential' meaning. This is precisely what Stevenson meant by the expression 'persuasive definition': the withholding of the commendatory force of 'self-determination' (and with it the protection afforded by the principle of client self-determination) from behaviour which would ordinarily be regarded as self-determined, but which the authors of these definitions wish to discourage.

A contributory factor to the shaping of the concept of self-determination in this fashion in social work theory was, perhaps, the influence on it of Idealist thought. If this is so it would not in any way weaken my contention regarding its persuasive character, since the Idealists were not renowned for any great respect for ordinary language when it threatened to get in the way of their moral or metaphysical systems. Consider Bernard Bosanquet, for instance, on what he, following Rousseau, calls 'the real will'; a concept that he uses to elucidate the meaning of 'self-determination':[8]

> In order to obtain a full statement of what we will, what we want at any moment must at least be corrected and amended by what we want at all other moments; and this cannot be done without also correcting and amending it so as to harmonise it with what others want, which involves an application of the same process to them. But when any considerable degree of such correction and amendment had been gone through, our own will would return to us in a shape in which we should not know it again . . . . Such a process of harmonising and readjusting a mass of data to bring them into a rational shape is what is meant by criticism. And criticism, when applied to our actual will, shows that it is not our real will.

This, it seems to me, is characteristic of the equivocations upon which persuasive definitions rely. It may be that if we were to try to be as rational as possible in all our actions, what we did would be very different from what we are now inclined to do. But this is a hypothetical statement about what things would be like under different conditions—a counter-factual conditional. As things are, some of us are not too bothered about the consistency of our actions, and even those who are, are not always very good at achieving it. So if it is our real wills we are talking about, not the will we might have had, then the things we really want and really will are often inconsistent, foolish and immoral. It is, of course, highly desirable that we should try to be rational and good. But it would be more honest, and in the long run perhaps more effective, if we were told exactly why, rather than being manoeuvred into believing that what we ought to do is in fact what we want to, or have in some obscure way already chosen to do.

The ordinary meaning of 'self-determination'

However, before the claim that any particular definition is persuasive can be accepted, it needs to be shown that there is a standard or ordinary meaning of the word defined from which the proposed usage is a departure. For it is only in so far as a definition represents a departure of this kind based on evaluative considerations that it is persuasive in the sense under discussion. What, then, is the ordinary meaning of 'self-determination'?

The answer, based on the literal meaning of its component terms, seems obvious: determination of oneself by oneself; or, paraphrasing it more freely, the making of one's own choices and decisions, as opposed to submission to those made by others. But in view of the tendency of some philosophers and social work theorists to disregard this as too superficial an interpretation, it would be as well to explore the matter a little further.

The *Shorter Oxford Dictionary* gives the relevant meaning of 'self-determination' as 'Determination of one's mind or will by oneself or itself'. But this is hardly an improvement on the literal paraphrase we already have: it does not clarify matters to have to deal with the obscure notion of the will's determining itself. So perhaps we should go behind the dictionary to actual usage. Unfortunately, what we discover here is that apart from its place in moral and political philosophy, where its meaning tends to change chameleon-like from theory to theory, and its more recent employment in social work, there seems to be no well established use in ordinary language for the word 'self-determination' as applying to individual human beings. What we do find in common use, however, is the expression 'national self-determination', and it might be useful to examine briefly what light it can throw on the question.

What unites those who join in demanding self-determination for their respective nations is not what they are for, which may be as varied as the political factions amongst them, but what they are against. To get the foreigner, the 'not-self', off their backs without coming under the domination of another equally foreign power is to have achieved national self-determination. It matters not that they may be disappointed with it when they have got it, that it fails to satisfy many of their more positive aspirations, e.g., for socialism or democracy. Provided they still have something recognisably like a government, they will have achieved national self-determination. In other words, the concept of national self-determination is what might be called a negative concept: the condition it refers to is best characterised by its negative rather than its positive features; by the absence of foreign domination rather than by the presence of a particular kind of government.

Interestingly enough, the negative role of 'self-determination' in this context is characteristic of a wide range of grammatically analogous expressions like 'self-regulation', 'self-propulsion', etc., which suggests that what we are dealing with here is not a peculiarity of the concept of national self-determination, but a typical function of the prefix 'self' when used in conjunction with verbs or their derivatives. To say that a machine is self-regulating is to deny that it needs constant supervision and attendance. Similarly, to say that a vehicle is self-propelling, in so far as one has a use for this expression in a highly mechanised age, is to deny that it needs, for instance, a horse to pull it. And that is all it means. There is no special way a machine has to operate to be self-regulating, or a vehicle driven to be self-propelling; nor do they have to attain any specially high standard of performance: provided it moves, a slow, noisy and uncomfortable motor-car can be just as self-propelling as the latest model off the assembly line.

What all this seems to show is that given the meaning of 'self-determination' in other contexts, and the function of the prefix 'self' in analogous expressions, there is a strong presumption that the concept of individual self-determination should be interpreted as essentially a denial that the actions of an individual so described are determined by anyone else. Of course, they must be 'determined', i.e. they must have direction and purpose, and this presupposes some degree of rationality—the rationality involved in choosing means towards ends, and being able to give reasons for one's actions in terms of one's own beliefs and values. But this is far from implying that self-determined actions must be socially acceptable. It excludes actions committed in a fit of rage or panic, compulsive acts, and possibly a large class of actions committed in a confused or ambivalent state of mind. But there will still remain a wide range of socially unacceptable behaviour, including fraud, theft, assault and murder, which must be regarded as perfectly capable of being self-determined. To do otherwise and to do it from fear of appearing to sanction such actions is, it seems to me, as clear a case of persuasive definition as one is ever likely to find.

Objections to the persuasive definition of 'self-determination'

Now it may be argued that even if the definition of 'self-determination' implicit in much social work theory is persuasive, this is not necessarily a cause for criticism or complaint. Just as theoreticians in other fields are permitted to stipulate the use to which they intend to put familiar words within their theories, in order to achieve the precision and coherence they desire; so, a similar liberty may be claimed for those engaged in the theory of social work.

The weakness in this argument is that the effect of stipulation in the two cases is not the same. The main effect of stipulation in persuasive definitions is not to promote clarity of thought, though it may do so incidentally in some cases and in some respects; but to bring about a change in attitude towards some of the things to which the word in question is customarily applied. In other words, the real issues are not the linguistic ones that are, as it were, staged in public, but those that are settled behind the scenes. And this is precisely what is wrong with persuasive definitions: they misrepresent the character of the debates in which they are involved. They present what is in fact a process of persuasion as if it were a matter of linguistic clarification. The result is that they lead to moral decisions being taken and moral positions being adopted without proper consideration having been given to the relevant facts and arguments, and possibly without any realisation on the part of those so committed that there were moral choices involved.

Consider the issues involved in client self-determination. One of the most important of these is whether the right of self-determination should be regarded as extending only to choices and decisions that are socialy acceptable, or to human choices and decisions as such. The case for excluding socially unacceptable choices and decisions is obvious. The very expression 'socially unacceptable' implies that they are undesirable and to be discouraged. On the other hand, it is unlikely that there should have been so much fuss about the right of self-determination if all it was intended to protect was what was socially acceptable. It is not when one is behaving in a perfectly respectable manner, basking in the approval of one's neighbours and society generally, that one's freedom of thought or action comes under threat. Except in the most arbitrary of tyrannies, it is only when one begins to deviate from accepted social norms that any real need for the protection afforded by a right of self-determination arises. This is why champions of freedom and self-determination, like John Stuart Mill, have sought to mark out a sphere of thought and action within which the individual is sovereign however much he may affront the expectations of society. It may be that the setting up of rigid boundaries of this sort is unworkable and not the best way of defending individual freedom; but that it does need to be defended even when the individual incurs the displeasure of society is what constitutes a belief in freedom as a fundamental value.

Yet the very existence and relevance of this issue to social work is liable to be obscured by definitions of 'freedom' and 'self-determination' that restrict the application of these terms to socially acceptable behaviour. For, equipped with such persuasively defined concepts, and guided by the social norms which they presuppose, what restraints would his professional values impose on a zealous social worker? He is not likely to see any dilemma in the question whether, for instance, a client's sexually promiscuous behaviour ought, so far as this is practicable, to be changed; certainly not a dilemma involving the principle of client self-determination. The persuasive definition of the word 'self-determination' will have carved up the relevant conceptual space in such a way that, the client's behaviour being regarded as immoral, there could be no room for doubts, based on this principle, about the justifiability of bringing about a change towards a more socially acceptable and, therefore, self-determining mode of conduct. And if it is not in defence of the client's freedom and self-determination, what other grounds are there for resisting constraints and pressures designed to promote social conformity? Thus the right of the client to go his own deviant but not illegal way will have been undermined or lost, not because of any deliberate decision to reject it, but as the result of the lack of conceptual framework within which the relevant issues could be properly articulated.

In criticising this widely held conception of the meaning of 'self-determination' I am not denying the validity of the ideal in terms of which it has been defined, i.e. the ideal of rational, constructive and responsible behaviour. Nor am I arguing, as Raymond Plant does[9] that commitment to this ideal of 'positive freedom'—as he, in keeping with current philosphical practice, calls it—is incompatible with other fundamental social work values. It would be, if the pursuit of 'positive freedom' necessarily entailed coercive or manipulative tenchiques; but this is far from being the case. Not only is it questionable whether rational, constructive and responsible behaviour can be promoted by such techniques; but even if it could, it does not follow that social workers must use them, or that such an ideal ought to be eschewed in case they are tempted to do so. In other words, provided they do it without violating, through the use of coercive or manipulative techniques, the client's right of self-determination in the ordinary sense of this word, it seems neither impossible nor undesirable that social workers should give their clients such help as they can to make wiser and more responsible choices and decisions, i.e. to achieve so called 'positive freedom'.

What is wrong, then, with the persuasively defined concept of self-determination that we have been discussing, is not that it embodies an ideal which is unacceptable or out of place in social casework, but that the ideal it embodies is not that of self-determination, in the ordinary, undoctored sense of this word. Moreover, by being called 'self-determination', it threatens to usurp the place of a more fundamental principle; one which, because it concerns the right of the individual to make his own choices and decisions as such, irrespective of their content, requires fewer linguistic contortions to pass as a principle of self-determination. It is not that they cannot both co-exist in due subordination the one to the other, but that they can hardly co-exist under the same name or title. And since there seem to be perfectly adequate alternative resources in the language to refer to the ideal or ideals embodied in the concept of self-determination as 'positive freedom', it would seem gratuitously confusing to persist in using the word 'self-determination' for the purpose.

Self-determination and other moral values

Now the acceptance of the literal interpretation of the meaning of 'self-determination' may well appear to put the status of client self-determination as a fundamental social work principle in jeopardy. For if the concept of self-determination includes choices and decisions that are plainly illegal or immoral, to elevate it into a principle or to recognise it as a right of clients would appear to involve the rejection of law and morality. And this would seem to confirm the worst suspicions of its critics as to the mischievous and subversive nature of the principle. Let me, therefore, try to meet some of the more obvious objections from this quarter.

One of the reasons why the principle of client self-determination seems on this interpretation to be so implausible is that it is often assumed that to be guided by a principle is to be committed to acting in accordance with it in any and every situation to which it is at all relevant. Thus the fact that social workers often find themselves obliged to act against their client's wishes, and to try to prevent them from carrying out their own self-determined plans, is adduced by some as grounds for dismissing the principle of client self-determination as illusory;[10] while others attempt to reconcile the apparent discrepancy between principle and practice by re-defining the word 'self-determination' in such a way that, as we have seen, it excludes such unacceptable plans from the scope of the principle. But that these drastic measures are not necessary is made abundantly clear by the way in which conflicts of obligation are dealt with in ordinary moral practice.

The fact that one sometimes has to break a promise does not necessarily lead one to question the reality of the promisee's rights, or to re-define what was originally promised in order to make it appear as if the promise has not, after all, been broken. One simply accepts that despite the validity of one's obligations to those to whom one has made promises, there are some situations in which the conflicting claims of others are so much stronger that they must be given priority. To subordinate some of one's obligations in this way is not to deny their existence. The compunction with which one breaks a promise, the steps one takes to make amends, explain or apologise, even when one knows one has done the right thing; all manifest one's continued recognition of and respect for the promisee's rights. The reason why this is not in any way self-contradictory is that it is not the function of rights to dictate in isolation what ought to be done in a particular situation. They present weighty considerations that have to be taken into account in deciding what ought to be done. But whether they are decisive or not depends on the strength of the other claims that might in a particular situation compete for satisfaction (Melden, pp. 217-23 below).

What these general observations show with regard to the principle of client self-determination is that even when it is interpreted as applying to all self-determined activity, whether moral or immoral, it does not require the social worker to stand idly by while his client brings disaster upon himself and all around him. The function of the principle is to remind the social worker that he is not morally free to compel or manœuvre another human being into acting against his own wishes without strong countervailing grounds for doing so. Exactly what does give one person the right to invade another's freedom in this way is too large a question to go into here (for a discussion of the subject see Hart, p. 192 below), but the fact that there are such grounds does not render the principle futile or illusory. It makes all the difference to the readiness with which one contemplates such actions, and the spirit in which one performs them, whether one violates another's rights knowing what one is doing, and why, regrettably, one has to do it; or forges ahead oblivious of any moral restraints that may bar one's way.

Secondly, there is a distinction which is liable to be overlooked, but is of some importance in understanding the peculiar relevance of the principle of client self-determination to social work. This is the distinction between the process of deliberation which culminates in a decision, and the implementation of that decision in action. If one considers that aspect of the concept of self-determination which has to do with the deliberative process and its control, rather than the physical and social circumstances in which choices and decisions are made and have to be implemented; if, in other words, one considers self-determination as the having of a will and purposes of one's own, and as responding in terms of one's own values to one's environment, be it a metropolis or a prison cell; then, to adapt the title of Bernstein's article (p. 33 above), there is something to be said for regarding it, if not as king, then, as a very special citizen in the realm of values.

For, although there have to be many restrictions on what a person may be allowed to do, there are few grounds on which the process of deliberation by which he arrives at his decisions may be justifiably subverted. It does not matter that he may through his deliberations arrive at foolish, self-destructive or anti-social decisions; he still has the right to make up his own mind, not necessarily without the aid of others, but certainly without being bullied or manipulated by them. It is a right so closely bound up with his status as a human being that it is as near to being inalienable and absolute as any right one could think of. This, together with the fact that it is especially relevant to the characteristic social work tasks of encouraging, advising and helping clients to gain more insight into their own motives and the consequences of their actions, helps explain the importance and centrality of the principle of client self-determination in social work.

Even when the distinction between deliberation and action is made, however, the client's right of self-determination may still seem unrealistic to those who associate it with such concepts as value neutrality, permissiveness and non-directiveness. For it then seems as if the main function of the principle is to protect clients from the influence of social workers; and since there can be no genuine human contact without some such influence taking place, the principle of client self-determination is made to appear as if it places impossible demands on social casework.

That such a view of the principle is unwarranted can be shown, I believe, by an examination of the liberal tradition within which the commitment to individual self-determination has developed. If, for instance, one examines Mill's essay *On Liberty,* one finds that, far from defending any sort of value neutrality, he is concerned to stress the need for 'a great increase of disinterested exertion to promote the good of others'; a theme which he develops as follows:[11]

> Human beings owe to each other help to distinguish the better from the worse, and encouragement to choose the former and avoid the latter. They should be for ever stimulating each other to increased exercise of their higher faculties, and increased direction of their feelings and aims towards wise instead of foolish, elevating instead of degrading, objects and contemplations. But neither one person, nor any number of persons, is warranted in saying to another human creature of ripe years, that he shall not do with his life for his own benefit what he choses to do with it. . . . Considerations to aid his judgement, exhortations to strengthen his will, may be offered to him, even obtruded on him, by others; but he himself is the final judge. All errors he is likely to commit against advice and

warning are far outweighed by the evil of allowing others to constrain him to what they deem his good.

I have quoted this passage at some length because it illustrates so strikingly how far from being identified with any form of moral *laissez-faire* was Mill's, and the general liberal commitment to personal freedom or self-determination. I am not, of course, proposing Mill's picture of zealous do-goodism as a model for contemporary social work. But in reaction against it we should be careful not to confuse the right of self-determination with a right to privacy, non-interference, or protection from the influence of others. However repugnant we may find the smug presumption, implicit in Mill's writings, that he and his like are equipped and entitled to busy themselves improving lesser mortals, there is nothing incompatible, once the proper distinctions are made, between his 'directiveness' (i.e. his holding of a definite view on how another should behave and trying to persuade him to behave accordingly) and his commitment to the individual's right of self-determination. If we object to being pursued, accosted and badgered by those who make it their business to rescue us from social or spiritual damnation, it is because we find it a nuisance, an invasion of our privacy, or insulting, not because it robs us of our liberty. The point at which these intrusions threaten our liberty or right of self-determination is when they are reinforced by the pressures of blackmail or threats of violence, or the more insidious powers of the 'hidden persuader' exploiting our fears and fantasies at the expense of our capacity for rational deliberation and choice.

If being self-determining, then, is not the same as being insulated from all normal exchange of ideas and influence between adult human beings, it follows that the client's right of self-determination cannot be regarded as necessarily incompatible with the social worker's commitment to certain values, his intervention into the client's affairs, or his attempting to persuade the client of the desirability of adopting or avoiding a particular course of action. There may be other reasons for avoiding such things, but not that they violate the client's right of self-determination. The real threat to this right comes not from his exposure to the social worker's values, but from the opportunities for manipulation available to the social worker in the exercise of his authority—both his legitimate authority, and the pseudo-authority with which he is often accredited. And this threat will be resisted, if at all, not by abandoning the principle of client self-determination as unrealistic and unworkable, or transforming it into something compatible with manipulation and coercion, but by a sustained effort to grasp in all its ramifications the moral significance of the client's right of self-determination, and its bearing on the various methods and approaches open to social workers in their dealings with their clients.

Conclusion

To conclude, let me restate the main points of this paper. I have sought to show that a tendency in social work thought to equate the concept of self-determination with that of rational, constructive and socially acceptable conduct, represents a departure from the literal or ordinary meaning of 'self-determination'. Moreover, and this is what makes it a process of persuasive definition, its effect, whether intentional or not, is to deny to certain actions and activities which would ordinarily be regarded as self-determining the commendatory force that that word had acquired in social work, and the protection of the principle of client self-determination, thus leaving the way open for the exercise of control over clients by social workers in such matters. A more literal interpretation of the meaning of 'self-determination' would reveal it in a profoundly different light. It would show that far from reinforcing the controlling aspects of social work, the main function of the principle of client self-determination is to provide a moral restraint upon social workers in the pursuit of their professional aims; a moral restraint springing from the client's right to go his own way not because it is constructive, good, or socially acceptable, but simply because it is his own. And my case against the persuasive definition of 'self-determination' is not just that it weakens this moral restraint, but that it tends to define it out of existence.

Notes

I wish to express my thanks to my colleague Mr W. D. Glasgow for helpful criticisms of an earlier draft of this paper.

1 F. P. Biestek, 'The principle of client self-determination', *Social Casework*, vol. 32, no. 9, 1951.
2 F. P. Biestek, *The Casework Relationship*, Allen & Unwin, 1961, pp. 100-19.
3 Biestek, 'The principle of client self-determination', p. 372.
4 C. L. Stevenson, *Ethics and Language*, Yale University Press, 1944.
5 *Ibid.*, p. 210.

6 B. Crick, *In Defence of Politics,* Weidenfeld & Nicolson, 1962, p. 51.
7 See W. D. Hudson, *Modern Moral Philosophy,* Macmillan, 1970, pp. 140-5.
8 B. Bosanquet, *The Philosophical Theory of the State,* Macmillan, 1951, pp. 111-12.
9 R. Plant, *Social and Moral Theory in Casework,* Routledge & Kegan Paul, 1970, pp. 25-34.
10 Neil Leighton, 'The myth of self-determination', *New Society,* no. 230, 23 February 1967.
11 J. S. Mill, *On Liberty,* Everyman's Library edition, p. 133.

Part two

Self-determination, freedom and related concepts

9   Two concepts of liberty[*]

Sir Isaiah Berlin

I

To coerce a man is to deprive him of freedom—freedom from what? Almost every moralist in human history has praised freedom. Like happiness and goodness, like nature and reality, the meaning of this term is so porous that there is little interpretation that it seems able to resist. I do not propose to discuss either the history or the more than two hundred senses of this protean word recorded by historians of ideas. I propose to examine no more than two of these senses— but those central ones, with a great deal of human history behind them, and, I dare say, still to come. The first of these political senses of freedom or liberty (I shall use both words to mean the same), which (following much precedent) I shall call the 'negative' sense, is involved in the answer to the question 'What is the area within which the subject—a person or group of persons—is or should be left to do or be what he is able to do or be, without interference by other persons?' The second, which I shall call the positive sense, is involved in the answer to the question 'What, or who, is the source of control or interference that can determine someone to do, or be, this rather than that?' The two questions are clearly different, even though the answers to them may overlap.

The notion of 'negative' freedom

I am normally said to be free to the degree to which no man or body of men interferes with my activity. Political liberty in this sense is simply the area within which a man can act unobstructed by others. If I am prevented by others from doing what I could otherwise do, I

*An extract from the revised version of his inaugural lecture 'Two concepts of liberty' published in *Four Essays on Liberty* by Isaiah Berlin, Oxford University Press, 1969, pp. 121-34. Reprinted by permission of the author and the Oxford University Press.

am to that degree unfree; and if this area is contracted by other men beyond a certain minimum, I can be described as being coerced, or, it may be, enslaved. Coercion is not, however, a term that covers every form of inability. If I say that I am unable to jump more than ten feet in the air, or cannot read because I am blind, or cannot understand the darker pages of Hegel, it would be eccentric to say that I am to that degree enslaved or coerced. Coercion implies the deliberate interference of other human beings within the area in which I could otherwise act. You lack political liberty or freedom only if you are prevented from attaining a goal by human beings.[1] Mere incapacity to attain a goal is not lack of political freedom.[2] This is brought out by the use of such modern expressions as 'economic freedom' and its counterpart, 'economic slavery'. It is argued, very plausibly, that if a man is too poor to afford something on which there is no legal ban—a loaf of bread, a journey round the world, recourse to the law courts—he is as little free to have it as he would be if it were forbidden him by law. If my poverty were a kind of disease, which prevented me from buying bread, or paying for the journey round the world or getting my case heard, as lameness prevents me from running, this inability would not naturally be described as a lack of freedom, least of all political freedom. It is only because I believe that my inability to get a given thing is due to the fact that other human beings have made arrangements whereby I am, whereas others are not, prevented from having enough money with which to pay for it, that I think myself a victim of coercion or slavery. In other words, this use of the term depends on a particular social and economic theory about the causes of my poverty or weakness. If my lack of material means is due to my lack of mental or physical capacity, then I begin to speak of being deprived of freedom (and not simply about poverty) only if I accept the theory.[3] If, in addition, I believe that I am being kept in want by a specific arrangement which I consider unjust or unfair, I speak of economic slavery or oppression. 'The nature of things does not madden us, only ill will does', said Rousseau. The criterion of oppression is the part that I believe to be played by other human beings, directly or indirectly, with or without the intention of doing so, in frustrating my wishes. By being free in this sense I mean not being interfered with by others. The wider the area of non-interference the wider my freedom.

This is what the classical English political philosophers meant when they used this word.[4] They disagreed about how wide the area could or should be. They supposed that it could not, as things were, be unlimited, because if it were, it would entail a state in which all men could boundlessly interfere with all other men; and this kind of 'natural' freedom would lead to social chaos in which men's minimum needs would not be satisfied; or else the liberties of the weak would be suppressed by the strong. Because they perceived that human purposes and activities do not automatically harmonise with one another, and because (whatever their official doctrines) they put high value on other goals, such as justice, or happiness, or culture, or security, or varying degrees of equality, they were prepared to curtail freedom in the interests of other values and, indeed, of freedom itself. For, without this, it was impossible to create the kind of association that they thought desirable. Consequently, it is assumed by these thinkers that the area of men's free action must be limited by law. But equally it is assumed, especially by such libertarians as Locke and Mill in England, and Constant and Tocqueville in France, that there ought to exist a certain minimum area of personal freedom which must on no account be violated; for if it is overstepped, the individual will find himself in an area too narrow for even that minimum development of his natural faculties which alone makes it possible to pursue, and even to conceive, the various ends which men hold good or right or sacred. It follows that a frontier must be drawn between the area of private life and that of public authority. Where it is to be drawn is a matter of argument, indeed of haggling. Men are largely interdependent, and no man's activity is so completely private as never to obstruct the lives of others in any way. 'Freedom for the pike is death for the minnows'; the liberty of some must depend on the restraint of others. 'Freedom for an Oxford don', others have been known to add, 'is a very different thing from freedom for an Egyptian peasant.'

This proposition derives its force from something that is both true and important, but the phrase itself remains a piece of political claptrap. It is true that to offer political rights, or safeguards against intervention by the state, to men who are half-naked, illiterate, underfed, and diseased is to mock their condition; they need medical help or education before they can understand, or make use of, an increase in their freedom. What is freedom to those who cannot make use of it? Without adequate conditions for the use of freedom, what is the value of freedom? First things come first: there are situations, as a nineteenth-century Russian radical writer declared, in which boots are superior to the works of Shakespeare;

individual freedom is not everyone's primary need. For freedom is not the mere absence of frustration of whatever kind; this would inflate the meaning of the word until it meant too much or too little. The Egyptian peasant needs clothes or medicine before, and more than, personal liberty, but the minimum freedom that he needs today, and the greater degree of freedom that he may need tomorrow, is not some species of freedom peculiar to him, but identical with that of professors, artists, and millionaires.

What troubles the consciences of Western liberals is not, I think, the belief that the freedom that men seek differs according to their social or economic conditions, but that the minority who possess it have gained it by exploiting, or, at least, averting their gaze from, the vast majority who do not. They believe, with good reason, that if individual liberty is an ultimate end for human beings, none should be deprived of it by others; least of all that some should enjoy it at the expense of others. Equality of liberty; not to treat others as I should not wish them to treat me; repayment of my debt to those who alone have made possible my liberty or prosperity or enlightenment; justice, in its simplest and most universal sense—these are the foundations of liberal morality. Liberty is not the only goal of men. I can, like the Russian critic Belinsky, say that if others are to be deprived of it—if my brothers are to remain in poverty, squalor, and chains—then I do not want if for myself, I reject it with both hands and infinitely prefer to share their fate. But nothing is gained by a confusion of terms. To avoid glaring inequality or widespread misery I am ready to sacrifice some, or all, of my freedom: I may do so willingly and freely: but it is freedom that I am giving up for the sake of justice or equality or the love of my fellow men. I should be guilt-stricken, and rightly so, if I were not, in some circumstances, ready to make this sacrifice. But a sacrifice is not an increase in what is being sacrificed, namely freedom, however great the moral need or the compensation for it. Everything is what it is: liberty is liberty, not equality or fairness or justice or culture, or human happiness or a quiet conscience. If the liberty of myself or my class or nation depends on the misery of a number of other human beings, the system which promotes this is unjust and immoral. But if I curtail or lose my freedom, in order to lessen the shame of such inequality, and do not thereby materially increase the individual liberty of others, an absolute loss of liberty occurs. This may be compensated for by a gain in justice or in happiness or in peace, but the loss remains, and it is a confusion of values to say that although my 'liberal', individual freedom may go by the board, some other kind of freedom—'social' or 'economic'—is increased. Yet it remains true that the freedom of some must at times be curtailed to secure the freedom of others. Upon what principle should this be done? If freedom is a sacred, untouchable value, there can be no such principle. One or other of these conflicting rules or principles must, at any rate in practice, yield: not always for reasons which can be clearly stated, let alone generalised into rules or universal maxims. Still, a practical compromise has to be found.

Philosophers with an optimistic view of human nature and a belief in the possibility of harmonising human interests (e.g. Locke or Adam Smith and, in some moods, Mill) believed that social harmony and progress were compatible with reserving a large area for private life over which neither the state nor any other authority must be allowed to trespass. Hobbes, and those who agreed with him, especially conservative or reactionary thinkers, argued that if men were to be prevented from destroying one another and making social life a jungle or a wilderness, greater safeguards must be instituted to keep them in their places; he wished correspondingly to increase the area of centralised control and decrease that of the individual. But both sides agreed that some portion of human existence must remain independent of the sphere of social control. To invade that preserve, however small, would be despotism. The most eloquent of all defenders of freedom and privacy, Benjamin Constant, who had not forgotten the Jacobin dictatorship, declared that at the very least the liberty of religion, opinion, expression, property, must be guaranteed against arbitrary invasion. Jefferson, Burke, Paine, Mill, compiled different catalogues of individual liberties, but the argument for keeping authority at bay is always substantially the same. We must preserve a minimum area of personal freedom if we are not to 'degrade or deny our nature'. We cannot remain absolutely free, and must give up some of our liberty to preserve the rest. But total self-surrender is self-defeating. What then must the minimum be? That which a man cannot give up without offending against the essence of his human nature. What is this essence? What are the standards which it entails? This has been, and perhaps always will be, a matter of infinite debate. But whatever the principle in terms of which the area of non-interference is to be drawn, whether it is that of natural law or natural rights, or of utility or the pronouncements of a categorical imperative, or the sanctity of the social contract, or any other concept with which men have sought to clarify and justify their convictions, liberty in this sense means liberty *from;* absence of interference beyond the shifting, but always recognisable, frontier. 'The only freedom which deserves the name is that of pursuing our own good in our own way', said the most celebrated of its champions. If this is so, is compulsion ever justified? Mill had no doubt that it was. Since justice demands that all indiviuals be entitled to a minimum of freedom, all other individuals were of necessity to be restrained, if need be by force, from depriving anyone of it. Indeed, the whole function of law was the prevention of just such collisions; the state was reduced to what Lassalle called contemptuously the functions of a night-watchman or traffic policeman.

What made the protection of individual liberty so sacred to Mill? In his famous essay he declares that, unless men are left to live as they wish 'in the path which merely concerns themselves', civilisation cannot advance; the truth will not, for lack of a free market in ideas, come to light; there will be no scope for spontaneity, originality, genius, for mental energy, for moral courage. Society will be crushed by the weight of 'collective mediocrity'. Whatever is rich and diversified will be crushed by the weight of custom, by men's constant tendency to conformity, which breeds only 'withered capacities', 'pinched and hidebound', 'cramped and warped' human beings. 'Pagan self-assertion is as worthy as Christian self-denial.' 'All the errors which a man is likely to commit against advice and warning are far outweighed by the evil of allowing others to constrain him to what they deem is good.' The defence of liberty consists in the 'negative' goal of warding off interference. To threaten a man with persecution unless he submits to a life in which he exercises no choice of his goals; to block before him every door but one, no matter how noble the prospect upon which it opens, or how benevolent the motives of those who arrange this, is to sin against the truth that he is a man, a being with a life of his own to live. This is liberty as it has been conceived by liberals in the modern world from the days of Erasmus (some would say of Occam) to our own. Every plea for civil liberties and individual rights, every protest against exploitation and humiliation, against the encroachment of public authority, or the mass hypnosis of custom or organised propaganda, springs from this individualistic, and much disputed, conception of man.

Three facts about his position may be noted. In the first place Mill confuses two distinct notions. One is that all coercion is, in so far as it frustrates human desires, bad as such, although it may have to be applied to prevent other, greater evils; while non-interference, which is the opposite of coercion, is good as such, although it is not the only good. This is the 'negative' conception of liberty in its classical form. The other is that men should seek to discover the truth, or to develop a certain type of character of which Mill approved—critical, original, imaginative, independent, non-conforming to the point of eccentricity, and so on—and that truth can be found, and such character can be bred, only in conditions of freedom. Both these are liberal views, but they are not identical, and the connection between them is, at best, empirical. No one would argue that truth or freedom of self-expression could flourish where dogma crushes all thought. But the evidence of history tends to show (as, indeed, was argued by James Stephen in his formidable attack on Mill in his *Liberty, Equality, Fraternity*) that integrity, love of truth, and fiery individualism grow at least as often in severely disciplined communities among, for example, the puritan Calvinists of Scotland or New England, or under military discipline, as in more tolerant or indifferent societies; and if this is so, Mill's argument for liberty as a necessary condition for the growth of human genius falls to the ground. If his two goals proved incompatible, Mill would be faced with a cruel dilemma, quite apart from the further difficulties created by the inconsistency of his doctrines with strict utilitarianism, even in his own humane version of it.[5]

In the second place, the doctrine is comparatively modern. There seems to be scarcely any discussion of individual liberty as a conscious political ideal (as opposed to its actual existence) in the ancient world. Condorcet had already remarked that the notion of individual rights was absent from the legal conceptions of the Romans and Greeks; this seems to hold equally of the Jewish, Chinese, and all other ancient civilisations that have since come to light.[6] The domination of this ideal has been the exception rather than the rule, even in the recent history of the West. Nor has liberty in this sense often formed a rallying cry for the greatest masses of mankind. The desire not to be impinged upon, to be left to oneself, has been a mark of high civilisation both on the part of individuals and communities. The sense of privacy itself, of the area of personal relationships as something sacred in its own right, derives from a conception of freedom which, for all its religious roots, is scarcely older, in its developed state, than the Renaissance or the Reformation.[7] Yet its decline would mark the death of a civilisation, of an entire moral outlook.

The third characteristic of this notion of liberty is of greater importance: liberty in this sense is not incompatible with some kinds of
autocracy, or at any rate with the absence of self-government.
Liberty in this sense is principally concerned with the area of
control, not with its source. Just as a democracy may, in fact,
deprive the individual citizen of a great many liberties which he
might have in some other form of society, so it is perfectly conceivable that a liberal-minded despot would allow his subjects a
large measure of personal freedom. The despot who leaves his subjects a wide area of liberty may be unjust, or encourage the wildest
inequalities, care little for order, or virtue, or knowledge; but provided he does not curb their liberty, or at least curbs it less than
many other régimes, he meets with Mill's specification.[8] Freedom in
this sense is not, at any rate logically, connected with democracy or
self-government. Self-government may, on the whole, provide a
better guarantee of the preservation of civil liberties than other
régimes, and has been defended as such by libertarians. But there is
no necessary connection between individual liberty and democractic
rule. The answer to the question 'Who governs me?' is logically
distinct from the question 'How far does government interfere with
me?' It is in this difference that the great contrast between the two
concepts of negative and positive liberty, in the end, consists.[9] For
the 'positive' sense of liberty comes to light if we try to answer the
question, not 'What am I free to do or be?', but 'By whom am I
ruled?' or 'Who is to say what I am, and what I am not, to be or do?'
The connection between democracy and individual liberty is a good
deal more tenuous than it seemed to many advocates of both. The
desire to be governed by myself, or at any rate to participate in the
process by which my life is to be controlled, may be as deep a wish as
that of a free area for action, and perhaps historically older. But it is
not a desire for the same thing. So different is it, indeed, as to have
led in the end to the great clash of ideologies that dominates our
world. For it is this—the 'positive' conception of liberty: not freedom
from, but freedom to—to lead one prescribed form of life—which
the adherents of the 'negative' notion represent as being, at times,
no better than a specious disguise for brutal tyranny.

II The notion of positive freedom

The 'positive' sense of the word 'liberty' derives from the wish on the
part of the individual to be his own master. I wish my life and

decisions to depend on myself, not on external forces of whatever kind. I wish to be the instrument of my own, not of other men's, acts of will. I wish to be a subject, not an object; to be moved by reasons, by conscious purposes, which are my own, not by causes which affect me, as it were, from outside. I wish to be somebody, not nobody; a doer—deciding, not being decided for, self-directed and not acted upon by external nature or by other men as if I were a thing, or an animal, or a slave incapable of playing a human role, that is, of conceiving goals and policies of my own and realising them. This is at least part of what I mean when I say that I am rational, and that it is my reason that distinguishes me as a human being from the rest of the world. I wish, above all, to be conscious of myself as a thinking, willing, active being, bearing responsibility for my choices and able to explain them by reference to my own ideas and purposes. I feel free to the degree that I believe this to be true, and enslaved to the degree that I am made to realise that it is not.

The freedom which consists in being one's own master, and the freedom which consists in not being prevented from choosing as I do by other men, may, on the face of it, seem concepts at no great logical distance from each other—no more than negative and positive ways of saying much the same thing. Yet the 'positive' and 'negative' notions of freedom historically developed in divergent directions not always by logically reputable steps, until, in the end, they came into direct conflict with each other.

One way of making this clear is in terms of the independent momentum which the, initially perhaps quite harmless, metaphor of self-mastery acquired. 'I am my own master'; 'I am slave to no man'; but may I not (as Platonists or Hegelians tend to say) be a slave to nature? Or to my own 'unbridled' passions? Are these not so many species of the identical genus 'slave'—some political or legal, others moral or spiritual? Have not men had the experience of liberating themselves from spiritual slavery, or slavery to nature, and do they not in the course of it become aware, on the one hand, of a self which dominates, and, on the other, of something in them which is brought to heel? This dominant self is then variously identified with reason, with my 'higher nature', with the self which calculates and aims at what will satisfy it in the long run, with my 'real', or 'ideal', or 'autonomous' self, or with my self 'at its best'; which is then contrasted with irrational impulse, uncontrolled desires, my 'lower' nature, the pursuit of immediate pleasures, my 'empirical' or 'heteronomous' self, swept by every gust of desire and passion, needing to be rigidly disciplined if it is ever to rise to the full height of its 'real' nature. Presently the two selves may be represented as divided by an even larger gap: the real self may be conceived as something wider than the individual (as the term is normally understood), as a social 'whole' of which the individual is an element or aspect: a tribe, a race, a church, a state, the great society of the living and the dead and the yet unborn. This entity is then identified as being the 'true' self which, by imposing its collective, or 'organic', single will upon its recalcitrant 'members', achieves its own, and therefore their, 'higher' freedom. The perils of using organic metaphors to justify the coercion of some men by others in order to raise them to a 'higher' level of freedom have often been pointed out. But what gives such plausibility as it has to this kind of language is that we recognise that it is possible, and at times justifiable, to coerce men in the name of some goal (let us say, justice or public health) which they would, if they were more enlightened, themselves pursue, but do not, because they are blind or ignorant or corrupt. This renders it easy for me to conceive of myself as coercing others for their own sake, in their, not my, interest. I am then claiming that I know what they truly need better than they know it themselves. What, at most, this entails is that they would not resist me if they were rational and as wise as I and understood their interests as I do. But I may go on to claim a good deal more than this. I may declare that they are actually aiming at what in their benighted state they consciously resist, because there exists within them an occult entity—their latent rational will, or their 'true' purpose— and that this entity, although it is belied by all that they overtly feel and do and say, is their 'real' self, of which the poor empirical self in space and time may know nothing or little; and that this inner spirit is the only self that deserves to have its wishes taken into account.[10] Once I take this view, I am in a position to ignore the actual wishes of men or societies, to bully, oppress, torture them in the name, and on behalf, of their 'real' selves, in the secure knowledge that whatever is the true goal of man (happiness, performance of duty, wisdom, a just society, self-fulfilment) must be identical with his freedom—the free choice of his 'true', albeit often submerged and inarticulate, self.

This paradox has been often exposed. It is one thing to say that I know what is good for X, while he himself does not; and even to ignore his wishes for its—and his—sake; and a very different one to say that he has *eo ipso* chosen it, not indeed consciously, not as he seems in everyday life, but in his role as a rational self which his empirical self may not know—the 'real' self which discerns the good, and cannot help choosing it once it is revealed. This monstrous impersonation, which consists in equating what X would choose if he were something he is not, or at least not yet, with what X actually seeks and chooses, is at the heart of all political theories of self-realisation. It is one thing to say that I may be coerced for my own good which I am too blind to see: this may, on occasion, be for my benefit; indeed it may enlarge the scope of my liberty. It is another to say that if it is my good, then I am not being coerced, for I have willed it, whether I know this or not, and am free (or 'truly' free) even while my poor earthly body and foolish mind bitterly reject it, and struggle against those who seek however benevolently to impose it, with the greatest desperation.

This magical transformation, or sleight of hand (for which William James so justly mocked the Hegelians), can no doubt be perpetrated just as easily with the 'negative' concept of freedom, where the self that should not be interfered with is no longer the individual with his actual wishes and needs as they are normally conceived, but the 'real' man within, identified with the pursuit of some ideal purpose not dreamed of by his empirical self. And, as in the case of the 'positively' free self, this entity may be inflated into some super-personal entity—a state, a class, a nation, or the march of history itself, regarded as a more 'real' subject of attributes than the empirical self. But the 'positive' conception of freedom as self-mastery, with its suggestion of a man divided against himself, has, in fact, and as a matter of history, of doctrine and of practice, lent itself more easily to this splitting of personality into two: the transcendent, dominant controller, and the empirical bundle of desires and passions to be disciplined and brought to heel. It is this historical fact that has been influential. This demonstrates (if demonstration of so obvious a truth is needed) that conceptions of freedom directly derive from views of what constitutes a self, a person, a man. Enough manipulation with the definition of man, and freedom can be made to mean whatever the manipulator wishes. Recent history has made it only too clear that the issue is not merely academic.

The consequences of distinguishing between two selves will become even clearer if one considers the two major forms which the desire to be self-directed—directed by one's 'true' self—has historically taken: the first, that of self-abnegaton in order to attain

independence; the second, that of self-realisation, or total self-iden-
tification with a specific principle or ideal in order to attain the self-
same end.

Notes

1 I do not, of course, mean to imply the truth of the converse.
2 Helvétius made this point very clearly: 'The free man is the man who is not in
  irons, nor imprisoned in a gaol, nor terrorized like a slave by the fear of punishment . . . it is not lack of freedom not to fly like an eagle or swim like a whale.'
3 The Marxist conception of social laws is, of course, the best known version of this
  theory, but it forms a large element in some Christian and utilitarian, and all
  socialist, doctrines.
4 'A free man', said Hobbes, 'is he that . . . is not hindered to do what he hath the
  will to do.' Law is always a 'fetter', even if it protects you from being bound in
  chains that are heavier than those of the law, say, some more repressive law or
  custom, or arbitrary despotism or chaos. Bentham says much the same.
5 This is but another illustration of the natural tendency of all but a very few thinkers
  to believe that all the things they hold good must be intimately connected, or at
  least compatible, with one another. The history of thought, like the history of
  nations, is strewn with examples of inconsistent, or at least disparate, elements
  artificially yoked together in a despotic system, or held together by the danger of
  some common enemy. In due course the danger passes, and conflicts between the
  allies arise, which often disrupt the system, sometimes to the great benefit of
  mankind.
6 See the valuable discussion of this in Michel Villey, *Leçons d'histoire de la
  philosophie du droit,* who traces the embryo of the notion of subjective rights to
  Occam.
7 Christian (and Jewish or Moslem) belief in the absolute authority of divine or
  natural laws, or in the equality of all men in the sight of God, is very different from
  belief in freedom to live as one prefers.
8 Indeed, it is arguable that in the Prussia of Frederick the Great or in the Austria
  of Josef II men of imagination, originality, and creative genius, and, indeed,
  minorities of all kinds, were less persecuted and felt the pressure, both of institutions and custom, less heavy upon them than in many an earlier or later
  democracy.
9 'Negative liberty' is something the extent of which, in a given case, it is difficult to
  estimate. It might, prima facie, seem to depend simply on the power to choose
  between at any rate two alternatives. Nevertheless, not all choices are equally free,
  or free at all. If in a totalitarian state I betray my friend under threat of torture,
  perhaps even if I act from fear of losing my job, I can reasonably say that I did not
  act freely. Nevertheless, I did, of course, make a choice, and could, at any rate in
  theory, have chosen to be killed or tortured or imprisoned. The mere existence of
  alternatives is not, therefore, enough to make my action free (although it may be
  voluntary) in the normal sense of the word. The extent of my freedom seems to
  depend on (a) how many possibilities are open to me (although the method of
  counting these can never be more than impressionistic. Possibilities of action are
  not discrete entities like apples, which can be exhaustively enumerated); (b) how
  easy or difficult each of these possibilities is to actualize; (c) how important in my
  plan of life, given my character and circumstances, these possibilities are when
  compared with each other; (d) how far they are closed and opened by deliberate
  human acts; (e) what value not merely the agent, but the general sentiment of the
  society in which he lives, puts on the various possibilities. All these magnitudes

must be 'integrated', and a conclusion, necessarily never precise, or indisputable, drawn from this process. It may well be that there are many incommensurable kinds and degrees of freedom, and that they cannot be drawn up on any single scale of magnitude. Moreover, in the case of societies, we are faced by such (logically absurd) questions as 'Would arrangement X increase the liberty of Mr A more than it would that of Messrs B, C, and D between them, added together?' The same difficulties arise in applying utilitarian criteria. Nevertheless, provided we do not demand precise measurement, we can give valid reasons for saying that the average subject of the King of Sweden is, on the whole, a good deal freer today than the average citizen of Spain or Albania. Total patterns of life must be compared directly as wholes, although the method by which we make the comparison, and the truth of the conclusions, are difficult or impossible to demonstrate. But the vagueness of the concepts, and the multiplicity of the criteria involved, are an attribute of the subject-matter itself, not of our imperfect methods of measurement, or incapacity for precise thought.

10 'The ideal of true freedom is the maximum of power for all the members of human society alike to make the best of themselves', said T. H. Green in 1881. Apart from the confusion of freedom with equality, this entails that if a man chose some immediate pleasure—which (in whose view?) would not enable him to make the best of himself (what self?)—what he was exercising was not 'true' freedom: and if deprived of it, would not lose anything that mattered. Green was a genuine liberal: but many a tyrant could use this formula to justify his worst acts of oppression.

10   A critique of the ideals of liberty *

H. J. McCloskey

Liberty now occupies a very secure and respected place as one of the great, and perhaps as the greatest and most important political ideals, and few would wish not to pay homage to it as such. Yet if we look at the writings of political philosophers, we find a widespread diversity of views as to the nature of liberty associated with the assumption that there is only one genuine concept and only one true ideal of liberty, whereas it might reasonably have been expected that the possiblity of a number of distinct, genuine ideals of liberty might have been entertained. In the relatively few cases in which various concepts have been distinguished as genuine concepts of liberty, one has usually been explained in terms of and reduced to the other; such that only one is viewed as being the basis of an ultimate, irreducible ideal. It is of course true that Mill and some other notable liberals treat a number of distinct concepts of liberty as ideals, but they do so without a clear awareness that they are operating with significantly different concepts. Some of Mill's apparent inconsistencies in *Liberty and Principles of Political Economy* are simply due to his moving from one concept of liberty to another. In the less common cases where a number of concepts of liberty are distinguished as irreducibly distinct, e.g. as with Berlin with his insistence on the fundamental distinction between negative and positive liberty, we find that one is represented as the real ideal, and the other very equivocally; as a less humane and even as a 'dangerous' ideal, i.e. presumably, as not really an ideal at all. He writes:[1]

> The 'negative' liberty that they strive to realise seems to me a truer and more humane ideal than the goods of those who seek in the great, disciplined, authoritarian structure the ideal of

*From *Mind*, vol. 74, no. 296, October 1965, pp. 483-508. Reprinted with the permission of the author and Basil Blackwell, publishers of *Mind*.

'positive' self-mastery by classes, or peoples, or the whole of mankind. It is truer, because it recognises the fact that human goals are many, not all of them commensurable, and in perpetual rivalry with one another. . . . It is more humane because it does not (as the system builders do) deprive men in the name of some remote, or incoherent, ideal, of much that they have found to be indispensable to their life as human beings.

These claims are equally compatible with positive liberty construed simply as self-determination. That Berlin speaks of 'negative' liberty, and not of both 'negative' and 'positive' liberty (construed as self-determination) as a truer and more humane ideal than the views of positive liberty noted here, suggests, as is the case, that he thinks that positive liberty, even when understood as self-determination, is a dangerous ideal because, and only because, it lends itself more readily than does negative liberty to development into untrue and inhumane ideals.

Now it has been a commonplace to distinguish positive and negative liberty, but usually those who have drawn this distinction have argued that one or the other is not really liberty, Berlin being unusual in acknowledging both as genuine concepts of liberty.

It is this whole trend of thought that I wish to question, and I propose to do so by noting and examining various concepts and arguing that several of them and not simply one or two are distinct concepts of liberty. I shall then go on to consider whether any or some of them are the bases of genuine, ulimate, irreducible, political ideals, arguing that the concepts of negative liberty are not such, and that there are difficulties, but not necessarily insurmountable difficulties, with various of the concepts of positive liberty.

Although the distinction between negative and positive liberty is drawn in many different and strange ways—some theorists explain positive liberty in such a way that it is properly called liberty, whilst others misleadingly call some other ideal, e.g. perfection of self, right conduct, good citizenship, etc., by the name liberty—this general distinction as drawn by Berlin may usefully be taken as our starting point. Berlin explains the distinction in various ways, but his basic distinction is between negative liberty interpreted as 'not being interfered with', 'being let alone', and positive liberty as self-determination. Berlin explains negative liberty by reference to Mill as follows: 'One is that all coercion is, in so far as it frustrates human desires, bad as such, although it may have to be applied to prevent other, greater evils; while non-interference, which is the opposite of coercion, is good as such, although it is not the only good. This is the "negative" conception of liberty in its classical form' (p. 12) [see p. 146 above]. Of positive liberty he writes: 'For the "positive" sense of liberty comes to light if we try to answer the question, not "What am I free to do or be?" but "By whom am I ruled?" or "Who is to say what I am, and what I am not, to be or to do?" (p. 15) [see p. 148 above]. And he goes on to speak of "the desire to be governed by myself. . .' and to state: 'The "positive" sense of the word "liberty" derives from the wish on the part of the individual to be his own master. I wish my life and decisions to depend upon myself, not on external forces of whatever kind' (p. 16). (See also pp. 6 and 7) [see p. 148 above]. All page references are to *Two Concepts of Liberty*. (I understand that Berlin would now omit all reference to desires in the analysis of negative liberty and would substitute for it 'range of unimpeded choices'.) Berlin also explains positive liberty in a range of ways—as self-mastery, true self-mastery, etc., but the origin of the range of accounts he gives is self-determination. Clearly Berlin is right as far as he goes but further important distinctions need to be drawn such that two distinct concepts of negative liberty and four concepts of positive liberty need to be distinguished as follows: (i) non-interference unqualified, (ii) non-interference with one's enjoyment of one's rights, (iii) self-determination, (iv) reasonable self-determination, (v) oppportunity to enjoy one's rights, (vi) opportunity to seek one's self-perfection. Additional, but less important, distinctions may be drawn within some of these concepts, but these appear to be the more important of the concepts which have reasonable claims to being considered to be concepts of liberty. These various concepts although distinct from one another, tend, both at the conceptual level and in the writings of political philosophers, to merge one into the other. It is their fluidity which makes any examination of them so difficult. It should also be noted here that, as Berlin points out, all concepts of liberty have in common the element of non-interference. However, it is not simply nor even primarily by virtue of this common element that each is thought to be a concept of liberty as is evident from a consideration of self-determination.

I shall not concern myself with those accounts of 'liberty' which confuse liberty with other, distinct political ideals, beyond noting that such confusions are not uncommon and take a multitude of forms, not the least important of which is that of calling some good a 'freedom from', e.g. security is equated with freedom from fear, health with freedom from disease, etc. Many of the goods which are so often confused with liberty are in fact pre-conditions of liberty, in certain senses of that expression, and this fact has no doubt encouraged the confusion of identifying them with liberty or with part of liberty. The concepts of liberty with which I shall be concerned, are concepts which seem to me to have a real claim to be called such, even though various of them are more attenuated and less satisfactoty than first appearances suggest; and I shall defend my view against suggestions such as that of Benn and Peters (if indeed it is one they do intend to make) that all concepts of positive liberty rest on a confusion of liberty with goods other than liberty, simply by elucidating the concept of positive liberty under consideration.[2] However, it must be noted and conceded that ordinary usage is so vague and muddled in the areas of the language of liberty, that it is without doubt true, as my subsequent discussion will bring out, that all the concepts of liberty that I have distinguished, except that of self-determination, could be questioned, but if questioned, I should not know of a more apt and illuminating general characterisation of the ideals to which they point, than the general characterisation as liberty. It is relevant to note that whilst many accounts of liberty amount to confusions between liberty and other ideals, probably all liberal and libertarian accounts of liberty confuse liberty with equal liberty or with fairly distributed liberty, whereas liberty is one thing or one group of things and equality and justice other things.

A. Negative liberty

(a) *Non-interference unqualified*

Many theorists have seemed to uphold non-interference as the ideal, and have even believed themselves to be doing so, but on close examination of their statements it becomes evident that few, if any, philosophers have argued for liberty in this sense of the expression, and that Hobbes, who is not remembered as a libertarian, and Humboldt and Spencer, are among the few philosophers who *seek* to *explain* liberty simply as non-interference. Of the others, Mill hankers after it in *Liberty,* but he is too acute a liberal and too much of a political realist, to settle for it. And whilst Berlin does not express himself with sufficient definiteness in *Two Concepts of Liberty* for it to be clear whether he associates his concept of negative liberty with a theory of rights (he gives no clear criteria as to what constitutes interference) it is probable that when he applies it, he does so on such a basis, for he does not seem to see the current recognition of a right to property as a major invasion of negative liberty, which it would be if negative liberty were to be explained simply as non-interference.

It is no accident that non-interference (unqualified) has not been embraced as a political ideal, for it cannot be given the rich full content that exponents of liberty wish to give to their ideal. If to enjoy liberty is simply to be let alone, i.e. not to be interfered with, where interference is not defined in terms of and on the basis of a theory of rights, liberty appears as a stunted, sterile thing, rather than as the glorious ideal it is so often portrayed as being. This is apparent if we consider what is implied by liberty conceived of as non-interference, in particular, what would be permitted and what would be condemned as an invasion of liberty, i.e. what constitutes an interference with another person.

We are free, in this sense of liberty, if we are let alone. So we are free if we are let to starve, or to die for want of means of subsistence. We are free to read, to write, to acquire learning in a state in which the only education available is private education at a cost beyond our means, provided that no one interferes with us and prevents us seeking education when and if we can afford it. Thus we can enjoy the fullest liberty, yet be unable to do anything we wish to do, for we may lack the means to realise our wishes, but be free because we are let alone. The illiterate, unemployed, starving, dying paralytic—who, in a modern welfare state would have been educated, treated and made well, employed and made a useful member of the community and such that he could realise his wishes—such an ineffective person, who cannot fulfil a single wish because of his disabilities and lack of training, is nevertheless completely free, he is enjoying the fullest liberty, in this sense of negative liberty, provided he is not interfered with, i.e. provided he is let alone; and letting him alone would not necessarily entail leaving his property, if any, alone, for exclusive property rights would seem to involve interference with the free actions of others. Again, it would seem that on this view, the labourer who, in a *laissez-faire* economy, bargains for his wages and hours and settles for the best he can get, an 80-hour week and below subsistence wage, is also enjoying the fullest liberty, for he is not being interfered with. If it is claimed that he is *really* being interfered with, then a gap opens between the concept of 'being let alone' and that of 'not being interfered with'. It is no doubt true that it is the actions of men which cause him to be faced by such an unpleasant choice; but it is none the less a choice that faces him. He could properly claim that he was not being let alone if, and only if, he were forced to work or not to work. It might of course be argued that much interference is indirect, unintended interference, and that liberty as non-interference still justifies much social legislation, being interference to prevent interference. But surely this is to switch to a concept of interference distinct from the concept of not letting a person alone. To suggest that the wage-earner in a *laissez-faire* economic state is being interfered with in being obliged to agree to unsatisfactory wages and conditions, is to change the concept of interference such that all who are obliged to pay for their goods more than they would wish to pay, are being interfered with, since prices are socially determined, i.e. ultimately determined by human action and are forced upon us to a greater or less extent. A view of liberty which would permit and even justify interference with all that is humanly determined or humanly affected is no longer the negative liberty of non-interference it is represented as being.

On first impression this appears to be the least questionable concept of liberty; yet even it might be questioned, and for the following reasons: (i) Not all interference is an invasion of liberty. If I strike my neighbour, not because he is not doing what I wish him to do, but simply from malice, that is not an invasion of his liberty: it is an interference with him. It is not letting him alone. It would be an invasion of liberty only if it were in the form of coercion designed to intimidate and influence future action. (ii) Too much is let in by such an account of liberty in other respects. Engaging in an act of gross immorality in the presence of a highly moralistic person might be 'forcing' that person to experience pain which he does not wish to experience, but it is hardly an invasion of his liberty. Yet it is significant that it is along the lines of such an argument that some liberal exponents of negative liberty have sought to justify intolerance of nudity. The same issue arose in respect of Sabbatarian legislation. This suggests perhaps that negative liberty should be explained simply as interference with action. Yet such a limitation leads to difficulties of the opposite kind, due to its being too narrow. (iii) Again, there are the borderline cases of interference; and how they are resolved bears significantly on whether negative liberty is really liberty. Are bribes and rewards interferences? Is a threat an interference? Is social pressure interference? Is it an interference to tell a person that you will not like him if he acts in a certain way? What in general are the marks of interference which is not in the form of direct force? Are all such interferences invasions of liberty? (iv) If no theory of rights is written into the concept of 'being let alone', then to set up a property system and restrict the movement of people is clearly to interfere with others, for a property system is a system of rights backed by sanctions; and the sanctions represent interference, perhaps justifiable interference, but interference none the less. This is most apparent to us when we contemplate property systems different from our own. Similarly with marriage systems, systems of justice, and the like. Only interference to prevent interference will be possible as dictates of negative liberty, and it is difficult to see how property and protection of property can be compatible with such liberty. What is true of property appears to be true of other rights such as family rights. It would seem that claims such as that considered above, that the labourer in a *laissez-faire* economy, is being interfered with in being obliged to accept below subsistence wages, is only plausible if and in so far as a right to life is written into the concept of non-interference. How then should we determine, without reference to rights, what is an interference? I suggest that this can be done, although it would be extremely difficult, and large areas of uncertainty would remain. But the conclusions as to the nature of liberty, negative liberty, would not be those one expects from such an ideal, and would be such as to give rise to some slight misgivings in continuing to call it liberty.

(b) *Liberty as non-interference with rights*

The other concept, and I suggest, the historically important concept of negative liberty is that of non-interference with rights, where rights, their content, nature and grounds are variously conceived and where liberty is usually thought of as one among other rights as well as consisting in liberty to enjoy rights in general. In spite of his allusions to Hooker, and his celebrated statement 'that ill deserves the name of confinement which hedges us in only from bogs and precipices' Locke, like so many who hold this view of liberty, speaks of liberty as consisting in non-interference with one's rights and *also* of it as a distinct right. This is a common liberal position: liberty is thought of as consisting in non-interference in the enjoyment of our rights to liberty of thought, speech, action, contract, property, happiness, etc., i.e. as consisting in the enjoyment of all our rights including the right to liberty. (The liberty in the right to liberty is variously represented as negative liberty in the sense of simple non-interference, and as positive liberty in the sense of scope to be self-determining. There are obvious difficulties in conceiving of liberty, in the right to liberty, as non-interference unqualified, when defence of the right to property, of contract, etc., are also firmly insisted on as part of the defence of liberty in the broader sense of that expression.) This view is also the view of most of those nineteeth-century liberals who favoured non-interference and *laissez-faire,* for such liberals have regarded the defence of the right to property as a vital part of the defence of liberty.

That there is a sense of the expression 'liberty' such that we can be said to enjoy liberty when we are not interfered with in the enjoyment of our rights is apparent from our charges, and our explanations of our charges, that our liberty has been invaded when our rights, e.g. to life, property, to marry, etc., are interfered with. We do not complain that our liberty is interfered with when we are prevented from using other people's property, or committing bigamy, or being cruel to animals, although it is true that there is a tendency to move from saying that there has been no invasion of liberty in *some* such cases to saying of *other* cases that there has been no unjust invasion of liberty.

This concept of liberty involves less difficulty concerning what constitutes interference. We are interfered with if we are prevented by human agency from enjoying our rights. Thus the nature of our rights determines how comprehensive this ideal of liberty is. If our rights are as they have so often been claimed to be, to life, property, happiness, family life, etc., then much is implied by this view of liberty. We enjoy liberty when we are not harmed in our life, person, property, happiness, family life. If we are diseased paupers, propertyless and wretched, unmarried because too poor, we are enjoying full liberty provided that we are not actively prevented from enjoying our rights. The helping of others to secure enjoyment of their rights is not enjoined by this ideal of liberty. Yet various of the difficulties of the other view of negative liberty arise here—for instance, it is doubtful if it is always an invasion of liberty to be made unhappy.

There are also special difficulties for this account of liberty. If our rights are as they are represented as being by say, the Thomists, e.g. by Leo XIII, then liberty interpreted in the sense of non-interference in the enjoyment of rights seems less plausible and indeed totally unplausible as a concept of liberty. And if we take other views about the nature and content of our rights it seems blatantly wrong to describe non-interference with rights as liberty. If we held the sorts of views about the rights of 'natural' slaves of the kind implicit in Aristotle's discussion of slavery, it would seem that slaves are free i' their rights are not interfered with, i.e. if they are treated well as slaves. And this is plain nonsense. Yet if we look closely at accounts of rights such as Locke's, and nineteenth-century exponents of it, we see that the insistence on the right to property, and talk about interference with it as an invasion of liberty, involves the same paradox, the more so as many of a general Lockean persuasion concerning the nature of liberty thought of the right to property as including the right to property in slaves, and hence, that interference with one's slave ownership was an invasion of liberty. Again, if the ground of rights is explained in terms of social recognition, social function, or utility, strange views about liberty will result from time to time.

If liberty, then, is to be explained as non-interference with rights—and there does appear to be an accepted usage of the expression according to which it is construed as such—then it must be based on only certain views concerning rights, and these need to be determined before liberty can satisfactorily be explained along these lines. Yet whatever view of rights is adopted, difficulties arise as to whether the account is fairly characterised as an account of liberty, for any one who denied and rejected the theory of rights, and who was punished for infringing the rights of others, could very reasonably and properly claim that the system of liberty resting on it was in fact a system denying him liberty. None the less, although *all* views identifying liberty with non-interference with rights involve coercion that could fairly be described as a denial of liberty, and although on many views of rights, non-interference with rights could not accurately and fairly be characterised as liberty, there seem to be at least *some* views of rights such that non-interference with rights is fairly and usefully to be characterised as liberty in a significant sense of that expression.

(c) *Evaluating negative liberties as political ideals*

1 *Non-interference unqualified*   (i) Most arguments for negative liberty seem to be arguments in terms of its utility, either as a pre-condition of self-determination, or of other goods such as self-

perfection, progress, happiness, knowledge, moral development, etc. Mill's celebrated infallibility argument, in so far as it is used in defence of negative liberty, is among the more important of these.[3] Berlin's defence of negative liberty on the basis of a denial that there is any 'final solution' is another such argument (p. 52), as is his suggested argument that negative liberty makes self-fulfilment and self-determination possible (p. 57).   All such arguments reduce negative liberty to a subsidiary ideal, the ultimate ideals being those by reference to which liberty is justified.

(ii) Mill and other liberals limit the demand for negative liberty, particularly in the political sphere, to mature adults. It has been put to me that this also suggests that negative liberty is valued for the self-determination it makes possible. However this is not clearly so, for some of those excluded, i.e. minors, seem to be capable of self-determination. In any event, a puzzle remains as to why, not only in the political sphere but more generally, libertarians are disinclined to describe negative liberty for minors as a good which they ought to enjoy. Parental direction and guidance are not thought of as necessary evils; they are not thought of as evils at all.

(iii) It is sometimes argued that negative liberty is a genuine ideal because others lack the right to interfere, or to interfere without good reason. It would seem to me true that we need a reason, and a good reason at that, to justify our interfering with others, and that this fact does create a prima facie case for a policy of non-interference. However, this fact does not provide a ground for regarding negative liberty, in the sense of being let alone, as a positive, real, ultimate, irreducible ideal. Liberals, by overstating the case that can be built on the need for reasons for interference, obscure this truth. It is to be noted that this fact does not make negative liberty even a prima facie ultimate ideal, for, to have a reason for interference, e.g. promotion of the general happiness, or of the individual's moral virtue, is not to have a clash of ideals, happiness versus liberty, virtue versus liberty, but simply one ideal or good in each case, happiness or virtue.

(iv) This brings out that negative liberty, in the sense of non-interference, cannot be an ideal on a par with ideals such as justice, equality, fraternity. Consider what follows if it is regarded as one among other prima facie ideals. A prima facie ideal is an ideal which can be weighed against other ideals, and may itself be outweighed. But how can we possibly weigh the claims of non-interference against the claims of justice? What we do in such cases is to weigh what negative liberty makes possible, or that which makes it valuable, against the claims of justice. In no other way is it meaningful to try to weigh non-interference against justice. And this confirms that negative liberty is not itself an ultimate ideal.

It might be replied that whilst non-interference may not be a good which we can weigh, interference is always evil and such that we can weigh its evilness against the goods we seek to promote by interference. However, the foregoing discussion, e.g. of interference with minors, suggest that it is very questionable whether interference *qua* interference is necessarily evil. I suggest that when it is so, it is an interference with self-determination (although it is not clear that all such interferences are evil *qua* interference) in which case it is the ideal of self-determination and not that of negative liberty which is being weighed against other ideals.

That interference is not necessarily evil in itself is apparent too if we consider useful activities of the state. On this view of liberty the state, in engaging in useful activities such as providing forms of bequeathing or transferring property, for recognising marriages and family relationships, etc., would be said to be invading liberty, negative liberty, and would be justified in so doing because and in so far as other ideals are being realised. Yet it is not at all clear that we are being deprived of something valuable by the state when it acts in these ways.

2 *Liberty as non-interference with rights*   Besides being exposed to various aspects of certain of the difficulties noted above, the following additional difficulties arise for negative liberty interpreted as non-interference with rights.

(i) Its value turns on the view of rights that is assumed and written into the concept of liberty. Both the content and the grounds of rights are vital. The views of rights assumed by exponents of this sort of view of liberty usually include a right to property. To limit liberty of property, by punishing theft, is severely to limit liberty in significant senses of that expression, as is evident if we consider property systems other than our own. If a right to property is recognised and breaches punished, so too, the same restriction could be imposed on the basis of other rights, and lack of them. For example, there could be punishment for adultery, bigamy (i.e. illegal polygamy), cruelty to animals, etc. The scope of liberty becomes more and more circumscribed, as more rights of these sorts are recognised and respect for them enforced. An equally serious difficulty arises over the grounds of our rights—if our rights arise from recognition by society, from our social function, or from their utility, the limits of liberty will vary drastically from society to society.

(ii) In the light of these difficulties, liberty, construed as one right among other rights, rather than simply as scope to enjoy rights in general, may be stressed. But what emerges if it is so stressed? The view would either remain that stated here or it would come to be interpreted as implying that every use of force to protect rights is an interference with liberty, a justifiable interference, but an interference none the less. We are then back with the first view of negative liberty, with all its difficulties, including that of the strangeness of saying of certain of the preventions of interferences with rights that they are justifiable invasions of liberty, for many such preventions of interference are normally not described as invasions of liberty at all.

(iii) On this general view of liberty, the value of liberty will spring from the rights which we are free to enjoy, or from that which is the source of our rights and which gives them their value. It should therefore follow that rights ought not simply to be protected; rather, conditions for their enjoyment ought to be promoted. The negative form—protection of rights, non-interference with rights, as opposed to promotion of conditions for enjoying rights—has no claim to be regarded as an ultimate ideal.

B. Positive liberty

(a) Self-determination

Clearly, to be self-determining is to enjoy liberty in an obvious and indisputable sense of liberty, yet in a sense which is distinct from that of negative liberty. We enjoy or 'possess' negative liberty if we are in a coma and are let alone. We possess liberty, in the sense of self-determination, if we are capable of directing our lives without impediment and hindrance from others. To be self-determining, and to enjoy liberty in this sense, does not imply right choice, nor even reasonable choice. It simply involves that our conduct be determined by us, whoever and whatever sort of person we may be. A stupid, or a dithering person is free if all his actions result from him and not from another. Again, with negative liberty, all interference is a deprivation of freedom; with liberty viewed as self-determination interference may be dictated by concern for it without any deprivation of liberty occurring, as for instance, if we have fallen into a coma, or become compulsives, neurotic, alcoholic, drug-addicted, etc. In these cases the interference need not be a depriva-tion of self-determination; and it is directed at restoring our self-determining powers. If we have not freely and knowingly caused ourselves to lose our power to be self-determining, such interference is enjoined by the ideal of self-determination. (Where our loss of power to be self-determining results from a deliberate decision of our own, it is less clear what concern for self-determination dictates.)

It has been suggested that self-determination as an ideal involves removing impediments imposed by men, and the formula summaris-ing this would be 'interference to frustrate interferences with self-determination'. In this way, liberals have sought to justify, as giving real liberty of choice, legislation involving compulsory education, limited hours and conditions of employment, minimum wage laws, etc. Consider the disagreement between Ritchie and Spencer con-cerning State education. Although Ritchie's view of true liberty is of positive liberty to be self-developing, his argument is one which has been used to this end by exponents of liberty viewed as self-deter-mination, Ritchie writes:[4]

> In this country no one is hindered by law from reading all the works of Mr. Herbert Spencer. This is negative liberty. But if a man cannot read at all, or if he can read but has not any money to spare for the purpose of buying so many volumes, or if he has no access to any public library, or if the managers of any library to which he has access refuse to permit such works on their shelves, or, if, having access to them, he has no leisure in which to read them, or if he has not had such an education as enables him to understand what he reads, he cannot be said to get much good out of the fact that the law of the land does not prohibit him from reading Mr. Spencer's works. Thus, in order that the great mass of the inhabitants of this country should really enjoy the privilege of appreciating the philosophical basis on which Mr. Spencer founds his objections to State education, State libraries, and all such forms of interference with individual liberty, it is necessary that such forms of State interference with individual liberty—and a good many others—should be in active operation.

However, concern for liberty as self-determination seems to call for more than the elimination of man-made obstacles. It would seem to entail that natural impediments which are removable should be removed, and that artificial aids should be provided if they extend the scope of self-determination. For example, if we regard self-determination as a good, we should act to restore good health, etc., whether or not the ill-health emanates from human action. Consider the case of the artist who, through disease, loses his sight, which can be restored, and who wishes to have it restored in order to continue as an artist; or that of the person born legless, who can be provided with artificial legs and thereby enabled to become capable of engaging in work in which he wishes to engage. Further, concern for liberty in this sense of liberty, involves not merely removing obstacles and compensating for privations, but also providing goods—e.g. providing education is hardly removing obstacles; rather it involves creating or cultivating powers and capacities. We should not know how to read or write if we were let alone and never interfered with, directly or indirectly, by other human beings. It is the activity of other human beings which makes this possible.

Those who espouse this liberty as an ideal usually suggest that the stupid person in his stupid actions, the ditherer in his ineffective dithering, the existentialist in his 'leaps in the dark' and the reasonable man in his thoughtful self-determination, are all exercising this liberty and enjoying this good of self-determination. This poses a puzzle as to what exactly constitutes self-determination. The expression 'self-determination' suggests the determining of one's own life, by one's own decisions. But when are we entitled to speak of decisions? Does the ditherer or even the stupid person really make decisions? When does a decision *qua* decision, become something valuable? In particular, if the ditherer and the stupid person are thought to be self-determining, as determining their modes of life, then there seems little of value in self-determination, in so far as it is manifested in the stupid decisions of the stupid person, or the foolhardy acts of the foolish person, or the ineffective dithering of the person incapable of making up his mind. However, it can perhaps be argued that not all such persons are really free and self-determining. After all, not all human beings are thought to be capable of self-determination—and perhaps the stupid in their stupid acts are incapacitated in a way similar to that of imbeciles. The stupid person experiences what he consciously does not want, directly as a result of his own decisions. He wants to choose the means and he wants to choose the end; and choice in both respects conflicts so that he cannot be fully self-determining. It is relevant here that error and ignorance are limitations to liberty, so it is perhaps wrong to take the stupid person's self-determination as genuine or full self-determination; and it would seem to depend on the circumstances of the case whether the choice of means or of ends makes the stupid person more self-determining. Again, with the ditherer we can hardly say that he *determines* his mode of existence. Rather, it is more accurate to say that things and events overtake him, or that they happen to him or befall him. Much of the case for claiming that self-determination is a genuine political ideal, and one which merits recognition as such, turns on these points.

The foregoing discussion shows that we can give some meaning to the concept of self-determination, where self-determination is not qualified by and explained in terms of a theory of rights. But if we try to become more definite and specific, difficulties arise. This comes out when we consider how we should try to determine when one person's self-determination interferes with another person's self-determination. When do we frustrate other people's self-determination? Do we do so only when we interfere with their enjoyment of their rights? What constitute hindrances, impediments, lacks, privations, which concern for self-determination dictates that we ought to deal with? Is any ability to satisfy our desires a lack of power to be self-determining? If so, should we act against and eliminate all or as many such obstacles as we can? For instance, the State activities mentioned by Ritchie might be claimed to be dictated, not by the claims of self-determination, but as Ritchie himself suggests, by liberty as scope to be self-developing. This general difficulty can be presented in another way. If the idea of rights (or of some general standard such as self-perfection) is not written into the concept of self-determination, then any interference with another's rights is only an invasion of his liberty in so far as it frustrates his self-determination. But is this obviously so? It is relevant here to consider how large a part enjoyment of our rights plays in the exercise of our liberty. A very great deal of our exercise of self-determination consists in its exercise in respect of our rights within legal systems which apply sanctions to enforce recognition of our rights—e.g. much liberty consists in our use of property (taking property to include money) and in exercising exclusive family rights. These are large areas of liberty, yet other property and family systems are possible, and the creation of the legal structures which make these activities possible and which secure us in our enjoyment of our rights, may in fact lessen the total self-determination of others, where self-determination is interpreted without reference to rights. Those who favour other family and property systems could reasonably think so.

It is also relevant here that we frequently talk about certain areas of self-determination as being more important than others. When we do this we again usually seem to be moving to a concept of liberty as self-determination qualified in a certain way, for the differences in importance are often not explicable in terms of self-determination alone.

(b) Evaluating self-determination as a political ideal

(i) Traditionally the notion of self-determination has been interpreted so as to include the ditherer, the stupid, and the immoral. To consider its value so interpreted. If we look at particular acts of self-determination, of the sort that the libertarian is most concerned to justify, such as ineffectual gropings after the truth, propagation of error, immoral acts, etc., it is difficult to see precisely what element of value is introduced by the fact that the acts are self-determined. Consider the ditherer, who hesitates and hesitates, and ends up simply drifting, doing what he does not wish to do and becoming what he does not wish to become, because he cannot make up his mind what he wants to do. What is there of value in this sort of drifting? There seems no greater element of value in the acts of the stupid and foolish. Consider the man who stupidly resists treatment which will restore his health, or the act of the foolhardy driver who recklessly speeds through traffic lights at 70 miles an hour. The same appears to be true of a trivial act such as that of choosing an orange when presented with a choice between an apple and an orange. So too, there seems little of value in the situation of the man who roughly and cruelly pulls out the claws of a stray cat which he plans to use in the training of his greyhounds. It is because the latter act is an act of self-determination that it is so evil; if it were accidental it would be much less evil. This is most apparent if we consider a self-determined life such as that of Eichmann. The notion of elements, components, ingredients of acts such that we might say that the self-determination element or ingredient is valuable is one which will not stand up to critical examination. The act is an integral whole such that we cannot separate parts in this way. Its being an act of self-determination is not an element but rather what makes it an act in the full sense of act. It is an act in that it is freely chosen. And our assessment of the evil act as an act of the kind it is, is shown by our endeavours to prevent its recurrence; and in so doing, we do not consider that we are eliminating any element of value in preventing such acts as those of Eichmann. This suggests that it is only certain kinds of acts of self-determination, i.e. only certain kinds of acts, which have value. In that case, the proper ideal would appear not to be self-determination unqualified, but self-determination of a certain kind—e.g. towards the good, or the reasonable, or towards self-perfection. It is perhaps significant that the passage in which Mill comes closest to defending self-determination for its own sake, he chooses to rest his defence on an appeal to a most favourable description of it, and not of vicious, ineffective, or harmful self-determination. He writes (p. 117):

> He who lets the world, or his own portion of it, choose his plan of life for him, has no need of any other faculty than the ape-like one of imitation. He who chooses his plan for himself, employs all his faculties. He must use observation to see, reasoning and judgement to foresee, activity to gather materials for decision, discrimination to decide, and when he has decided, firmness and self-control to hold to his deliberate decision. And these qualities he requires and exercises exactly in proportion as the part of his conduct which he determines according to his own judgement and feelings is a large one. It is possible that he might be guided in some good path, and kept out of harm's way, without any of these things. But what will be his comparative worth as a human being? It really is of importance, not only what men do, but also what manner of men they are that do it. Among the works of man, which human life is rightly employed in perfecting and beautifying, the first in importance surely is man himself. Supposing it were possible to get houses built, corn grown, battles fought, causes tried, and even churches erected and prayers said by machinery—by automatons in human form— it would be a considerable loss to exchange for these automatons even the men and women who at present are but starved specimens of what nature can and will produce. Human nature is not a machine to be built after a model and set to do exactly the work prescribed for it, but a tree, which requires to grow and develop itself on all sides, according to the tendency of the inward forces which make it a living thing.

Part of Mill's contention is that to be a person we must be self-determining; that self-determination is not a means to being a person, but a large part of it, and that persons are of value. I shall later briefly consider arguments from the dignity of man, but it is sufficient to note here that the contrast is not between being a person and being an automaton as Mill suggests, but between being self-determining and being coerced but still a person. Those coerced by fear of the sanctions of the law are still persons. Further, when we challenge the claim that to be a person is to be something of value, the value of persons is usually explained, largely or entirely, in terms of their self-determining nature and the value of self-determination, i.e. the argument, not simply by chance, is usually circular.

(ii) As with the ideals of negative liberty, liberty construed as self-determination is commonly defended for its utility. Mill and many others praise self-determination not so much for itself as for the goods, other than self-determination, that it makes possible and/or of which it is simply a part—goods such as knowledge, rational and vital belief, happiness, security, self-perfection, moral excellance, etc. And in so far as it is defended *only* in this way, it is not being espoused as an ulitmate, irreducible ideal. Thus such arguments must give rise to the doubt as to whether it would be valued at all if it were thought that it would always be unwisely and unprofitably used, and entered only into complex wholes which were evil.

(iii) It is equally significant that we tend to restrict self-determination to those who are thought to be capable of exercising it profitably—in the political sphere we confine it to mature adults, and elsewhere we foster it much less than we might among those who are capable of being self-determining. The fact that the 12 to 20 year-old group would be less wise in their voting than the 21 pluses is generally accepted as constituting a conclusive reason for denying them their political self-determination; but what is most significant about the use and acceptance of such an argument is that it rarely seems to be felt, even by libertarians, that a great good is being denied the adolescent group.

It is often suggested that the exclusion of minors, as well as lunatics and animals, is a limitation of liberty to those capable of being self-determining; but this seems not to be the case as adolescents seem completely capable of self-determination but are suspect on the score of wisdom, i.e. it is doubted whether they are capable of right self-determination. This is even more true of younger children who are capable of being self-directive in an

obvious sense of that expression. When we deny them the right to be
self-determining, e.g. in such matters as to whether to attend or not
to attend school, to watch television until close of transmission, etc.,
we seem not be faced by a conflict of goods, the good of self-determination against the good of the child's future happiness, etc. The
only relevant considerations seem to be those relating to what will be
for the child's good and happiness, and for the parents' convenience.
If it is claimed that self-determination in children is not real self-
determination, the concept of self-determination then seems to
come to be explained so as to be akin to rational, right, self-
determination—at the very least rationality is being written more
explicitly into the concept than it appears to be when stupid adults
are considered and when self-determination is urged as a good which
all adults should be allowed to enjoy.

(iv) Liberty as self-determination is sometimes defended as a
dictate of the dignity of man, sometimes on the grounds that we are
all God's creations, sometimes simply from the lack of right of any
one to interfere with the self-determination of others.

The latter argument can be dismissed without much difficulty.
Political life, except in a democracy in which there is real and not
merely tacit consent would be incompatible with acceptance of this
argument and of this ideal on these grounds. Further, such an
argument makes liberty *a negative ideal* which will not do the job
liberal exponents of self-determination have wanted to do, namely
justify aid rather than simply prevent interferences. Consider legislation such as that of setting up a government health service which
helps give added powers to those suffering privations and ill-health.
If such an argument is not interpreted as entailing the banning of all
interference, it will not provide effective grounds for resisting interference, for it will merely call for reasons for interference, and of
course, reasons are usually available. People interfere with others to
safeguard the individual's happiness, moral excellence, right belief,
or to prevent harm to others.

If we were indeed God's creatures, this might suggest that we are
all in a sense equal. We should be equal in the kind of trivial sense of
equality according to which all members of a species, canines,
felines, *homo sapiens,* are all equal with other members of their
species, i.e. equal in the sense of all being members of the same
species. This equality is compatible with real inequality. The
inequality may imply, as a dictate of justice, inequality in respect of
liberty such that some be self-determining and some directed by

others. Possession of souls, and being created by God, are as irrelevant to liberty (and to equality) as is the fact that all humans have hair, eyes, and a nose. Sentient beings have much in common with one another such that we could say that all sentient beings are equal, but obviously nothing follows from this fact about liberty and equality for sentient beings. An awareness of the real inequalities compatible with this trivial equality suggests that self-determination is not, in all its instances, of one value but rather of different values according to who is self-determining and the level of the self-determination, for it seems to make sense to talk of levels of self-determination such that one level is more or less valuable than another. But here again we begin to move towards another, and different concept of liberty.

The argument in terms of the dignity of man is usually set out in terms of man *qua* man meriting respect. Respect is said to involve not forcing the will. But surely it is virtuous men and talented men who merit respect; and different men merit different degrees of respect. Further, respect for one's fellows involves helping them—aiding them if they are blind, preventing them from harming themselves or falling over precipices or into bogs, from falling into error and evil, even if coercion is required. (And notice, few deliberately choose ignorance and error in preference to true knowledge—error is more usually due to unavoidable 'accidents'; and where people do deliberately choose to ignore or deny unpalatable truths, it would not be claimed that we are interfering with their liberty in confronting them with incontrovertible evidence for the unpalatable truth.) I suggest that talk about the dignity of man neither solves nor illuminates anything and is simply another, emotive, confusing way of raising the same problem. Instead of asking: Is liberty an ultimate, irreducible ideal? we now have to ask two questions: Is liberty in the sense of self-determination dictated by respect for the dignity of man? And are there sound reasons for claiming that man, rather than particular men, has dignity and worth such that *qua* man, he merits respect? It is not without importance that Kant based his claim to the dignity of man on man's rational nature, and suggested that it is rational beings that merit respect, and further, that he thought of the completely rational being as having a holy will and as being incapable of immorality.

Telling as these various considerations are against the view that self-determination alone is valuable for its own sake, because of the complexity of the issues involved, and the exploratory nature of this enquiry, it would be unwise to construe them as completely conclusive without much lengthier argument than is possible here.

(c) Reasonable self-determination

This may be treated of briefly as it raises few issues over and above those raised by self-determination unqualified. A person is not free if he does not know what he is doing. Hence stupid, unreasonable behaviour can, with some point, be said not to be fully free. If a person is not reasonable in his self-direction, if he stupidly yields to impulses, etc., he is not free or not fully free. This is not to say that he becomes free by being forced to act in a reasonable way. To be forced to be reasonable is not necessarily to be reasonable or self-directing, although coercion and reasonable self-determination are not necessarily incompatible as is apparent from our own reactions to the criminal law.

This concept of liberty, if taken as an ideal, enjoins positive action to make it possible. Education, information, etc., are obvious preconditions for its exercise; and interference with unreasonable conduct, e.g. foolish, stupid acts would not be interference with genuine exercises of liberty so understood.

(d) Evaluating reasonable self-determination

(i) As with self-determination, reasonable self-determination is defended for its utility. Such defences amount to the valuing of it as a means to the realisation of other goods or for the valuable complex wholes which it makes possible and into which it enters.

(ii) Many of the difficulties of self-determination, in particular the problem of the value of self-determination as exercised by the viciously immoral, remain. The activity of coldly calculating how to extract vengeance most cruelly and effectively and acting on the basis of such calculations is hardly more valuable an activity of self-determination for its being reasonable—on the contrary it is worse. It is the calculated, reasoned character of their acts of self-determination which makes the acts of individuals such as Eichmann as shocking as they are— i.e. the reasoned nature of an act of self-determination makes it worse than if it were a thoughtless act, and both are worse than unintended 'acts'.

(iii) Whatever value, if any, reasonable self-determination has over and above that possessed by self-determination unqualified, is due to the evaluation of rationality rather than to self-determination (if as is arguable, rationality and full self-determination can properly be distinguished); in that case it would seem to be rationality and not liberty which would be the ideal suggested here. But as the above examples suggest, it is not clear that reasonable self-determination is valuable apart from its useful instances and those instances in which it enters into a valuable complex whole as in a moral act or in intellectual enquiry, etc.

(e) Liberty as having scope to enjoy one's rights

This, by contrast with negative liberty interpreted as non-interference with rights, is the having of a positive and real opportunity to enjoy rights, hence it calls for positive action to promote conditions in which rights may be enjoyed. It might be questioned whether it is properly called liberty and whether it is not perhaps some distinct but important ideal. I suggest that it does have a real claim to be called liberty in at least some of its forms, since it has been so called in the literature of liberalism and is one of the most important concepts of positive liberty in liberal writings and in day to day talk about liberty. It is for instance the concept of liberty of socialistic liberals such as Tawney and Laski[5] and of forerunners of socialistic liberalism. Hobhouse often adopts this view as does Green. This is no accident. We complain that we are not free if we cannot enjoy our rights. We describe the situation as our not being free to do so. By contrast, we do not complain in the same way about coercion which does not impinge on the enjoyment of a right. Again, we speak of the creation of opportunities to enjoy our rights as enlargements of our liberty, e.g. where legislative action makes it possible for us and others to acquire property, to share in the cultural heritage, to marry, to rear one's offspring as judged best, etc. Laski saw liberty, in this sense of liberty, as entailing a great deal of State interference and activity directed towards greater equality and providing necessary facilities for all, such as reliable news sources, adequate medical and legal aid, etc. Laski was clearly right, for we have liberty to enjoy our rights only when the conditions are such that it is possible for us to do so; and this does entail special aids to the needy and less fortunate. These aids are not part of liberty but rather conditions for its existence; and to view them as part of liberty would be to confuse goods other than liberty with liberty.

(f) Evaluating liberty viewed as scope to enjoy rights

Many of the points made concerning negative liberty viewed as non-interference with rights also hold here and may be restated thus:

(i) Since this liberty is explained in terms of rights, whether it is in fact a kind of liberty depends on the nature and grounds of our rights. If rights are only to what is good and true, it would be compatible with much coercion, for the suppression of evil would then not be an invasion of liberty. If rights are created by social function, utility, or by social recognition, liberty would vary drastically from time to time, and from community to community. Also, the points made earlier concerning how even systems of property, marriage and justice set up in accord with or in recognition of rights, may properly be charged by those holding other views of rights, with invading and restricting liberty. None the less, for the reasons set out above and in the discussion of negative liberty, it still remains true that some forms of this view of liberty are properly and illuminatingly called views of liberty.

(ii) The value of such liberty would be derivative from the rights or from that which gives rights their value. If rights are grounded on a good such as perfection of self, the ultimate ideal would be perfection of self, not liberty.

(iii) Usually liberty is explained also as a right among other rights, as well as consisting in scope to enjoy rights. It is included as a right among other rights in lists which include such rights as liberty of speech, action, association, property, happiness, etc. If this lesser right to liberty plays a key part in the explanation of liberty, this liberty seems to become a combination of two concepts—on the one hand either negative liberty, or positive liberty to be self-determining (the liberty in the right to liberty can be explained in either way) and on the other, liberty to enjoy rights. The combination then either amounts to one of the views already examined, or it is interpreted in a way which makes no difference to this view.

(g) Liberty as opportunity to be self-perfecting

Here I mean to include the whole family of distinct but closely related theories which relate liberty and self-perfection, self-realisation, self-fulfilment, self-development, moral and intellectual excellence, etc. Liberty, so viewed, is more open to being rejected as not a real concept of liberty, and as some other good of which a factor is self-determination. It is no doubt true that these theories are nearer to being accounts of what constitutes permissible liberty than to being accounts of liberty as such. In so far as they avoid being theories of permissible liberty, they seem to move towards being simply persuasive presentations of self-determination as an ideal, noting as they do the goods which may be realised through the exercise of self-determination. However, there is a strong case for including opportunity to be self-perfecting as a concept of liberty. The element of free decision and self-determination is an essential component of this account. It is an account which has figured prominently as a liberal ideal of liberty—it is that of Ritchie and it is one about which Mill becomes most eloquent. To be self-frustrating or self-destructive or self-stultifying is to be unfree in a significant sense. Further, it is commonly assumed that people really want to be self-developing, or self-perfecting, and if liberty is defined simply as consisting in scope to do what we want to do, there is no clear guide as to which obstacles and hindrances should be removed and which aids brought into being. Clearly, different aids and the removal of different hindrances and obstacles are dictated by concern for self-perfection, from those dictated by self-determination alone. A person claiming liberty only in the former sense can claim only provision of what is needed for his self-perfection, not for realising any at all of his wishes (subject to not interfering with others) as would apparently be the case on the latter ideal. Again, if it is treated as a distinct, non-liberty ideal, self-perfection is in danger of being confused with the very different non-libertarian ideal of perfection of self. Perfection of self is interpreted by liberals as involving self-perfection, but it is not universally so interpreted, and the two ideals need to be clearly distinguished. Perhaps the least misleading way of pointing to the libertarian ideal of self-perfection would be to distinguish two views of self-determination, self-determination unqualified and self-determination to be self-perfecting. And to hold the latter as an ideal would involve fostering self-determination only when it led or was likely to lead on balance to self-perfection rather than to evils such as ignorance, error, immorality and harm.

Liberty in the sense of scope to be self-perfecting is far removed from the concepts of negative liberty, and entails positive acts by the state to make its realisation possible. Many things are noted by exponents of this theory as demanded by it, e.g. educational facilities, vocational guidance, reliable news sources, employment, adequate wages, satisfactory conditions or work, participation in management of industry, provision of facilities for the useful employment of leisure hours, medical and legal facilities, etc. These goods of course are not part of liberty but simply means to liberty and dictated by liberty interpreted as opportunity to be self-perfecting. What is dictated by this liberty could coincide with what is dictated by the rights view of positive liberty; but equally it could involve much more State action. The two views do however, tend to merge into one another in the writings of particular political philosophers.

(h) Evaluating liberty as opportunity to be self-perfecting

(i) There are difficulties in determining precisely what is implied by self-perfection, and this bears significantly on its evaluation. Self-perfection either involves some reference to an independent standard of self-perfection—in which case this liberty is a narrower, more limited liberty than the other positive liberties, or self-perfection is thought to be what the individual takes to be so, in which case it is not significantly different in nature and value from self-determination. The only difference would be that the exponent of this view would be demanding liberty to do what he thinks will contribute to his self-perfection, whereas the exponent of self-determination is appealing for liberty to be self-determining, whether it be towards self-perfection, self-destruction, or self-frustration. However, this leads to little difference in their evaluations.

(ii) We need therefore to consider whether there is a *right* self-perfection for each of us, or whether Berlin is right, that there are simply different ways of working out our lives. This view is suggested but not firmly nor explicitly stated in *Two Concepts of Liberty*, pp. 53-4. It is possible that all that Berlin wishes to argue for is the view developed there, that there are a variety of right self-perfections for each person. If there were no right and no wrong ways of working out our lives, this view would, as indicated above, be tantamount to equating liberty to be self-perfecting with liberty to be self-determining. However, it would take a bold thinker to assert that all ways of working out our lives are equally sound from the point of view of self-perfection. Obviously, some modes of life will stunt us, others will give wide scope to our capacities. Some modes of life will lead to moral excellence, wisdom, and knowledge. And the latter modes of life are obviously more self-perfecting than the former. Thus whilst it is not the case that for each man there is *one* right road to self-perfection and one terminus, it is true that there are a number of possible roads with equally good termini, and a multitude of wrong roads and wrong termini.

(iii) Talk about self-perfection does seem then, to have some point. We need to consider now whether the value of liberty to be self-perfecting emanates from the value of the perfection of self to which it leads. If this is the case, then liberty to be self-perfecting would not be an ultimate ideal—and it would only be a derivative ideal if it could be shown by empirical arguments that liberty to be self-perfecting in fact did lead to perfection of self. Here I should wish to argue further that any concept of perfection of self which was distinguished from self-perfection would be of something of comparatively little value. Self-perfection is a good, and a very great good, made up as it is of goods as intellectual and artistic activities and achievements, moral endeavour and moral achievements, physical activities and physical achievements, i.e. of goods which are complexes in which the activity of self-determination is usually and perhaps always a vital factor. However, it is to be noted that the liberty that is valued here is not liberty to be ignorant, vicious, or slothful—it is liberty to be self-perfecting. And it is also to be noted that attainment of many of the goods which seem to be part of self-perfection and which require the factor of self-determination, seem not neccessarily to be incompatible with the presence of threats and coercions. Moral excellence, for instance, is compatible with the presence of legal sanctions against immorality, and indeed it would appear that much less moral evil and little less moral value results from such legal sanctions. This, in the light of the other grounds for uneasiness over calling this a concept of liberty, might encourage the view that it should not be called liberty; yet, since self-determination is such an important contributing factor to and aspect of self-perfection, and since the latter involves recognition of the need for choice between a variety of equally good modes of self-perfection I should still incline towards regarding it as a concept of liberty, and as one which is the basis of a genuine, ultimate, irreducible ideal. But the ideal is not necessarily an egalitarian one, for if different self-perfections are of different values, the more valuable might in justice be preferred.

To conclude.   Our enquiry suggests that neither of the concepts of negative liberty survives as a sound basis for ultimate, irreducible ideals of liberty, and further, that only some forms of the view equating non-interference with rights can be accepted as views of liberty, whilst non-interference (unqualified) is seen to be a genuine but seriously attenuated concept of liberty when properly understood. Positive liberty in the senses of self-determination and reasonable self-determination are clearly genuine concepts of liberty, but our enquiries suggest grounds for grave doubts as to whether self-determination can properly be viewed as an ultimate, irreducible ideal. As with its negative counterpart, positive liberty in the sense of opportunity to enjoy rights can be regarded as a concept of liberty only in some of its forms; and even then it is not an ultimate, irreducible ideal of liberty. On the other hand, positive liberty in the sense of opportunity to be self-perfecting seems to emerge as a genuine, irreducible ideal, but not without encountering difficulties concerning its claims to be regarded as a genuine concept of liberty.

Notes

1 I. Berlin, *Two Concepts of Liberty,* Clarendon Press, Oxford, 1958, pp. 56-7.
2 Stanley I. Benn and R. S. Peters, *Social Principles and the Democratic State,* Allen & Unwin, London, 1959, p. 212. It is not clear from the context precisely how far Benn and Peters wish to press this suggestion, in particular whether they would wish to exclude positive liberty interpreted as self-determination.
3 J. S. Mill, *On Liberty,* Everyman's Library, Dent, London, p.79. All subsequent references to *On Liberty* are to this edition.
4 D. G. Ritchie, *Natural Rights,* Allen & Unwin, London, 1894, p. 139.
5 E.g. in *Grammar of Politics* Allen & Unwin, London, 1925, ch. 4.

Marx's concretization of the concept of freedom *

Iring Fetscher
Translated by R. Dunayevskaya

The young Marx encountered the question of individual freedom in society in two conceptual forms: the liberal concept, most concisely formulated philosphically by Kant, and Hegel's metaphysics of freedom. Both conceptual forms appear as expressions of historically concrete thought within the limitations of a given social and political reality. From the very outset, Marx's theoretical structure and political intention were to surmount, theoretically and practically, the limitation of these conceptions and their complementary abstraction. It is therefore impossible to understand adequately Marx's original political aim without a grasp of how he analysed these concepts as 'bourgeois conceptions of freedom'.

For Kant, the principle of political freedom is[1]

> that no one can force me (in so far as he considers another person's welfare) to be happy in his way, but *each must seek his own happiness* in the way that suits him best provided that he permits *another the freedom* to pursue a similar goal; it is therefore possible to *formulate* a universal law for *the freedom of all* which does not interfere with *the freedom of each.*

Freedom is thus the scope for the individual's pursuit of happiness, which is limited only by another individual's equally legitimate pursuit. The obvious deficiency of this concept is that it refers only negatively to one's fellow man, viewing him solely as the unavoidable legal *barrier* to one's own individual whim or caprice. This concept necessarily follows if, as with Hobbes and Kant, thought starts from the assumption that man's 'unsocial social existence' is an unyielding fact. If we proceed from the supposition that spontaneous,

* From *Socialist Humanism: an International Symposium*, edited by Erich Fromm, Allen Lane, 1967, pp. 238-49. Copyright © 1965 by Doubleday & Co. Inc. Reprinted with the permission of the publishers. This essay has also been published under the title 'Liberal, democratic and Marxist concepts of freedom', in *Marx and Marxism*, by Iring Fetscher, Herder & Herder, New York, 1971.

natural man is necessarily hostile to others until a state law forces him to consider the voice of conscience that leads him to respect the freedom claims of his fellow men, then we can find no other but this restrictive relationship between men.

For Marx, however, this antagonism of individuals—imputed to 'nature' since Hobbes—is the characteristic only of capitalistic competitive society. Jean-Jacques Rousseau preceded Marx in recognising the historical nature of '*homo lupus*' when he explained that Hobbes's statements could be legitimately applied only to contemporary man and not to man in general.[2] In contrast to Rousseau, however, Marx saw that the free development of the human individual in all societies is tied to the active cooperation of the other individuals. A recognition of this could not break through to full consciousness until the advent of modern, highly specialised society with its division of labour. Whereas Rousseau yearned to turn back to an earlier age, to escape from the mercantilist division of labour of the pre-capitalist society of essentially self-sufficient rural families which he knew, Marx looked ahead to a cooperative civilisation in which each man would take satisfaction in his own accomplishments because they contributed to the gratification of others and would accept the work of others as contributing to his own gratification. Instead of dissolving the mutual relations which corresponded to the ideal of the city-state, Marx preferred their universalisation, and a radical transformation of their character.

Marx was not, however, the first to stress the limitations of Kant's conception of the liberal state. Whereas Kant developed the position that the function of the liberal state is to help the individual fulfil himself by securing the peaceful coexistence of naturally egoistical individuals, Hegel sought the freedom of rational citizens not in laws guaranteeing individual freedom of opportunity, but in the state structure itself.

In the *Philosophy of History* Hegel turned specifically against all liberal concepts of freedom, as Marx did later, and condemned them as mere 'negativity' and formalism: The state is[3]

> not an assemblage of people *wherein the freedom of all individuals must be limited.* Freedom is only negatively comprehended when it is represented *as if the individual* in his relations to other individuals thus limited his freedom in order that this universal limitation—the mutual constraint of all—might secure a small space of liberty for each.

Already in the *Jenenser Realphilosophie* Hegel explained 'formal freedom' as that 'whose substance is external to itself'.[4] The substance of freedom, for Hegel, is the 'Spirit', or, more precisely, what is objective in the living spirit of the commonwealth's institutions and laws. Although idealistically and mystically embellished, these thoughts were nevertheless perceived by Marx as an essential advance over the Kantian standpoint.

To see this, one has only to define 'Substance' as the real society of cooperating people, where the individual's truly human development can occur. The positive relation of the individual to all his fellow men (first of all incorporated into a state) becomes, with Hegel, a mere identification of the 'subjective Spirit' of each man with the 'objective Spirit' of the state. With Hegel, dialectical identification, which does not exclude the independent existence of both the individual and the state as fixed poles in relation to each other, remains merely a thing of ideal dimensions. The living man and the living society (Hegel's 'necessary and rational state') remain below this lofty sphere 'in insubstantial appearance'. Fundamentally, Hegel has only exchanged one abstraction for another. Whereas the liberal concept of freedom is based on the positive relationship between people and expresses the restraints determined by the psychic demands of people in competitive society, the Hegelian state metaphysic says that man finds and can exercise freedom in the Ideal realm, not in his workaday personal relationships. Indeed, Hegel asserted, the 'state is the reality in which the individual has his freedom',[5] but the ideal state is not the human environment; in real 'civil society', it is the world of production, exchange and industry and here man must seek his freedom.

Marx's critique demonstrated the historical basis of the liberal concept of freedom and showed that it remained confined within the socially and temporally limited horizon of bourgeois thought. In the case of the Hegelian concept, Marx indicated that its illusory and complementary character becomes apparent against the reality of bourgeois society. His most thoroughgoing critique of the bourgeois thesis of freedom and the rights of man is found in *Capital:*[6]

> This sphere (of circulation and commodity exchange) that we are deserting, within whose boundaries the sale and purchase of labour-power goes, is in fact a very Eden of the innate rights of man. There alone rule Freedom, Equality, Property and Bentham. Freedom, because both buyer and seller of a

commodity, say of labour-power, are constrained only by their own free will. They contract as free agents, and the agreement they come to is but the form in which they give legal expression to their common will. Equality, because each enters into relation with the other, as with a simple owner of commodities, and they exchange equivalent for equivalent. Property, because each disposes only of what is his own. And Bentham, because each looks only to himself. The only force that brings them together and puts them in relation with each other, is the selfishness, the gain and the private interests of each. Each looks to himself only, and no one troubles himself about the rest, and just because they do so, do they all, in accordance with the pre-established harmony of things, or under the auspices of an all-shrewd providence, work together to the mutual advantage, for the common weal and in the interest of all.

Marx showed that the freedom and equality guaranteed in the French Constitution as the Rights of Man, and taken over in similar form by all liberal democratic constitutions, was an adequate expression of human relations in a market society, where no one's social condition is fixed by the privileges of birth, and everyone, as a 'commodity owner', is free to dispose of his goods and is bound only by the terms of the contract to which he agreed. But the sale of the labour-power commodity, this apparent equality and freedom, is actually false. The actual inequality of ownership lies in the fact that the owners of labour-power have nothing to sell but their labour-power and are therefore compelled, although not by law, to part with it, or—as German so graphically puts it—'to contract oneself out' (*sich zu verdingen*). Their labour-power, unlike the objective goods a craftsman brings to market, is not an objective part of their being but objective *ability* itself. Man's essence is his ability to transform Nature creatively and to shape it to his wishes and ends. When he is forced to sell this ability he renounces his humanity and an alienated relationship to mankind and humanity results. The liberal conception of freedom is limited because it attributes man's calculated special interests to his essence, whereas, in actuality, this characterisation only reflects man in competitive society and may be wrong about both the past and the future. Marx shows Hegel's metaphysics of the state as the abstract complementary of the idea of freedom already expressed by bourgeois *democracy* in the Constitution of the French Revolution.

Marx's criticism of the Hegelian Philosophy of Right was that it explained the bourgeois democratic state which Hegel, as a German, first encountered only in its theoretical (ideological) form. The superiority of the Hegelian conception over the liberal was, as we have already seen, its ability to grasp the dialectical relationship of the individual to society. We find the same recognition again in Marx—no matter whether he gained it from Hegel or from the experience of social reality itself:[7]

> It is above all necessary to avoid postulating 'society' once again as an abstraction confronting the individual. The individual *is* the *social being*. The manifestation of his life—even when it does not appear directly in the form of a communal manifestation, accomplished in association with other men—is therefore a manifestation and affirmation of social life.

As we have already seen, for Marx the Hegelian conception fails because it presents the social individual only in the idealistic abstract form of subjective and objective Spirit and relegates concrete man (the sensuous real being), as well as the civil society formed by him, to a sphere of lower rank. Man as a socially related being is suspended in an illusory and imaginary sphere beyond civil society with its calculated intelligence, its private egoism, its work, its law and its competition. But Marx realised that the abstraction of Hegelian philosophy from concrete daily life was no accident: it was only possible for 'German thought to abstract its notion of the modern state from natural man while, and in so far as, the modern state was itself abstracted from actual people, or the whole man gratified himself only in an imaginary manner'.[8] Man lived in this 'modern state' only in the abstract form of *citizen* (*citoyen*) during the course of his real sensuous existence as a member of the bourgeois (competitive) society. As a citizen he might be part of the civil society and imagine himself dialectically united with the rest of the citizens in the community, but in his real sensuous existence he is unfree and isolated, subject to alien laws ('contingency') and can relate himself to his fellow men only negatively (e.g. as competitor).[9]

> The completed political state [Marx writes in 1843], is in its essence the *species-life of man* in opposition to his material life. All presuppositions of his egoistical life continue to exist *outside of the state sphere* in civil society. Where the political state has

reached its true development, man leads a double life, heavenly and earthly, not only in thought, in consciousness, but in actuality, in life, life in the political community *in which he recognises himself as a social being,* and life in civil society where he acts as a *private person,* looks upon *other people as means,* and is *himself degraded into a means* and becomes the plaything of alien forces.

Man's 'true life' should be in community with his fellow men, each fulfilling himself and relating to the others in enriching accomplishment; but this 'true life' exists in the modern world only as the illusory and transcendental form of the community of citizens that is first tangibly experienced when it closes ranks and is brought into hostile relations with the community of citizens of *another* state.[10] In their real daily existence, on the other hand, individuals lead an 'untrue life', a life of deliberate isolation and hostility against their fellow men: 'actual man is first recognised in the form of egoistical (untrue) individuals, true man, in the form of abstract (unactual) citizen'.[11] This analysis posed the task of developing the actual (untrue) person of civil society into a true person (conscious of his dialectical relationship with his fellow men).

In his early writings Marx formulated the task in this way:

Only when actual man takes back into himself the abstract citizen of the state and, *as individual man in his empirical life. in his individual work, in his individual relations,* has become species-essence, only when man has recognised and reorganised his *forces propres* as social powers, and therefore no longer separates from himself social power in the form of political power, *only then is human emancipation completed.*

In his works of the 1840s and 1850s, particularly in the *Extracts* (*Exzerptheften*) and in the *Outline to the Critique of Political Economy* (*Grundrisse der Kritik der politischen Oekonomie*), Marx left us detailed information about this concrete free man who, 'in his individual work, in his individual relations, has become species-essence'. Man is 'species-essence' when he no longer projects his inherent qualities into an otherworldly Being—as, according to Feuerbach, happened with religious reification—or, as in political alienation, no longer poses a world beyond the existing everyday bourgeois 'state'. According to his natural abilities, then, every individual has acquired *all-roundedness* which, for him and with him, living humanity has realised by humanised work. Only when he is liberated from the 'idiocy' of life-long fixation to a trade, and from the slavery of wage labour, will such all-rounded appropriation of species-life by the individual be possible. Only when this is realised can the state (and religious ideology) wither away as the necessary complement to the incomplete actuality of society and its members. The state's becoming superfluous is specifically linked, above all, to the abolition of economic class privileges; with their abolition the necessity for the forcible protection of the privileged against the underprivileged is also abolished. The superfluity of the (democratic) state is dependent on the rise of a society in which the individuals have become 'species-beings' (*Gattungswesen*) who relate themselves totally and positively to their fellow men.

The barriers to individual freedom in the 'political state' were and remain necessary so long as real inequality in the opportunity for individual development remains, and the 'alienation' of all is not overcome. With the elimination of property privileges a decisive step is taken but the end not yet attained. As long as it is not yet possible to reduce working time so that that necessary tasks of all can be fulfilled voluntarily and the productivity of all suffices to satisfy the total needs of each, inequality remains the real prospect and therewith the 'unfreedom' of the concrete individual remains. As long as the gratification of my needs remains mediated not through my claim as man but through my purse—and this is surely the case today even in the 'socialist states'—there can be no talk that the human development of which the young Marx spoke has come true.

In the *Excerpts* as well as the *Economic Essays,* originating in the years 1844 and 1845, Marx opportunely worked out the idea of alienated, commodity-producing society pregnant with the future, unalienated human society. In these formulations one can clearly gather the sense which the concept of 'human emancipation', the liberation of concrete man, had for Marx. Division of labour in the technical sense is the prerequisite of both forms of society; but in the one it is tied to the egoistical isolation of each individual, and in the other to the loving relationship of each for all. The following description is valid, according to Marx, for commodity society:[12]

I have produced for myself and not for you, as you have produced for yourself and not for me. The result of my production has, in and of itself, just as little direct relation to you as the result of your production has to me, i.e. our production is (*not*) *production of people for people as people,* i.e. not social production. As human beings thus, none of us has a relationship of gratification to the product of the other. *Our mutual production has no existence for us as people.* Our exchange can therefore also not be the mediating movement wherein it is acknowledged that *my product* is for you, at the same time as it is *a materialization of your being, your needs.* For not the human essence is the bond of our production for each other.

The simple commodity system, and even more the expanding capitalistic one, is already exposed here as one in which the universal dependence of all on the products of work, differentiated by division of labour, does not appear as a spontaneous joyous, beneficent working of each for the others, the actualisation of the 'fundamental nature of man' for the human needs of other people, but as an egoistical working of each only for himself. Only indirectly—through the compulsion to exchange on the market—and 'behind the back', does production also become production for others. It is certainly not a relation between people, but only between 'solvent buyers'. Every single person (or group of people) satisfies the human needs of other people according to 'aesthetic laws' and other such characteristically established rules: great poetry is meaningful to the poetic understanding, a symphony to the musical ear, painting to the cultured taste, etc. But these appropriate attributes of people, the ability to enjoy, hear and see, do not mediate their 'appropriation' but only the dispostion of money. Specific products are not for me or you as people, but for you and me only in so far as we are commodity owners, money owners. They are also not created for us, but for our money, not for socially related men, but for the objectified embodiment of society: money.

In a truly 'human' society, where individuals are not mutual barriers to their freedom, but discover their essence as fulfilled and enriched beings, the following description would become valid:[13]

Granted, we have produced as people: in his production each of us has *twice affirmed* himself and the other. 1) In production I found my individuality, and my particularity materialised, and therefore, in the course of the activity I enjoyed a personal expression of life as well as a sense of the individual joy in the contemplation of my personality as objective, sensually perceptible and indubitable power. 2) *In your satisfaction,* or your use of my products, I had immediate *satisfaction as well as consciousness that my* work satisfied a human need. Therefore I, as an *objective human being,* have produced an object corresponding to another human being's need. 3) I became, *for you, the mediator between you and the species,* thus I became a necessary, self-conscious and sentient part of your fulfilment of your essence. Thus, *I knew I was affirmed in your thought as well as in your love.* 4) In my individual expression of life I directly created your expression of life. Thus, my true essence, my *actualised species-essence,* was confirmed *in my immediate individual activity.* Our productions were so many mirrors reflecting our being.

Here the evil magic of commodity-producing society, of exchange mediated through egoism, of products fragmented and losing their specific character (even disregarding the real transformation in labour itself) is dissolved. The variegated world of human products is transformed from a distorted mirror, where alienated man meets his likeness as a materialised commodity, into a true mirror of social humanity. The effort of all men becomes dependent upon the needs of others as is the effort of the lover who composes a song for his beloved.

Marx was no dreamer who expected the immediate realisation of his ideal of the human world. But I am convinced that, despite many cautious remarks at a later period, he always held fast to that concept of human potential. The mastery of nature by associated mankind and the increase in labour productivity are certainly necessary preconditions for such emancipation from the alienated and reified world, but they are not yet liberation itself. Never did Marx see in the mere mastery of man over nature the meaning of history and the essence of liberation to which socialism summons. One may almost cite the biblical phrase: 'For what is a man profited, if he shall gain the whole world and lose his own soul?' Also for Marx, it would have helped little to achieve a perfect mastery of nature without bringing about the society in which freely associated people remould their nature. The mastery over nature is not 'anti-nature', but 'prohumanity'. The goal is the elimination of egoism and of the rule of man over man.

However, as long as freedom and happiness have *not yet* become concrete realities, the two abstract concepts of freedom retain an actual importance, notwithstanding the valid reservations we have become acquainted with. In all countries—including the socialist countries—an inevitable bit of democratic metaphysics lies hidden, inevitable ideology. Precisely because individual labour output results, not from joyous spontaneity and love of fellow man, but from 'material interest', the picture of an antagonistic society, the state, must appear as the complement of the still unsocial society. Nor may it be identified with that communistic society which alone connects spontaneous human beings producing for each other. Each state, including the 'Peoples' Democracies', remains an 'illusory social essence' that can 'become superfluous' and then 'wither away' only when a true social essence, in the sense Marx outlined, originates underneath. But the liberal conception, to which we were introduced in the classical Kantian formulation, retains its relative significance during this entire time. It appears necessary and correct because it secures a scope of freedom for egoistical unsocial individuals. It appears in optimal form when an enforceable law separates the freedom of the individual, not only from another individual, but also from the superior power of the government. The liberal ideology which believes the maximum of human freedom to be attained with this kind of guarantee must certainly be opposed. Hegel and Marx clearly enough stressed the narrowness and abstractness of this concept of freedom. But as long as the human society described by Marx is not realized and the majority of individuals, even in the 'socialist countries', are driven by egoistical motives in the performance of their work, those liberal guarantees can in no way be dispensed with. They need, above all, to be concretized by supplementary measures guaranteeing the right of usufruct (education, medical care, universal social security, etc.). These measures are not superfluous as long as competitive envy and real inequality continue as essential characteristics of society. Misuse of freedom must also be prevented by the suitable interpretation of the Kantian formula. Freedom for the economic enslavement of fellow men does not belong to those actions 'which can coexist with the freedom of the will of each and all according to a universal law'.

As long as concrete freedom is not realised, the two complementary abstract forms of freedom retain their restricted and historically limited validity.

Notes

1 Kant, 'On the maxim: good in theory, but bad in practice', in *Werke*, Vorlander (ed.), vol. 4, pp. 87ff.

2 Cf. Rousseau's expression in the fragment *State and War:* 'Hobbes's error . . . is to confuse natural man with the men under his eyes. . . .' (Vaughan, *Rousseau's Political Writings*, vol. 1, p. 305). C. B. Macpherson, in his recent book *Political Theory of Possessive Individualism*, Oxford University Press, 1962, convincingly traced the relationship between antagonistic market society and political theory from Hobbes to Locke.

3 Hegel, *Philosophie der Weltgeschichte*, Lasson (ed.), vol. I, p. 90. (The translation used here is from the last revision of the Sibree translation as given in *Philosophy of History*, Dover, New York, 1956—*Translator.)*

4 Hegel, *Jenenser Realphilosophie*, Hoffmeister (ed.), vol. 2, p. 28.

5 Hegel, *Philosophy of History*, Lasson (ed.), vol. I, pp. 89ff.

6 Marx, *Capital*, Kerr edn, p. 195. (In the original the citation is from *Das Kapital*, Volksausgabe, Berlin, 1947, vol. 1, p. 184 — *Translator.)*

7 Marx-Engels-Gesamtausgabe, I/iii, p. 117. (The translation used here is from T. B. Bottomore's translation of Marx's essay, 'Private Property and Communism', as it appears in *Marx's Concept of Man*, by Erich Fromm, Frederick Ungar, New York, 1963, p. 130 — *Translator.)*

8 Marx-Engels, *Werke*, Berlin, 1955ff., vol. 1, pp. 384ff.

9 *Ibid.*, pp. 354ff., (excerpt from 'On the Jewish Problem' — *Translator*).

10 Hegel drew this consequence, and in *Philosophy of Right* he elaborated on this very point of the higher ethical nature of the idealistic concept of the state as against the civil state: 'An entirely distorted account . . . results from regarding the state as a merely civil society and from regarding its final end as only the security of individual life and property. . . . The ethical moment in war is implied in what has been said . . . . War is not to be regarded as an absolute evil. . . . War is the state of affairs which deals in earnest with the vanity of temporal goods and concerns. . . . This is what makes it the moment in which the ideality of the particular attains its right and is actualized. War has the higher significance that by its agency . . . the ethical health of peoples is preserved in their indifference to stabilization of finite institutions; just as the blowing of the winds preserves the sea from the foulness which would be the result of a prolonged calm. . . .' (*Rechtsphilosophie* §324, in *Werke*, Jubiläumsausgabe, vol. 7, p.434. [*Philosophy of Right*, §324. The translation used here is by T. M. Knox, Oxford University Press, 1942 — *Translator*]). Hegel saw empirical confirmation of his philosophical deduction of the usefulness of foreign war in the fact that successful wars have checked domestic unrest and consolidated the power of the state at home' *(loc. cit.).*

11 Hegel, *Rechtsphilosophie*, in *Werke*, Jubiläumsausgabe, vol. 7, p. 379.

12 Marx-Engels-Gesamtausgabe, I/iii, p. 544.

13 *Ibid.*, p. 546.

12   Are there any natural rights?*[1]

H. L. A. Hart

I shall advance the thesis that if there are any moral rights at all, it follows that there is at least one natural right, the equal right of all men to be free. By saying that there is this right, I mean that in the absence of certain special conditions which are consistent with the right being an equal right, any adult human being capable of choice (1) has the right to forbearance on the part of all others from the use of coercion or restraint against him save to hinder coercion or restraint and (2) is at liberty to do (i.e., is under no obligation to abstain from) any action which is not one coercing or restraining or designed to injure other persons.[2]

I have two reasons for describing the equal right of all men to be free as a *natural* right; both of them were always emphasised by the classical theorists of natural rights. (1) This right is one which all men have if they are capable of choice: they have it *qua* men and not only if they are members of some society or stand in some special relation to each other. (2) This right is not created or conferred by men's voluntary action; other moral rights are.[3] Of course, it is quite obvious that my thesis is not as ambitious as the traditional theories of natural rights; for although in my view all men are *equally* entitled to be free in the sense explained, no man has an absolute or unconditional right to do or not to do any particular thing or to be treated in any particular way; coercion or restraint of any action may be justified in special conditions consistently with the general principle. So my argument will not show that men have any right (save the equal right of all to be free) which is 'absolute', 'indefeasible', or 'imprescriptible'. This may for many reduce the importance of my contention, but I think that the principle that all men have an equal right to be free, meagre as it may seem, is probably all that the

*From *Philosophical Review*, vol. 64, 1955, pp. 175-91. Reprinted by permission of the author and the *Philosophical Review*.

political philosopshers of the liberal tradition need have claimed to support any programme of action even if they have claimed more. But my contention that there is this one natural right may appear unsatisfying in another respect; it is only the conditional assertion that *if* there are any moral rights then there must be this one natural right. Perhaps few would now deny, as some have, that there are moral rights; for the point of that denial was usually to object to some philosophical claim as to the 'ontological status' of rights, and this objection is now expressed not as a denial that there are any moral rights but as a denial of some assumed logical similarity between sentences used to assert the existence of rights and other kinds of sentences. But it is still important to remember that there may be codes of conduct quite properly termed moral codes (though we can of course say they are 'imperfect') which do not employ the notion of *a* right, and there is nothing contradictory or otherwise absurd in a code or morality consisting wholly of prescriptions or in a code which prescribed only what should be done for the realisation of happiness or some ideal of personal perfection.[4] Human actions in such systems would be evaluated or criticised as compliances with prescriptions or as *good* or *bad, right* or *wrong, wise* or *foolish, fitting* or *unfitting,* but no one in such a system would have, exercise, or claim rights, or violate or infringe them. So those who lived by such systems could not of course be committed to the recognition of the equal right of all to be free; nor, I think (and this is one respect in which the notion of a right differs from other moral notions), could any parallel argument be constructed to show that, from the bare fact that actions were recognised as ones which ought or ought not to be done, as right, wrong, good or bad, it followed that some specific kind of conduct fell under these categories.

I

(A) Lawyers have for their own purposes carried the dissection of the notion of a legal right some distance, and some of their results[5] are of value in the elucidation of statements of the form 'X has a right to . . .' outside legal contexts. There is of course no simple identification to be made between moral and legal rights, but there is an intimate connection between the two, and this itself is one feature which distinguishes a moral right from other fundamental moral concepts. It is not merely that as a matter of fact men speak of their moral rights mainly when advocating their incorporation in a legal system, but that the concept of a right belongs to that branch of morality which is specifically concerned to determine when one person's freedom may be limited by another's[6] and so to determine what actions may appropriately be made the subject of coercive legal rules. The words *'droit'*, *'diritto'*, and *'Recht'*, used by continental jurists, have no simple English translation and seem to English jurists to hover uncertainly between law and morals, but they do in fact mark off an area of morality (the morality of law) which has special characteristics. It is occupied by the concepts of justice, fairness, rights, and obligations (if this last is not used as it is by many moral philosophers as an obscuring general label to cover every action that morally we ought to do or forbear from doing). The most important common characteristic of this group of moral concepts is that there is no incongruity, but a special congruity in the use of force or the threat of force to secure that what is just or fair or someone's right to have done shall in fact be done; for it is in just these circumstances that coercion of another human being is legitimate. Kant in the *Rechtslehre,* discusses the obligations which arise in this branch of morality under the title of *officia juris,* 'which do not require that respect for duty shall be of itself the determining principle of the will', and contrasts them with *officia virtutis,* which have no moral worth unless done for the sake of the moral principle. His point is, I think, that we must distinguish from the rest of morality those principles regulating the proper distribution of human freedom which alone make it morally legitimate for one human being to determine by his choice how another should act; and a certain specific moral value is secured (to be distinguished from moral virtue in which the good will is manifested) if human relationships are conducted in accordance with these principles even though coercion has to be used to secure this, for only if these principles are regarded will freedom be distributed among human beings as it should be. And it is I think a very important feature of a moral right that the possessor of it is conceived as having a moral justification for limiting the freedom of another and that he has this justification not because the action he is entitled to require of another has some moral quality but simply because in the circumstances a certain distribution of human freedom will be maintained if he by his choice is allowed to determine how that other shall act.

(B) I can best exhibit this feature of a moral right by reconsidering the question whether moral rights and 'duties'' are correlative. The contention that they are means, presumably, that every statement of the form 'X has a right to . . .' entails and is entailed by 'Y has a duty (not) to . . .', and at this stage we must not assume that the values of the name-variables 'X' and 'Y' must be different persons. Now there is certainly one sense of 'a right' (which I have already mentioned) such that it does not follow from X's having a right that X or someone else has any duty. Jurists have isolated rights in this sense and have referred to them as 'liberties' just to distinguish them from rights in the centrally important sense of 'right' which has 'duty' as a correlative. The former sense of 'right' is needed to describe those areas of social life where competition is at least morally unobjectionable. Two people walking along both see a ten-dollar bill in the road twenty yards away, and there is no clue as to the owner. Neither of the two are under a 'duty' to allow the other to pick it up; each has in this sense a right to pick it up. Of course there may be many things which each has a 'duty' not to do in the course of the race to the spot—neither may kill or wound the other—and correspondingly to these 'duties' there are rights to forbearances. The moral propriety of all economic competition implies this minimum sense of 'a right' in which to say that 'X has a right to' means merely that X is under no 'duty' not to. Hobbes saw that the expression 'a right' could have this sense but he was wrong if he thought that there is no sense in which it does follow from X's having a right that Y has a duty or at any rate an obligation.

(C) More important for our purpose is the question whether for all moral 'duties' there are correlative moral rights, because those who have given an affirmative answer to this question have usually assumed without adequate scrutiny that to have a right is simply to be capable of benefiting by the performance of a 'duty'; whereas in fact this is not a sufficient condition (and probably not a necessary condition) of having a right. Thus animals and babies who stand to benefit by our performance of our 'duty' not to ill-treat them are said *therefore* to have rights to proper treatment. The full consequence of this reasoning is not usually followed out; most have shrunk from saying that we have rights against ourselves because we stand to benefit from our performance of our 'duty' to keep ourselves alive or develop our talents. But the moral situation which arises from a promise (where the legal-sounding terminology of rights and obligations is most appropriate) illustrates most clearly that the notion of having a right and that of benefiting by the performance of a 'duty' are not identical. X promises Y in return for some favour that he will look after Y's aged mother in his absence. Rights arise out of this transaction, but it is surely Y to whom the promise has been made and not his mother who *has* or *possesses* these rights. Certainly Y's mother is a person concerning whom X has an obligation and a person who will benefit by its performance, but the person *to whom* he has an obligation to look after her is Y. This is something *due to* or *owed* to Y, so it is Y, not his mother, whose right X will disregard and to whom X will have done *wrong* if he fails to keep his promise, though the mother may be physically injured. And it is Y who has a moral *claim* upon X, is *entitled* to have his mother looked after, and who can *waive* the claim and *release* Y from the obligation. Y is, in other words, morally in a position to determine by his choice how X shall act and in this way to limit X's freedom of choice; and it is this fact, not the fact that he stands to benefit, that makes it appropriate to say that he has *a right*. Of course often the person to whom a promise has been made will be the only person who stands to benefit by its performance, but this does not justify the identification of 'having a right' with 'benefiting by the performance of a duty'. It is important for the whole logic of rights that, while the person who stands to benefit by the performance of a duty is discovered by considering what will happen if the duty is not performed, the person who has a right (to whom performance is *owed* or *due*) is discovered by examining the transaction or antecedent situation or relations of the parties out of which the 'duty' arises. These considerations should incline us not to extend to animals and babies whom it is wrong to ill-treat the notion of a right to proper treatment, for the moral situation can be simply and adequately described here by saying that it is wrong or that we ought not to ill-treat them or, in the philosopher's generalised sense of 'duty', that we have a duty not to ill-treat them.[8] If common usage sanctions talk of the rights of animals or babies it makes an idle use of the expression 'a right', which will confuse the situation with other different moral situations where the expression 'a right' has a specific force and cannot be replaced by the other moral expressions which I have mentioned. Perhaps some clarity on this matter is to be gained by considering the force of the preposition 'to' in the expression 'having a duty to Y' or 'being under an obligation to Y' (where 'Y' is the name of a person); for it is significantly different from the meaning of 'to' in 'doing something to Y' or 'doing harm to Y', where it indicates the person affected by some action. In the first pair of expressions, 'to' obviously does not have this force, but indicates the person to whom the person morally bound is bound. This is an intelligible development of the figure of a bond (*vinculum juris: obligare*); the precise figure is not that of two persons bound by a chain, but of *one* person bound, the other end of the chain lying in the hands of another to use if he chooses.[9] So it appears absurd to speak of having duties or owing obligations to ourselves—of course we may have 'duties' not to do harm to ourselves, but what could be meant (once the distinction between these different meanings of 'to' has been grasped) by insisting that we have duties or obligations *to* ourselves not to do harm to ourselves?

(D) The essential connection between the notion of a right and the justified limitation of one person's freedom by another may be thrown into relief if we consider codes of behaviour which do not purport to confer rights but only to prescribe what shall be done. Most natural law thinkers down to Hooker conceived of natural law in this way: there were natural duties compliance with which would certainly benefit man—things to be done to achieve man's natural end—but not natural rights. And there are of course many types of codes of behaviour which only prescribe what is to be done, e.g., those regulating certain ceremonies. It would be absurd to regard these codes as conferring rights, but illuminating to contrast them with rules of games, which often create rights, though not, of course, moral rights. But even a code which is plainly a moral code need not establish rights; the Decalogue is perhaps the most important example. Of course, quite apart from heavenly rewards human beings stand to benefit by general obedience to the Ten Commandments: disobedience is wrong and will certainly harm individuals. But it would be a surprising interpretation of them that treated them as conferring rights. In such an interpretation obedience to the Ten Commandments would have to be conceived as due to or owed to individuals, not merely to God, and disobedience not merely as wrong but as *a wrong to* (as well as harm to) individuals. The Commandments would cease to read like penal statutes designed only to rule out certain types of behaviour and would have to be thought of as rules placed at the disposal of individuals and regulating the extent to which *they* may demand certain behaviour from others. Rights are typically conceived of as *possessed* or *owned by* or *belonging to* individuals, and these expressions reflect the conception of moral rules as not only prescribing conduct but as forming a kind of moral property of individuals to which they are as individuals entitled; only when rules are conceived in this way can we speak of *rights* and *wrongs* as well as right and wrong actions.[10]

II

So far I have sought to establish that to have a right entails having a moral justification for limiting the freedom of another person and for determining how he should act; it is now important to see that the moral justification must be of a special kind if it is to constitute a right, and this will emerge most clearly from an examination of the circumstances in which rights are asserted with the typical expression 'I have a right to . . .'. It is I think the case that this form of words is used in two main types of situation: (A) when the claimant has some special justification for interference with another's freedom which other persons do not have ('*I* have a right to be paid what you promised for my services'); (B) when the claimant is concerned to resist or object to some interference by another person as having no justification ('*I* have a right to say what I think').

(A) *Special rights.* When rights arise out of special transactions between individuals or out of some special relationship in which they stand to each other, both the persons who have the right and those who have the corresponding obligation are limited to the parties to the special transaction or relationship. I call such rights special rights to distinguish them from those moral rights which are thought of as rights against (i.e., as imposing obligations upon)[11] everyone, such as those that are asserted when some unjustified interference is made or threatened as in (B) above.

(i) The most obvious of special rights are those that arise from promises. By promising to do or not to do something, we voluntarily incur obligations and create or confer rights on those to whom we promise; we alter the existing moral independence of the parties' freedom of choice in relation to some action and create a new moral relationship between them, so that it becomes morally legitimate for the person to whom the promise is given to determine how the promisor shall act. The promisee has a temporary authority or sovereignty in relation to some specific matter over the other's will which we express by saying that the promisor is under an obligation *to* the promisee to do what he has promised. To some philosophers the notion that moral phenomena—rights and duties or obligations—can be brought into existence by the voluntary action of individuals has appeared utterly mysterious; but this I think has been so because they have not clearly seen how special the moral notions of a right and an obligation are, nor how peculiarly they are connected with the distribution of freedom of choice; it would indeed be mysterious if we could make actions morally good or bad by voluntary choice. The simplest case of promising illustrates two points characteristic of all special rights: (1) the right and obligation arise not because the promised action has itself any particular moral quality, but just because of the voluntary transaction between the parties; (2) the identity of the parties concerned is vital—only *this* person (the promisee) has the moral justification for determining how the promisor shall act. It is *his* right; only in relation to him is the promisor's freedom of choice diminished, so that if he chooses to release the promisor no one else can complain.

(ii) But a promise is not the only kind of transaction whereby rights are conferred. They may be *accorded* by a person consenting or authorising another to interfere in matters which but for this consent or authorisation he would be free to determine for himself. If I consent to your taking precautions for my health or happiness or authorise you to look after my interests, then you have a right which others have not, and I cannot complain of your interference if it is within the sphere of your authority. This is what is meant by a person surrendering his rights to another; and again the typical characteristics of a right are present in this situation: the person authorised has the right to interfere not because of its intrinsic character but because *these* persons have stood in *this* relationship. No one else (not similarly authorised) has any *right*[12] to interfere in theory even if the person authorised does not exercise his right.

(iii) Special rights are not only those created by the deliberate choice of the party on whom the obligation falls, as they are when they are accorded or spring from promises, and not all obligations to other persons are deliberately incurred, though I think it is true of all special rights that they arise from previous voluntary actions. A third very important source of special rights and obligations which we recognise in many spheres of life is what may be termed mutuality of restrictions, and I think political obligation is intelligible only if we see what precisely this is and how it differs from the other right-creating transactions (consent, promising) to which philosophers have assimilated it. In its bare schematic outline it is this: when a number of persons conduct any joint enterprise according to rules and thus restrict their liberty, those who have submitted to these restrictions when required have a right to a similar submission from those who have benefited by their submission. The rules may provide that officials should have authority to enforce obedience and make further rules, and this will create a

200 H. L. A. HART

structure of legal rights and duties, but the moral obligation to obey
the rules in such circumstances is *due to* the co-operating members
of the society, and they have the correlative moral right to obedience.
In social situations of this sort (of which political society is the most
complex example) the obligation to obey the rules is something
distinct from whatever other moral reasons there may be for
obedience in terms of good consequences (e.g., the prevention of
suffering); the obligation is due to the co-operating members of the
society as such and not because they are human beings on whom it
would be wrong to inflict suffering. The utilitarian explanation of
political obligation fails to take account of this feature of the
situation both in its simple version that the obligation exists because
and only if the direct consequences of a particular act of disobedience are worse than obedience, and also in its more sophisticated version that the obligation exists even when this is not so, if disobedience increases the probability that the law in question or other
laws will be disobeyed on other occasions when the direct consequences of obedience are better than those of disobedience.

Of course to say that there is such a moral obligation upon those
who have benefited by the submission of other members of society to
restrictive rules to obey these rules in their turn does not entail either
that this is the only kind of moral reason for obedience or that there
can be no cases where disobedience will be morally justified. There is
no contradiction or other impropriety in saying 'I have an obligation
to do X, someone has a right to ask me to, but I now see I ought not
to do it'. It will in painful situations sometimes be the lesser of two
moral evils to disregard what really are people's rights and not perform our obligations to them. This seems to me particularly obvious
from the case of promises: I may promise to do something and
thereby incur an obligation just because that is one way in which
obligations (to be distinguished from other forms of moral reason for
action) are created; reflection may show that it would in the
circumstances be wrong to keep this promise because of the suffering it might cause, and we can express this by saying '*I ought not to*
do it though *I have an obligation to him* to do it' just because the
italicised expressions are not synonyms but come from different
dimensions of morality. The attempt to explain this situation by saying that our real obligation here is to avoid the suffering and that
there is only a prima facie obligation to keep the promise seems to
me to confuse two quite different kinds of moral reason, and in
practice such a terminology obscures the precise character of what is

at stake when 'for some greater good' we infringe people's rights or do not perform our obligations to them.

The social-contract theorists rightly fastened on the fact that the obligation to obey the law is not merely a special case of bene-volence (direct or indirect), but something which arises between members of a particular political society out of their mutual relationship. Their mistake was to identify *this* right-creating situa-tion of mutual restrictions with the paradigm case of promising; there are of course important similarities, and these are just the points which all special rights have in common, viz., that they arise out of special relationships between human beings and not out of the character of the action to be done or its effects.

(iv) There remains a type of situation which may be thought of as creating rights and obligations: where the parties have a special natural relationship, as in the case of parent and child. The parent's moral right to obedience from his child would I suppose now be thought to terminate when the child reaches the age 'of discretion', but the case is worth mentioning because some political philosophies have had recourse to analogies with this case as an explanation of political obligation, and also because even this case has some of the features we have distinguished in special rights, viz., the right arises out of the special relationship of the parties (though it is in this case a natural relationship) and not out of the character of the actions to the performance of which there is a right.

(v) To be distinguished from special rights, of course, are special liberties, where, exceptionally, one person is *exempted* from obliga-tions to which most are subject but does not thereby acquire a *right* to which there is a correlative obligation. If you catch me reading your brother's diary, you say, 'You have no right to read it'. I say, 'I have a right to read it—your brother said I might unless he told me not to, and he has not told me not to'. Here I have been specially *licensed* by your brother who had a right to require me not to read his diary, so I am exempted from the moral obligation not to read it, but your brother is under no obligation to let me go on reading it. Cases where *rights*, not liberties, are accorded to manage or interfere with another person's affairs are those where the licence is not revocable at will by the person according the right.

(B) *General rights.* In contrast with special rights, which consti-tute a justification peculiar to the holder of the right for interfering with another's freedom, are general rights, which are asserted defensively, when some unjustified interference is anticipated or threatened, in order to point out that the interference is unjustified. 'I have the right to say what I think'.[13] 'I have the right to worship as I please'. Such rights share two important characteristics with special rights. (1) To have them is to have a moral justification for determining how another shall act, viz., that he shall not interfere.[14] (2) The moral justification does not arise from the character of the particular action to the performance of which the claimant has a right; what justifies the claim is simply—there being no special relation between him and those who are threatening to interfere to justify that interference— that this is a particular exemplification of the equal right to be free. But there are of course striking differences between such defensive general rights and special rights. (1) General rights do not arise out of any special relationship or transaction between men. (2) They are not rights which are peculiar to those who have them but are rights which all men capable of choice have in the absence of those special conditions which give rise to special rights. (3) General rights have as correlatives obligations not to interfere to which everyone else is subject and not merely the parties to some special relationship or transaction, though of course they will often be asserted when some particular persons threaten to interfere as a moral objection to that interference. To assert a general right is to claim in relation to some particular action the equal right of all men to be free in the absence of any of those special conditions which constitute a special right to limit another's freedom; to assert a special right is to assert in relation to some particular action a right constituted by such special conditions to limit another's freedom. The assertion of general rights directly invokes the principle that all men equally have the right to be free; the assertion of a special right (as I attempt to show in Section III) invokes it indirectly.

III

It is, I hope, clear that unless it is recognised that interference with another's freedom requires a moral justification the notion of a right could have no place in morals; for to assert a right is to assert that there is such a justification. The characteristic function in moral discourse of those sentences in which the meaning of the expression 'a right' is to be found—'I have a right to . . .', 'You have no right to . . .', 'What right have you to . . .?'—is to bring to bear on interferences with another's freedom, or on claims to interfere, a type of moral evaluation or criticism specially appropriate to interference with freedom and characteristically different from the moral criticism of actions made with the use of expressions like 'right', 'wrong', 'good', and 'bad'. And this is only one of many different types of moral ground for saying 'You ought . . .' or 'You ought not . . .'. The use of the expression 'What right have you to . . .?' shows this more clearly, perhaps, than the others; for we use it, just at the point where interference is actual or threatened, to call for the moral *title* of the person addressed to interfere; and we do this often without any suggestion at all that what he proposes to do is otherwise wrong and sometimes with the implication that the same interference on the part of another person would be unobjectionable.

But though our use in moral discourse of 'a right' does presuppose the recognition that interference with another's freedom requires a moral justification, this would not itself suffice to establish, except in a sense easily trivialised, that in the recognition of moral rights there is implied the recognition that all men have a right to equal freedom; for unless there is some restriction inherent in the meaning of 'a right' on the type of moral justification for interference which can constitute a right, the principle could be made wholly vacuous. It would, for example, be possible to adopt the principle and then assert that some characteristic or behaviour of some human beings (that they are improvident, or atheists, or Jews, or Negroes) constitutes a moral justification for interfering with their freedom; *any* differences between men could, so far as my argument has yet gone, be treated as a moral justification for interference and so constitute a right, so that the equal right of all men to be free would be compatible with gross inequality. It may well be that the expression 'moral' itself imports some restriction on what can constitute a moral justification for interference which would avoid this consequence, but I cannot myself yet show that this is so. It is, on the other hand, clear to me that the moral justification for interference which is to constitute a *right* to interfere (as distinct from merely making it morally good or desirable to interfere) is restricted to certain special conditions and that this is inherent in the meaning of 'a right' (unless this is used so loosely that it could be replaced by the other moral expressions mentioned). Claims to interfere with another's freedom based on the general character of the activities interfered with (e.g., the folly or cruelty of 'native' practices) or the general character of the parties ('We are Germans; they are Jews') even when well founded are not matters of moral right or obligation. Submission in such cases even where proper is not *due to* or *owed to* the individuals who interfere; it would be equally proper whoever of the same class of persons interfered. Hence other elements in our moral vocabulary suffice to describe this case, and it is confusing here to talk of rights. We saw in Section II that the types of justification for interference involved in special rights was independent of the character of the action to the performance of which there was a right but depended upon certain previous transactions and relations between individuals (such as promises, consent, authorisation, submission to mutual restrictions). Two questions here suggest themselves: (1) On what intelligible principle could these bare forms of promising, consenting, submission to mutual restrictions, be either necessary or sufficient, irrespective of their content, to justify interference with another's freedom? (2) What characteristics have these types of transaction or relationship in common? The answer to both these questions is I think this: If we justify interference on such grounds as we give when we claim a moral right, we are in fact indirectly invoking as our justification the principle that all men have an equal right to be free. For we are in fact saying in the case of promises and consents or authorisations that this claim to interfere with another's freedom is justified because he has, in exercise of his equal right to be free, freely chosen to create this claim; and in the case of mutual restrictions we are in fact saying that this claim to interfere with another's freedom is justified because it is fair; and it is fair because only so will there be an equal distribution of restrictions and so of freedom among this group of men. So in the case of special rights as well as of general rights recognition of them implies the recognition of the equal right of all men to be free.

Notes

1 I was first stimulated to think along these lines by Mr Stuart Hampshire, and I have reached by different routes a conclusion similar to his.
2 Further explanation of the perplexing terminology of freedom is, I fear, necessary. *Coercion* includes, besides preventing a person from doing what he chooses, making his choice less eligible by threats; *restraint* includes any action designed to make the exercise of choice impossible and so includes killing or enslaving a person. But neither coercion nor restraint includes *competition*. In terms of the distinction between 'having a right to' and 'being at liberty to', used above and further discussed in Section I(B), all men may have, consistently with the obligation to forbear from coercion, the *liberty* to satisfy if they can such at least of their desires as are not designed to coerce or injure others, even though in fact. owing to scarcity, one man's satisfaction causes another's frustration. In conditions of extreme scarcity this distinction between competition and coercion will not be worth drawing; natural rights are only of importance 'where peace is possible' (Locke). Further, freedom (the absence of coercion) can be valueless to those

victims of unrestricted competition too poor to make use of it; so it will be pedantic to point out to them that though starving they are free. This is the truth exaggerated by the Marxists whose *identification* of poverty with lack of freedom confuses two different evils.

3 Save those general rights (cf. Section II(B)) which are particular exemplifications of the right of all men to be free.

4 Is the notion of *a* right found in either Plato or Aristotle? There seems to be no Greek word for it as distinct from 'right' or 'just' *(dikaion)* , though expressions like *ta ema dikaia* (my rights) are, I believe, fourth-century legal idioms. The natural expressions in Plato are *to heauton (echein)* (what one has, what is in one's possession) or *ta tini opheilomena* (what is owing, or due, to one), but these seem confined to property or debts. There is no place for a moral right unless the moral value of individual freedom is recognized.

5 As W. D. Lamont has seen: cf. his *Principles of Moral Judgement,* Oxford, 1946; for the jurists, cf. Hohfeld's *Fundamental Legal Conceptions* New Haven, 1923.

6 Here and subsequently I use 'interfere with another's freedom', 'limit another's freedom', 'determine how another shall act', to mean either the use of coercion or demanding that a person shall do or not do some action. The connexion between these two types of 'interference' is too complex for discussion here; I think it is enough for present purposes to point out that having a justification for demanding that a person shall or shall not do some action is a necessary though not a sufficient condition for justifying coercion.

7 I write 'duties' here because one factor obscuring the nature of a right is the philosophical use of 'duty' and 'obligation' for all cases where there are moral reasons for saying an action ought to be done or not done. In fact 'duty', 'obligation', 'right' and 'good' come from different segments of morality, concern different types of conduct, and make different types of moral criticism or evaluation. Most important are the points (1) that obligations may be voluntarily incurred or created, (2) that they are *owed* to special persons (who have rights), (3) that they do not arise out of the character of the actions which are obligatory but out of the relationship of the parties. Language roughly though not consistently confines the use of 'having an obligation' to such cases.

8 The use here of the generalized 'duty' is apt to prejudice the question whether animals and babies have rights.

9 Cf. A. H. Campbell, *The Structure of Stair's Institutes,* Glasgow, 1954, p. 31.

10 Continental jurists distinguish between *subjektives* and *objektives Recht,* which corresponds very well to the distinction between *a* right, which an individual has, and what it is right to do.

11 Cf. Section (B) below.

12 Though it may be *better* (the lesser of two evils) that he should: cf. p. 200 below.

13 In speech the difference between general and special rights is often marked by stressing the pronoun where a special right is claimed or where the special right is denied. 'You have no right to stop him reading that book' refers to the reader's general right. '*You* have no right to stop him reading that book' denies that the person addressed has a special right to interfere though others may have.

14 Strictly, in the assertion of a general right both the *right* to forbearance from coercion and the *liberty* to do the specified action are asserted, the first in the face of actual or threatened coercion, the second as an objection to an actual or anticipated demand that the action should not be done. The first has as its correlative an obligation upon everyone to forbear from coercion; the second the absence in any one of a justification for such a demand. Here, in Hohfeld's words, the correlative is not an obligation but a 'no-right'.

Self-determination and human equality*

John Wilson

It is an observable and demonstrable fact that certain entities in the world possess powers to which we refer when we use words like 'will', 'choice', 'intention', 'intelligence', and many others. These powers are no doubt causally connected with certain physiological facts, and because of our ignorance of many of these facts they seem mysterious. This gives us no reason to place the powers in another 'super-natural' or 'transcendent' world, though in speaking of them we have to use language quite different from the language we use in speaking of entities that lack these powers. Just as in the history of evolution the inorganic merges almost imperceptibly into the organic, and non-life gradually produced what we call life, so the non-rational and non-intelligent may by slow degrees have thrown up certain entities that are rational and intelligent. There is a differ-ence in kind, that has to be marked in language, between the rational and the non-rational, as between life and non-life. But there is no sort of *magic* about it. There is no logical reason why we should not be able to produce a rational creature by artifical methods, just as we now create children by the natural processes of procreation.

What is uniquely important about these powers is that they enable every person who shares them—we might simply say, every *person*—to create his own values and his own rules. Meaningful disagree-ments can only arise within the framework of created human agree-ment: in particular, agreement about language and about the criteria of value. In order to dispute significantly, we depend on accepted rules of one kind or another: if we did not, we could fight or impede each other, as animals do, but we could not disagree. There are some rules, to which we usually refer as 'laws of thought', which it would be very hard to conceive as anything but essential for any rational creature: perhaps the most basic of these is the law of

*Reprinted with the permission of the author and publisher from *Equality* by John Wilson, Hutchinson, 1966, pp. 95-106.

non-contradiction. Other rules seem basically due to the fact that human beings share a common biological inheritance and common sense experience, so that it is natural for us to agree on a common language to denote these experiences. Other rules again, of a logically different kind, denote fairly widespread agreement about values, and seem to depend upon desires and dislikes which are widely shared amongst human beings.

Think again of a Martian, rational as ourselves, but with a totally different body, sense-organs, and desires. Let us indulge in science fiction, and imagine him to consist of waves and electrons: able to perceive what he would call 'colours' on the infra-red level and below: without what we call a sense of hearing: desiring things that to us seemed almost incomprehensible, such as a certain type of radio-wave, or to be bathed in cosmic rays. Such a creature would, as we might say, live in a different world from ourselves. We could not say that his world was 'less real' than ours, or that the 'colours' he perceives are 'not really' colours: or at least we could say this, but we should simply be reiterating our own ideas of what is real, or what really is a colour, in a language based on those ideas. Anything below the infra-red level, or above the ultra-violet, is not a colour, because it would not be what we meant by the word 'colour': but we have framed this criterion for the application of the word because it happens to suit our own particular sense-perceptions. The Martian's world is as real as our own: and this is simply to say that he suffers from no more delusions or hallucinations than we do, that he has built up a world out of his experience just as we have.

It seems equally plain that we cannot disagree with the Martian's criteria of value either, and for just the same reason: we have no common ground. If we care to stand on his ground and accept his ultimate ends—to experience radio-waves and cosmic rays—then we may be able to argue with him about what he actually does and thinks. We can point out certain facts to him, or criticise flaws in his reasoning, where these facts and flaws bear on his achievement of these ends. We might even think that his criteria were curiously disconnected from his actual nature—it might be that radio-waves tended to make him ill, and cosmic rays were liable to kill him. But it might be characteristic of Martians that they like being ill and running the risk of being killed. In any case, it would be his choice, and if we want to say that he had chosen wrongly, we should find ourselves at a loss for any criteria of value that would be common between him and ourselves.

This somewhat fantastic example brings home a truth which we are apt to forget when dealing with fellow-humans, though it applies equally to them: namely that if two people differ in their ultimate criteria of value or rules for behaviour, then—precisely because these criteria and rules are ultimate—they have no higher criteria or rules by which to settle their difference. This is a point which both analytic and existentialist philosophers have hammered home in the last few decades. It does not follow that we have to abandon any idea that ethics can be rational, but it does follow that our criteria of value are in the last analysis based upon human choice: and this has consequences for the notion of equality which are of the greatest importance.

The point can be made roughly by saying that all human beings have the same *status* as choosers and creators of value. When we disagree with somebody about ultimate criteria, it becomes important to notice what language we can intelligibly use. We can certainly disapprove of, or condemn, or show hostility towards his ultimate values: we can say words to the effect of 'I'm against them' or 'I choose quite differently', or 'I shall fight that tooth and nail'. But it is only in this sense intelligible to say that his values are not *good* or not the *right values*. For both 'good' and 'right' are normally used, not simply as terms of purely personal preference, but in reference to certain criteria in virtue of which we count things as good or right. We can question our criteria of goodness up to a certain point, by referring them to higher criteria: but the time comes when we run out of ammunition. The point here is not substantially different from the impossibility of talking about 'the right time' unless we already have agreed rules about what counts as the right time. If it is five o'clock in the USA and ten o'clock in England, what is 'the right time'? The question is unintelligible.

It seems unintelligible to say, therefore, that one person is a better valuer or a better chooser of values than another, if we press the matter to its limits. If two clocks run consistently but at different speeds the only justification we have for saying that one is better as a time-keeper than the other lies in a common agreement to refer the issue to Greenwich Observatory, or the sun, or some other accepted standard of measurement. It is sense to say that one tape-measure measures more accurately than the other, because we can compare them with the metre bar in Paris, but to ask whether the metre bar is a good measurer of metres is not sense— the metre bar *defines* the metre.

Because each man can shape his own ends and can choose his own values (despite the fact that many men accept values rather than choose them), there comes a point at which it is impossible to say that one man is superior or inferior to another: for 'superior' and 'inferior' only make sense in terms of some rule or criterion which is itself man-made. We cannot find any exact parallel here, for all other cases of human judgement or activity fall short of this point: but their inadequacies may perhaps help to make the point.

One sovereign law-making body, for instance, cannot be said to behave in a more legal or law-abiding way than another when it makes laws: for such a body does not follow the law, but defines it. One umpire or referee is less observant or well informed than another, thereby referring the issue to higher criteria. But the decisions of all umpires and referees are equally 'final'. Since they create their own values, men are rather more like bidders in an auction, who do not guess or judge the value of the objects, but make that value by their bids. In this vital respect, then, men are—to quote the dictionary definition of 'equal' again—'neither less nor greater' but 'on the same level': and it seems quite unexceptionable to describe them as equals in this respect. This is a natural and not an artificial equality: the whole point, indeed, is that it does not depend on any status which we give to particular people as creators of value, but upon the natural abilities of rational beings. The practical moral implication of this, which we shall draw more fully in subsequent parts, are not hard to see. For if one's morality pays any attention at all to the facts of human nature, to the actual powers and capacities of men, and also to the principle that similar cases demand similar treatment, then this particular similiarity amongst men is plainly one of the most important. It will be the most reasonable basis for the belief that men have the equal right to decide their own destinies, since they have an equal capacity to do so: and for the belief they have an equal right to make their wills and purposes felt—to actualise them in the world—since the will and purposes of each man are ultimately as valid as those of his neighbour.

Moreover this kind of equality can be pressed much further than other forms of natural equality. There is a rough similarity between men in many respects: they are all in some degree intelligent, liable to pain, and so on. But they do not have these characteristics to the same degree: we have to be content with general similarities. This also applies to certain empirical characteristics which have a moral aspect, such as those qualities to which we refer by such names as 'will-power', 'purposiveness', and 'determination'. These are in some loose sense measureable: one man possesses more of them than another. But the ability to form intentions and to value, to choose, and to have purposes, although it is empirically observable, is not in the same way quantitive. There is no difficulty about saying that one man is more purposive, or determined, or responsible than another; but it would be odd to say that one man is more able to form intentions or make choices than another.

It is not nonsense to say this, however. We could imagine ourselves saying of a man who, for instance, spent most of his time asleep or in intense pain that he was less able to make choices and decisions: though we should probably say that he had less *chance* of doing so. We could say of a madman, or even of somebody highly neurotic, perhaps, that he was less able: certainly we would use phrases like 'he can never make up his mind', 'he doesn't really value anything', 'he just drifts', 'he never seriously intends to do anything', 'he doesn't really choose, he just finds himself doing things', and so on. But these are extreme cases: and we should feel inclined to say that, to the extent that a person's powers of choice and decision were diminished, he was less of a person. Madmen are people only by courtesy: and prolonged pain can reduce people to the level of animals. In so far as human beings remain human, therefore, they possess these powers to an equal degree.

This is not just a logical sleight-of-hand, an attempt to prove this absolute equality by a pre-emptive definition of what it is to be human. For it is not a mere accident that we should continue to count as human such people as possessed *other* human characteristics (such as the capacity to love or feel pain) in a very slight degree, or not at all. We could call such people 'inhuman', but we would not mean it literally. In considering when to count children as people, or whether to count robots, animals, morons, Martians, and madmen as people, it is this central characteristic, the ability to choose and decide, that we always have in mind. We are concerned with whether the entity, as we say, 'has a will of its own'; and this is not a quantitative matter, though there may be borderline cases. Either it has a will of its own, or it has not.

If somebody chooses to do something which we think to be very silly or wicked, such as becoming an opium addict or a mass murderer, we are often tempted to deny that his powers of choice and deliberation are equal to our own. This denial may take the unsophisticated form of assuming that since our own values are so obviously correct, there must be something wrong with the person who overlooks or transgresses them: this is simply to miss the point made earlier, that intrinsic equality *lies behind* each man's values. But we might make a more subtle objection: the objection that, since each man's choices are necessarily limited by the language he uses and the facts available to him, some people are more able to choose, or able to choose more widely or more freely, than others. Thus if I am a member of a primitive tribe that follows a very narrow pattern of moral behaviour and has no contact with the outside world, I shall have neither the language nor the knowledge to make choices which fall far outside this pattern: and my imagination is also likely to be restricted by the limitations imposed by my environment.

This objection fails, however, because it assumes that a wide range of choices is to be preferred to a narrow one. Most of us would probably accept such an assumption: but it is not logically necessary, and it is quite possible to hold that human beings ought to consider only a narrow range of choices. The primitive tribe might easily claim that their moral choices and behaviour were the best possible, and that it was a waste of time—or positively dangerous—to look further afield. We could only persuade them otherwise by referring them to some criterion that they already had—perhaps the desire to make progress, improve their society, increase their power, or whatever—and show that they needed a wider range of choices in order to satisfy that criterion: but then we should be treating them as equals, by arguing on their criteria rather than writing them off as 'inferior' or 'limited' and imposing our own criteria on them. Similarly, in considering those very silly or very wicked people whom we feel inclined to dismiss as 'mad', 'not in their right mind', or 'in no position to choose for themselves', we must carefully distinguish between strongly disagreeing with their choices on the one hand, and denying that they have the power of choice on the other.

Exactly what tests we should employ in deciding whether someone had the power of choice or not is a hard question. Certainly he would need to be able to use language, and to represent his intentions to himself, if not to others. It seems also as if he would have to possess, in however small a degree, the power to reflect and deliberate: otherwise (to put it roughly) he would not be really *choosing,* but just reacting. In psychological terms, we should try to establish that the man had some kind of ego, a part of himself which was not just a swirling battleground of conflicting fears and desires but was capable of some sort of deliberate control and decision. Those with severe mental illness might well make us hesitate before deciding one way or the other. I incline to think, however, that even a faint flicker of genuine choice would be sufficient to establish the existence of a person, possessed of intrinsic equality (and whatever rights we might accept as following from this). A person who was only sane on Monday, and behaved like an animal for the rest of the week, would still be a person: after all, we count ourselves as people even though for a third of our life we are incapable of choice because we are asleep.

We must also remember that, in the practical workings of society, choices are rarely presented to individual people with that degree of clarity which my examples may have suggested. For instance, by industrialising a primitive agricultural society we do far more than merely change the economy and the technology: we transform the whole way of life of that society, because the behaviour appropriate to a new means of production inevitably spills over into other forms of behaviour. Thus a capitalistic and technological culture may perhaps demand certain kinds of responsibility and certain virtues in the individual—thrift, punctuality, self-discipline, independence —and the importance of these virtues is likely to be reproduced in the morality and religion of that society. My point here is that this process is likely to be unrecognised by the individuals: they will find themselves unconsciously adopting new values, and taking new things for granted. But this is not to say that they do not have the power of choice, in the sense I have been trying to give to the phrase: it is rather to say that, due to limitations on their understanding and their unconscious acceptance of the forms of life with which this economic process has saddled them, they have not realised their power of choice in this particular area.

The notion of 'having a will of one's own' is also importantly ambiguous. There are plenty of cases where people suffer, either on occasions or permanently, from what we may call atrophy of the will: but it is not this sense of 'will' on which intrinsic equality is based. A man may lack will-power or determination, or may not be able to make an effort: but we cannot for that reason count him as an inferior, or claim that he does not choose or that his choices should not count. Certainly, he will have to do more than merely *imagine* some state of affairs to himself or merely *feel a desire* for something: he must *will* it, in the sense of setting himself to some course of action: he must specifically desire to actualise it. There may not be any actual steps which he can take (either because he lacks will-power or for some other reason): but the position must be such that he would take some steps if he could. Given such a position—and this is usually not hard to verify—we must allow him to have chosen.

It is worth reminding ourselves of the relevance of these points to the possible interpretations of 'All men are equal' which we might use in reference to intrinsic equality. If we use the first defence mentioned in the last section, whereby we are measuring the class of men against other classes of entities, then we can represent intrinsic equality as an equality of powers, abilities or capacities. In this sense we must admit that *within* the class of men, all men are *not* equally capable of choice, desire, will-power, determination, effort, rational reflection, and so forth. But they may be allowed a comparative equality, as measured against the powers of other creatures. On the other hand, if we use the second defence, whereby we refer simply to a common characteristic, we have to distinguish carefully between two possiblities. First, we can say that all men are, equally, capable of will-power, effort, and rational reflection (though not in the same degree): and secondly, we can describe this equality without using adjectives of degree at all. Thus there is a sense to words and phrases like 'rational', 'conscious', 'having a will of one's own', 'choosing', 'purposive', and 'self-regulating' which does not permit one intelligibly to say that one person is more rational, conscious, etc., than another. Thus there is a sense in which one machine (a computer) may be more self-regulating than another (a simple thermostatic device): but there is also a sense in which a machine is either self-regulating or not. This is not to deny the possibility of borderline cases, about which we might feel doubtful and which we would have to settle by a decision. But amongst men such borderline cases are very rare.

All these interpretations can be accepted: but the real importance of intrinsic equality lies in the last; for as we have seen, the key point is that the equality which derives from the powers of choice, of creating one's own values, of having purposes, and of following rules has a significance quite unlike the significance of accidental similarities amongst men. For these former characteristics are the basis for language, and for the whole apparatus of judgement which depends on the criteria of language. Intrinsic equality rests on the fact that all human beings come into a particular category or mode of being. Their varying abilities to reflect and deliberate, to state their values or the rules they follow and to exercise will-power or effort, do not constitute the major issue. The point is rather that no human being can escape from his general category (except by suicide or by being reduced to an animal level), and above all that inclusion in this category gives all human beings a similar status *vis-à-vis* their fellows.

Moreover, no other conceivable power or ability can seem so important to us as the ability to choose and create value, because it is in terms of this ability that the importance of other abilities is defined. We might imagine super-beings that had all sorts of powers—they might be strong, telepathic, clairvoyant, all-wise, benevolent, and so forth; and yet there would still be a sense in which we were their equals, for we should have our wills and purposes, just as they had. In order to regard ourselves as wholly inferior, we should have to be able to conceive of some ability which somehow transcended the ability to choose, in the same sort of way that the ability to choose transcends our other abilities, and the abilities of animals: and such a conception seems impossible. Various religious writers have laid claim to it, but I have not found any way in which the will of God, for example, can be intelligibly shown to be a different *sort* of will from our own, or more valid than our own—unless we choose to count it as more valid, which is, of course, simply to reaffirm the primacy of our own choice and hence our own will. Since language and its concepts are based on human choice, they cannot allow any intelligibility to the notion of a super-choice or a super-will: all such notions will merely be projections of our own wills in a new form.

We may use this notion to pick up a point made earlier in this part. The accidental equality of men depended on the existence of certain similarities: but the existence of these, as we saw when considering man and nature, itself depends on a particular way of looking at the world, the use of particular contexts, and so on. The claim of intrinsic equality is essentially the claim that every man has an equal ability to frame his own world-view and his own criteria of similarity. This claim is a factual one: but it is closely allied to the claim that every man has an *equal* right to do this. In other words, not only does every man *have* a will just as much as every other man, but also his will *should count for as much as* the other's. The difficulty of denying this latter claim is simply that there seems to be no reason *outside* the wills and criteria of individual men, so to speak, for believing that the will of any one man is superior. It seems that we have to accept the claim in order to start on any process of argument or morality at all.

Many people may be disposed to accept this outright: but I think this would be premature. For, again, the *relevance* of the fact that other people have wills just like my own depends on my own values and criteria. I might think that their wills should not count, because they are stupid or neurotic. It is true that my criteria for stupidity and neurosis are *my* criteria, and may not be shared by them: but then I might think that these facts about them are more important: and to convince me you would have to prove this on my criteria of importance.

There is also another reason of a rather different kind why we cannot step so rapidly from the fact of intrinsic equality to some moral position about human rights. We must not forget that the powers on which we base our intrinsic equality are only actualised by a social environment: in particular, by the human infant being brought up in a society which teaches it a language. Now it would be quite possible for an anti-egalitarian to admit that all adults—let us say more precisely, children over the age of about three or four— had these powers, and hence the rights that went with them: but also to claim that there was no particular reason why we should give these powers to all infants. Thus suppose that for some odd moral reason I prefer a world consisting solely of whites or Aryans, I might treat existing Negroes and non-Aryans with perfect propriety as equals, but refuse to allow Negro or non-Aryan infants to be turned into people by the normal processes of upbringing. In other words, I might accept that people are equals, but fail to see why it should be a good thing to turn infants (or all infants) into people.

We may also remind ourselves of a third objection which is even more radical. Suppose a man's world-view, including his language and criteria of similarity, simply does not take into account the differences between creatures that have wills of their own and creatures that do not. Why should we make the distinctions we make? Why, to put it dramatically, should a super-being from some other galaxy distinguish between men and ants, in the way we want him to distinguish? Is the distinction between intelligent and non-intelligent life one which all intelligent beings are bound to make, and if so what binds them?

These and other difficulties are real ones, although they may seem to us—who share, for the most part, a common outlook and a common language—to be somewhat fantastic. Earlier we saw that the notion of accidental equality needed to be backed by a more general picture, and the picture painted by intrinsic equality is certainly more general, and may provide more common ground. But it is still not general enough to be as universally convincing as we should wish. For the egalitarian to bring everyone into his fold, he will have to show that everyone's criteria are such that, given due attention to facts and logic, they will be bound to admit the overwhelming importance of intrinsic equality.

14   Rights and right conduct *

A. I. Melden

A parent's right to special consideration can be honoured by his son in very many different sorts of ways; and by doing these things his son will meet his obligation to his parent. I shall now examine the question whether or not such obligation-meeting actions of the son are obligatory in the sense in which a failure to do what is obligatory is a failure to do one's duty and hence blameworthy (equivalently, a failure to do what is morally required in the specific situation in which the agent finds himself). In general, philosophers who discourse about rights assume that every obligation-meeting action is in this sense obligatory, so that whether or not they regard locutions about the rights of agents as replaceable without loss of meaning by locutions about right action, they assume that such locutions are equivalent. In any case they assume that it follows from the fact that an action is obligation-meeting that it is obligatory. They often express themselves as if they thought that if, for example, a person were to give up his theatre ticket to his parent and in that way meet the obligation which he has to his parent, then it would be his bounden duty to do so. Now it is this assumption that has led philosophers to hedge claims to the possession of rights with qualifications and even to heap ridicule upon those who subscribe to doctrines of 'natural', 'inalienable' or 'human' rights. For surely, they argue, we can imagine circumstances in which anything to which a person might lay claim as his right, must of moral necessity be withheld from him. So it is tempting to say, not that parents have the right to special consideration from their sons, but that they have 'presumptive' rights, the thought being that they will *have* rights only in specific circumstances and just to the extent to which these circumstances render the obligation-meeting actions obligatory.

*Reprinted with the permission of the author and publisher from A. I. Melden, *Rights and Right Conduct*, Basil Blackwell, 1959, pp. 9-16.

This seems to me to be as confused and as mistaken a view as any in moral philosophy. It confuses two quite distinct notions—obligation meeting action and obligatory action, and that these are distinct albeit related notions can be shown by means of the following considerations.

(1) We speak of a person demanding, asserting or standing on his rights. Conceivably one could say 'I demand my right . . .' when one has no such right. Fraud and even mistake are possible, at least in unusual cases. Jacob asked for and received the blessing due to Esau and so A may deceive B into supposing that he is the latter's parent and thus stand on rights he does not have at all. Or, he may be mistaken; he is C's parent, but not seeing B clearly thinks he is C, and afterwards say apologetically, 'I thought you were C, my son.' Or, supposing neither fraud nor mistaken identity, he might make another sort of mistake and subsequently excuse himself by saying, 'I thought you could have met your obligation to me, but I see now that you were in no position to do so.' A parent can, in good faith, mistakenly demand his rights. But not only are such errors possible, one can also be ill-advised in employing the language and demeanour of one who demands his rights. It is not always the prudent thing to make an issue of one's privileged moral position and, when what is at issue is of minor consequence, one can be offensive in making an unseemly fuss about little or nothing at all. Indeed, cases of this latter sort are apt to puzzle us when we see them occur; we may not understand a person when we observe him standing on his rights about something trifling. What is such a person trying to do? And if no answer can be given, we should write him off as either mad or bewildering. But there are cases in which a person would be intelligible but morally unjustified in standing on his rights, when there is neither fraud nor mistake of the sorts mentioned above, when there is no disputing the relevance of the right to the specific circumstances of the case, when there is no question of prudence or distasteful fuss about trifles, and when, granted that he has a right that can be honoured, it would be morally desirable to waive, without losing or forfeiting, the right he does have. For a parent not only has a right *vis-à-vis* his son, but also responsibilities and obligations to him, not only a moral interest in the relations in which he stands to him, but also in the moral relations in which his son stands to others. Moral rights and their correlative obligations do compete for satisfaction. To favour one's parent in this or that situation *may* entail a needless sacrifice of the development of one's own talents or

render it impossible to meet an enormously important obligation one has incurred to other persons. Surely it would be moral folly in such circumstances for a parent to stand on his rights and thus ignore the sometimes complex maze of rights and obligations that often surrounds all of the parties concerned. But if every obligation-meeting action is necessarily obligatory, it would be trivially true that one is morally justified in standing on one's rights, and self-contradictory to say that one ought not, by doing this or that specific action, to meet one's obligation.

(2) If every obligation-meeting action were obligatory, every case in which a parent waives his right would be a failure of moral nerve and a contribution to the moral delinquency of one's offspring by encouraging him to turn his back on his manifest duty. On this view, moral apologies and excuses, not explanations, would be required in order to mitigate the blameworthiness involved in waiving one's right (perhaps, by citing the motive, 'It was a case of pardonable parental affection that led me to encourage him not to meet his obligation to me'), but we not only excuse or pardon parents for waiving their rights, we even praise them for doing so, and not only because of the otherwise commendable love and affection they display towards their offspring but sometimes because of the superior moral wisdom they exhibit. If it is not self-contradictory to say that one is morally justified in waiving one's rights, then it does not follow from the fact that an action is obligation-meeting that it is obligatory. If it is possible to be morally justified in waiving one's moral right, then we can state what would count as a case of this sort. And surely there are cases in which a parent would be morally justified in waiving his right, on insisting that, in the specific circumstances then on hand, his son must not meet his obligation to him, if by doing so he puts himself in moral jeopardy with others or sacrifices the development of his own talents. Surely, in other words, one may be morally justified in waiving one's right. Least of all is it true that one is blameworthy in waiving one's right.

(3) If every obligation-meeting action were obligatory then those cases in which rights (and their correlative obligations) compete for satisfaction present no mere practical problems to be resolved by the moral wisdom of the persons concerned but, rather, logical absurdities. If both A and C have rights as against B, then B will have obligations to both A and C. If, as it sometimes happens, B finds himself in a situation in which he can perform either action x or action y, but not both, then supposing that actions x and y are

obligation-meeting with respect to A and C respectively, on the present view both actions x and y will be obligatory. If he performs action x, he will then be doing and not doing his duty; and the same holds true about the action y. It will not do to say that in such cases all moral bets are off on the ground that if he is morally damned if he does and morally damned if he does not, he is enmeshed in tragedy and deserves not censure but understanding and sympathy. Conflicting obligations are not instances of tragedy. Neither are they like instances in which all bets are off when the coin lands on its edge. They are, rather, familiar incidents in our common moral life which, in the great majority of cases, are easily comprehended by a not uncommon moral wisdom. There is no logical repulsion between rights or between obligations and it is, one must insist, the mark of the Pharisee to stand on all his rights, to view rights as if they were notes payable on demand, and obligations which one person may have to another as the inflexible decrees or air-tight directives of a quasi-legal tribunal.

All of this might well seem to be a case of belabouring the obvious were it not for the persistent confusions with which the topic of rights is surrounded in the philosophical literature. Not only do writers commonly assume that every obligation-meeting action is a case of obligatory action, they often confound these quite distinct concepts. This is apparent in the attempt of Maritain, for one, to derive the right which a person has from that which he is obliged to do; for example, the right to life from the duty he has to preserve and achieve the fullness of his being—his good.[1] What precisely this means is not at all clear. What seems to be asserted is that I ought to preserve my being because that is good, further that I have a right to do that which I ought to do, and since what I ought to do is to continue living, I have a right to live, i.e. a right to life. But this is in effect to translate locutions about rights into locutions about what it is right to do, and the best that can be said for this way of speaking (ignoring some of the curious steps in the argument) is that it simply ignores those areas of moral discourse in which we speak of a right which one person has *as against another* and, correlatively, the obligation which the latter has *to* the former. For what it substitutes for this language of rights is the different albeit related discourse about what it is right to do. It is this confusion that mars Bradley's discussion of rights and duties in his addendum to the essay 'My Station and its Duties' and, as I shall now show, much of the current talk about rights as claims.

A right, we are often told, is a claim.[2] But it is clear that since a person might have a right without registering a claim, i.e. claiming, we are to think of a claim as something a person has, whether or not he makes it, i.e. claims. Briefly, a right is a claim which a person may have even though he does not make it. But this surely renders unilluminating the statement that a right is a claim, for what on earth is a claim one does not make? Clearly, it can only be a right, and of course the word 'claim' is often used in legal contexts as a synonym for 'right'; but in that case we have not advanced a single jot. Surely, it will be replied, these writers are not simply advancing a synonym for 'right'. Of course not. If they were, they would not quickly add, as does Ritchie, for example, that the claim has to be sanctioned by society in the form of the approbation and disapprobation of private persons (in contrast to the sanctions imposed by society for the violation of the legal rights of persons). For the point of this specification is to distinguish claims that are justified and which, as justified, are rights from claims that stand in need of such justification and are not entitled, in consequence, to being designated as 'rights'. Thus it is that Garvin, to consider another writer, speaks of a moral right as a claim to something in so far as it is a just one. But such a move has the unfortunate effect of rendering the term 'claim' either too narrow or altogether unintelligible. Too narrow, because a justified claim would seem to be something claimed justly; hence no provision is made for rights that are not asserted—cases in which although A has a right to *x,* for one reason or another he or anyone else fails to claim *x* as justly his. (It will be noted that if need be I depart from ordinary usage in taking 'asserting one's right' and 'demanding one's right' to be equivalent.) Alternatively, if the application of 'justified claim' is to coincide with that of 'right', 'claim' cannot mean right; if it did, 'justified' would be redundant and in any case it would have the unhappy consequence of enabling us to speak of a 'justified right' and what this would mean is surely obscure. Would a justified right be a right the claim to the possession of which is justified? Every right is justified in this odd sense; that is to say, if whenever A has a right, his statement or claim that he has the right is capable of being justified, not by repeating 'I have the right' but by stating the facts which justify his claim that he has the right. Thus, if he has the right to special consideration from B, his claim that he has this right would be justified by showing that he is B's parent. By a 'justified right' one would mean, therefore, a right one actually has; so construed, the term 'justified' qualifies not the right that one has but the claim that one has the right. If, however, 'justified' in the expression 'justified claim' does qualify a claim as distinct from a right, then it is difficult to see what this claim could be if it is not the claim that an action is morally required or obligatory, in which case we have, once more, the familiar thesis that every obligation-meeting action is obligatory, this time in the extreme form according to which statements about rights are merely covert statements about right conduct. So it is in the case of Garvin's remarks. He tells us that 'rights are simply claims of individuals or of certain groups to certain goods and privileges such as are properly theirs in accordance with . . . social or distributive justice'.[3] Since, on Garvin's view, justice has to do with apportionment of goods, i.e. with *doing* things in such a way that individuals receive and enjoy goods and privileges, the justified claim by individuals *to* such enjoyments turns out to be the justified claim *that* they ought to receive them. Put simply, the thesis is that to say that an individual has a right to x is to say that it is right that the individual be given x. As this stands (although the difficulty might be rectified by counting a *possible* claim as a claim) this would deny that a person had rights unless he asserted them (or others for him), but asserting a right presupposes that there is a right to support the demand made. And it is by no means true that the possessor of a right must stand to benefit (to receive goods and privileges) from the actions that honour his right.[4] But the radical objections to this account of the matter are the ones cited in the preceding section of this essay. (1) Every justification of such a claim on the basis of the agent's right would turn out to be no justification at all, but an unavailing stutter. 'You ought to give me x, because it is mine in accordance with the requirements of justice', and this is only to say that 'you ought to because you ought to'. (2) One could not, on this view, speak of a parent having a right as against his son except in the case in which he was duty-bound to assert it and his son duty-bound to honour it. But it is not self-contradictory, it may even be morally commendable, to say, 'I have a right but I ought not to .assert it', and 'I have a right to special consideration from B, but it would be wrong for B to give me special consideration at this time'. For, having a right is not the only consideration relevant to the claim that the relevant action is morally required. Hence a right may be waived without being relinquished or forfeited. (3) Every case of competing rights and, correlatively, obligations would give rise not to tragedy but to logical absurdity. The plain fact of the matter, too often obscured by the philosophical ruts that constrict our ways of speaking, is that attempted 'reductions' of statements about rights into statements about right action do violence to the actual procedures of moral reflection. Here we need to be reminded of Aristotle's observation that 'the truth in practical matters is discerned from the fact of life; for these are the decisive facts.'[5] And the facts do stare us in the face: Agents have rights. Rights compete for moral satisfaction. Moral wisdom consists not only in recognising that a right may operate as a consideration that supports the claim that an action is right, but also in recognising how to weigh such supporting considerations whenever they compete and how in such cases to arrive at a determination of what it is that one is morally required to do.

Notes

1 Cf. *Man and the State,* University of Chicago Press, 1951, ch. 4.
2 By innumerable writers from D. G. Ritchie in *Natural Rights,* Allen & Unwin, London, 1894, p. 78, down to textbook writers like Lucius Garvin in *A Modern Introduction to Ethics,* ed. M. K. Munitz, Free Press, Chicago, 1958, p. 478.
3 Garvin, *op. cit.,* p. 479 (Garvin's italics are omitted).
4 This has been noted by H. L. A. Hart, 'Are there any natural rights?' *Philosophical Review,* vol. 64, 1955 [see pp. 192-205 above].
5 *Nicomachean Ethics,* book 10, 8. Translation by W. D. Ross, Oxford University Press, 1954.

15   Freedom and persuasion *

Stanley I. Benn

I

Some time in the 1950s everyone became conscious of the menace of
the hidden persuaders. Whether as commercial advertisers or as
political propagandists, they formed, it was said, an invisible power
élite, corrupting taste and manipulating opinion for private gain or
sectional power. We learnt with alarm that having the sense of
choosing freely was no guarantee that one really had a free choice;
choices could be rigged by skilful operators who could make us want
what they or their clients wanted us to want.

This scandal of our age seems to have been exaggerated. It is now
the fashion to take a more sober view of the claims of the persuasion
industry and its supporting 'motivational research'. Propaganda
and advertising, we are assured, can shape beliefs and attitudes
only within limits; people resist suggestions that run counter to their
basic personality characteristics.[1] So a film intended to counter a
prejudice may actually reinforce it. Though authoritarian personalities can be readily switched from fascism to communism, they
make poor liberals. 'Brain-washing' is effective only with alienated
and anomic individuals—and its effects even on them are relatively
short-lived once they leave the reinforcing environment.

All the same, although mass persuasive techniques are less
successful in changing attitudes than the alarmists would have us
suppose, they seem to be very effective in reinforcing already existing
tendencies to change. Furthermore, all the research done so far has
been on 'campaign effects'[2] i.e. on the kind of short-term effects
which are typically the goals of publicity and advertising; little is

*Reprinted with the permission of the author and the editor from *Australasian
Journal of Philosophy,* vol. 45, 1967, pp. 259-75. An earlier version of this paper was
read to the Eighth Annual Conference of the Australasian Political Studies
Association, at Canberra, August 1966.

known as yet of the long-term effects of mass persuasive influences. Besides, the reassurances that have been given amount only to saying that not much progress has been made so far. As yet, our minds cannot readily be made up for us unless we are initially indifferent (as, for instance, between one kind of soap and another, or, maybe, between one brand of authoritarianism and another); altering basic attitudes is very much more difficult. Propaganda may 'boomerang'; human personality is not infinitely plastic; psychologists have much to learn about the formation of human attitudes and propagandists about how to manipulate them. In much the same way one might have been assured at the end of last century that fear of aerial warfare was fantastic—pioneers had barely succeeded in getting a heavier-than-air machine off the ground. For the fact remains that there are interested people who are spending a great deal to find out what makes a man believe and behave as he does, and who clearly live in hope that out of it will come more efficient ways of influencing both. Discovering why primitive techniques have only limited effectiveness is the first step to more effective ones.

My intention here, however, is not to assess the claims of the persuasion industry, but rather to examine what the expressions of alarm that these claims evoke presuppose about freedom and the social interactions of aims and influences, and to gain from this an insight into certain liberal ways of thinking about politics and society. For the persuasion industry presents liberals with a new problem, which requires a re-examination of such basic concepts as freedom, choice, interest, and interference. Neither of Berlin's two concepts of liberty[3] are really adequate to express the kind of uneasiness that the liberal experiences when confronted by opinion-manipulation. The central questions of politics, according to Berlin,[4] are

> the questions of obedience and coercion. 'Why should I (or anyone) obey anyone else?' 'Why should I not live as I like?' 'Must I obey?' 'If I disobey, may I be coerced? By whom, and to what degree, and in the name of what and for the sake of what?'

These questions presuppose a conflict of will between the authority and the subject, the coercer and the coerced. The classic discussions of political obligation have all been concerned with what constitutes a good reason for requiring a man to put aside his own wishes or opinions and to act instead in accordance with someone else's. The problem presented by propagandists, advertisers and public relations experts is quite different. They aim not at overruling contrary intentions by threats of coercion but, by persuasion, to create a willing—if possible an enthusiastic—accord. They seek to avoid or dissolve conflict, not to overtake it. The task I have set myself in this paper, therefore, is to extend the application of the classical concepts of liberalism so that they can function coherently in the discussion of persuasive techniques. This exercise has, I believe, the added value that in discovering how to do new things with these concepts, one comes to a better understanding of their meaning in the traditional contexts. Finally, having found a way of re-stating liberal principles that will distinguish what is consistent with freedom from what is not, I shall try to elicit from them criteria for both the use and the control of persuasive and manipulative techniques.

According to Berlin, 'I am normally said to be free' (i.e. in the negative sense) 'to the degree to which no human being interferes with my activity. Political liberty in this sense is simply the area within which a man can do what he wants' (p. 7) [see p. 142 above]. But liberalism has never taken much notice of how men come to want what they do want—or rather, the traditional target for liberal critics like Milton, Jefferson, and Mill, has been censorship, the monopolistic control of the supply of ideas, not the techniques used to persuade people to adopt some ideas rather than others. Pinning their faith to human rationality, they believed that to drive out error truth needed no special privilege beyond the opportunity to be heard: the shoddy tricks of those who exploited credulity could not survive exposure to rational criticism. This faith never faced the challenge that there might be non-rational techniques for persuading a person to believe certain things or to adopt certain desired attitudes—that is, techniques for inducing him to want to do or be something that someone else had decided upon, even though arguments and evidence to the contrary remained fully accessible. Would the classical liberals have said that a person who was able to do what he wanted without interference, but whose preferences had been shaped by such techniques, was free because he was 'left to do or be what he wanted to do or be, without interference by other persons'?[5]

The classical liberals might have objected that the techniques of persuasion that modern liberals fear do in fact 'interfere'—not, certainly, with a man's doing what he wants to do, but with his freely *deciding* what he wants to do. But making this move commits the liberal to some way of distinguishing forms of persuasion that interfere from those that do not. For in defining social and political freedom, the liberal relies on a conception of a free market in ideas, a conception which actually presupposes that men will attempt to influence one another's beliefs. Accordingly, he must allow that there are some ways at least of getting people to change their minds that are not in his sense interferences.

The positive sense of 'freedom', according to Berlin, is the sense that 'derives from the wish on the part of the individual to be his own master' (p. 16) [see p. 148 above]. I am free, in this sense, if 'my life and decisions . . . depend on myself, not on external forces of whatever kind', if I am 'the instrument of my own, not of other men's, acts of will . . . a subject, not an object . . . moved by reasons, by conscious purposes, which are my own, not by causes which affect me, as it were, from outside . . . deciding, not being decided for, self-directed and not acted upon by external nature or by other men as if I were a thing, or an animal, or a slave incapable of playing a human role, that is, of conceiving goals and policies of my own, and realising them' (p. 16) [see p. 149 above]. This 'positive' concept of freedom seems more likely than the 'negative' concept to be what the liberal needs for framing his objections to certain persuasive techniques. It is no more apt, however, for distinguishing those that are consistent with freedom from those that are not. For there are certainly instances of one man prevailing upon another to do what he wants him to do, and so being a cause of his actions, without his acting on him as if he were a thing, or an animal, or an object, not a subject. The problem here is to decide what kinds of influence on a person are compatible with autonomy. A similar problem arises, indeed, in the classical area, in relation to coercion, and it will help in dealing with the relation of freedom to persuasion to look again at some loose ends of classical theory.

Hobbes argued that 'All actions that men do in commonwealths for fear of the law are actions which the doers had liberty to omit'. For to give a man an additional motive for action (i.e. fear of punishment) to set against whatever others he may have, makes him no less free; he may choose to disobey if he will and take the consequences. This looks, to a liberal, like a wilfully perverse account of freedom. Action under coercion or threat is, for the liberal, the very paradigm of unfreedom, of not being 'the instrument of my own act of will'. The incompatibility of freedom and coercion is what classical liberalism is all about. If Berlin is suspicious of the concept of positive freedom it is precisely because it has been abused in attempts to dissolve the concept of coercion, either by representing it as self-administered, and therefore not really coercion after all, or (the sour grapes method) by representing the forbidden object as not worth wanting, and therefore not really wanted. Both devices, however, are ways of denying the reality of coercion—they do not pretend, as the Hobbesian does, that coercion and freedom are compatible.

Hobbes's paradox can be highly suggestive, however, in distinguishing the problems of freedom in relation to persuasion, from the problems of freedom in relation to coercion. The standard situation Hobbes envisages is of a man wanting to do X and forbidden to do it by a law under threat of penalties. Now there is, of course, a normative sense of 'freedom.' which makes it analytically true to say that a man is not free (i.e. is not permitted) to do whatever is prohibited by a rule. But of course he may succeed in doing it all the same. And this is not really a paradox, because he may have been free to do it, in a second, material sense, if he was not actually hindered or impeded, as, for instance, by being locked in a cell. A legal prohibition is not in itself a material impediment, any more than is the rule in chess that one may not move a pawn backwards. One *can* do it, even though one must not. But now suppose the legal rule is supported by threat of a penalty P? One might now say 'I am not free to do X' (e.g. worship as I want, or refuse military service) meaning that X + P is so unattractive that it would no longer be sensible to choose to do X. Hobbes might argue that this is not inconsistent with freedom—the man would have chosen X had it been open to him, but has decided that since not X, but only X + P is open, he prefers to abandon X. Moreover, there may be some people who do deliberately choose X + P rather than not-X. It would seem absurd for a gaoled conscientious objector to say that he was not free (in a material sense) to refuse military service—he has refused it.[6] On the other hand, one less resolute or less dedicated, might obey the call-up order, giving as a reason for not refusing that he was not free to refuse. He would mean by that not only the law did not permit such a refusal (i.e. that he was not free in a normative sense) but that the threatened penalty constituted a material impediment to his refusing. But he could hardly give this as a reason unless he was prepared to argue that no one could rationally prefer X + P to not-X, i.e. that only someone with a disordered scale of values, a fanatic, would make such a choice—'No one is his senses would'.[7]

Even someone who argues in this way, however, could admit that the Hobbesian view of action under threat does presuppose a *kind* of freedom. For it depends on something like the economic model of a rational man choosing between alternative courses with different net utilities. The choice, it is true, may be rigged against him by some-one with the power to allot rewards or penalties (analogous to a monopolistic price-fixer), but given the conditions, he makes his own choice, and by virtue of his rationality he is his own master. If he could be said to be the instrument of another man's will, it is because the objective conditions of choice have been manipulated, not because he is not able to choose. And this concept of freedom in relation to threats is worth analysing because there are other ways of influencing action which are, in a much stricter sense, ways whereby men can use others as the instruments of their will. Hypnotic suggestion is one; brain-washing and Pavlovian conditioning tech-niques are others. In these cases it is the subjective conditions of choosing which are manipulated; the subject is evidently not master of himself. But this is not because he does what he does reluctantly or under a sense of constraint, or because he feels that the conditions of choice have been rigged against him; neither is it because he does not know what he is doing, or does not act deliberately—for once a suggestion is implanted, he may plan to realise it with normal prudence and circumspection. Still the deliberation is restricted. It can extend perhaps to the 'how', not to the 'why' of action. We say that his freedom has been infringed to the extent that some part of the deliberative process has been inhibited, or some element of action put beyond the possibility of rational criticism.

Now while persuasive influence is not like coercion, neither is it in every case like hypnosis or brain-washing. Suppose B changes his mind after listening to A's advice, or is moved by his exhortations, or converted by his sermon; is B on that account not master of himself? But suppose now that A studies B closely until, knowing precisely the kind of appeal that will move him, he can administer the stimulus that will induce the required response. If this is an invasion of B's freedom, is it because B cannot resist A's suggestion? But why can he not? If it is only that A has found a way of making him not want to, could one not say as much for a good argument? To say that a man cannot resist because he is in chains, or because someone else is standing over him with a gun, would be to say what kind of impediment there is to his doing what he would otherwise do, and that it is by virtue of this impediment that he is unfree. But in the case of persuasive manipulation there is no such impediment, only a set of causal conditions deliberately created by another person so that B should choose one thing rather than another.

I want to argue that, in the instance just cited, it is impossible to say whether A has invaded B's freedom, because not enough is yet known about the situation. Indeed, not only do we not know whether B could have resisted A's suggestion; we have first to decide what account to give of being able to withstand or resist a suggestion. How are we to distinguish forms of influence consistent with autonomy from those that are not?

II

The liberal emphasis on rationality may suggest that the distinction sought for, between persuasion that is consistent with autonomy and persuasion that is not, would be the distinction between rational and non-rational persuasion. This distinction can indeed be made, and, as I hope to show, can be useful, but it will not take us the whole way we have to go. Persuasion is rational in so far as the persuasiveness lies in the substance of the arguments rather than in the manner of presentation, the authority of the persuader, or some other special relationship by virtue of which one party is particularly susceptible to suggestions from the other. Rational persuasion, in short, is impersonal, in the sense that it is the argument not the person that persuades—the same argument advanced by anyone else would be as effective. Of course, not any kind of reason will do. To give as a reason the injury you will do to me if I reject your suggestions is to threaten me, not to use rational persuasion. However, some neutral or disinterested person with no control over your behaviour would be using rational persuasion if *he* warned me of what you would do to me if I disobeyed you. The distinctive feature of rational persuasion is that it invites and responds to criticism. The would-be persuader is committed to changing his opinion too if the persuadee gives sufficient reasons for rejecting it. Rational persuasion is therefore essentially a dialogue between equals. Although the man who warns me of the probable consequences of what I am doing may be trying to stop me doing it, and perhaps succeeds, he is not acting inconsistently with my autonomy; for though I might have preferred to remain ignorant of the inconvenient facts—or even to have gone on disregarding what I already really knew—still, he has not made my mind up for me, but, on the contrary, has made it more possible for me to make a rational decision for myself. Indeed, by offering reasons why I should make one decision rather than another, so far from abusing my rational autonomy he recognises and respects it.[8] It was because the liberal classics took this as the paradigm of persuasion that they never felt that necessity for defining the relation between persuasion and power.

Persuasion, as I said, is rational *in so far as* it seeks to convince by giving reasons, and consequently in so far as it is impersonal. This is not to say that we can distinguish sharply between the case of pure rational persuasion and others. Most cases combine rational and non-rational elements; any argument, however good, can be spoilt by bad presentation, and its effect heightened by fitting eloquence. Still, we can envisage a case of successful persuasion in which the persuader is so distasteful to the persuadee, his presentation so graceless and his whole demeanour so repellent, that almost anyone else could have done it better. Unless the persuadee is over-compensating for his personal dislike, we shall have to attribute the persuader's success entirely to the rational merits of his argument.

The possibility of distinguishing rational and non-rational persuasion does not imply, however, that an instance of persuasion is an invasion of personal freedom or autonomy precisely to the extent that it involves non-rational elements, like appeals to emotion or prejudice. The pretty girl in the toothpaste advertisement may be captivating, but do her charms really make slaves of us? While, therefore, we can confidently say that rational persuasion is consistent with freedom, we still have to distinguish among different forms of non-rational persuasion those that are not.

A is not unfree merely because his conduct is influenced (i.e. affected) by someone else's actions or communications of some kind other than rational arguments. Suppose, for instance, that he confides in B a plan from which he has great hopes: B, while offering no criticism, treats it scornfully; A, discouraged, gives up. Should we say that A's freedom had been infringed? Has B interfered with A, because B's non-rational influence upon A has put him off? Or should we not rather say that A must have been unusually weak-minded to be put off so easily?

This example suggests that whether a man is really master of himself or whether he is being interfered with, does not depend solely on the kind of influence another man exerts, not on its actual effects; it depends *also* on whether it would be reasonable to expect him, in the given conditions, to withstand influence of that kind.

I suggested earlier that to say that a man was not free to do what he would certainly be punished for doing is not to say that no one, faced with the same consequence, has ever chosen to do such a thing, but rather that the choice is not one we could reasonably expect a man to make. Similarly a temptation or a provocation is not irresistible merely because someone has in fact failed to resist it; but neither is the fact that someone has resisted it proof that it is not irresistible. A temptation is said to be irresistible only if a man *could not reasonably be expected to* resist it, even though others might actually have resisted it in the past.[9]

These are instances of a class of judgements which cannot be satisfactorily elucidated without using some standard of 'the normal man'. Judgements about freedom, influence, power, and interference are, I believe, of the same class. What does it mean to say that a man does not withstand an influence? It is not simply that he falls in with what is proposed. For the idea of withstanding it suggests some inner source of strength, some kind of disposition, interest, or motive for not falling in with it. It is not merely that the influence fails in its intent, but that it fails on account of something about the patient, not simply on account of the ineptitude of the agent. Consider the following dialogue:

Customer   I want a cake of soap, please.
Shopkeeper   Which brand?
Customer   Which do you recommend?
Shopkeeper   Pongo. (Aside) It's no different from any of the others, and I make a quarter cent more profit per bar.
Customer   Very well, I'll take *Pongo*.

Clearly, he could have said no. But why should he have done so? To say that he failed to withstand the suggestion seems to presuppose, what is not the case in this example, that he had some contrary interest or disposition, that he knew, for instance, that he was allergic to *Pongo*. Even then, one would not say that the grocer's influence was irresistible. For any other customer in his place would have said: 'No, not that one—I'm allergic to it'.

Bribery raises similar issues. If A asks B for a service in return for a sum of money, there is no reason prima facie why B should be expected to refuse the offer; and if B accepts it, we should not say that he failed to withstand or resist it. If, however, he accepts, having an interest that could provide a counter-motive, or a duty e.g. as a public official, not to do what A asks, one could properly say that he did not resist. Furthermore, if we wanted to plead irresistible temptation in his defence, we should have to argue that no one under the exceptional conditions in which B was placed (whatever they may have been) *could reasonably be expected* to resist. That a man has been provided with a counter-motive is not enough to make it impossible for him to do his duty, though it may sufficiently explain why he did not do it. In the absence of exceptional conditions, attempting to corrupt him does not deprive him of free choice. On the contrary, his freedom is an indispensable condition for his being held responsible should he give in to the temptation. Similarly one cannot plead by way of excuse that a man has been subject to non-rational persuasive influence, unless one can also maintain that no one, despite an interest counter to the suggestion, could reasonably have been expected not to fall in with it.

The problem for the liberal, then, is to establish tests by which to identify non-rational influences that a person could not reasonably be expected to resist, supposing that he has some interest in doing so. One such test is whether the patient can be aware of what is happening to him. For if one cannot know that an attempt is being made to manipulate one's preferences, and if one has no way of distinguishing a manipulated preference, one cannot be on one's guard against it. Subliminal suggestion would probably prove objectionable by this test (though there appear to be subconscious censors operating even here to inhibit out-of-character repsonses). An extension of the same principle would cover propaganda, supported and protected by censorship. For supposing the subject to have some initial disposition, presumed interest, or duty not to accept it, an apparently well-supported suggestion in the complete absence of any counter-evidence might fairly be called irresistible. Beyond these rather obvious criteria we should have to rely on the results of psychological research. If we want to discuss whether protection from mass persuasive techniques is necessary or even desirable, we must first have some idea of the kinds of influence that a person of normal firmness of purpose and with normal interests could reasonably be expected to withstand in a given situation. Moreover, there may be classes of persons, like children, who are peculiarly vulnerable to particular techniques, or to suggestions of particular kinds; principles of protection may very possibly have to use different norms for different puposes. Information like this is as important to the defenders of freedom as it is to the manipulators, and may well be among the fruits of psychologists' investigations into the effectiveness of advertising and propaganda techniques.

III

To what extent can such criteria for distinguishing forms of persuasion inconsistent with freedom suggest moral criteria for the use and control of persuasion and manipulative techniques? The liberal presupposition that every man has a right not to be interfered with unless he is doing something that itself interferes with the freedom or well-being of someone else, applies as much to the persuader as to the persuadee. Unless a form of persuasion itself interferes with the freedom or interests either of the persuadee or someone else, to interfere with it would be an invasion of the rights of the persuader. On the other hand, the persuadee can properly claim as a condition for *his* freedom, that he be protected from hidden manipulation aimed at political or economic exploitation.[10] From these considerations we can elicit, in the first place, criteria for any advertising or propaganda that is designed to promote the interests of the persuaders. We can say, provisionally, that there is no ground for objecting to such influences if they do not infringe the freedom of the persuadee, and constitute no threat to the interests of anyone else. It is up to the persuadee to determine whether his own interests would be served or impaired by letting himself fall in with what is suggested to him. It is not consistent, in other words, with liberal presuppositions about human nature and its characteristic excellence that he should be protected from every kind of influence that might lead him to do things against his own interests.[11] If men allow themselves to be exploited, through lack of reasonable caution or of the exercise of normal critical judgement, they have only themselves to blame. As rational and autonomous beings, they are responsible within reason for safeguarding their own interests— *caveat emptor* applies to ideas and tastes as well as to goods. There is a case, of course, for protection against misrepresentation of both ideas and goods. But this is not to protect the consumer against freely choosing what is damaging to his own interests; it is rather that in determining where his interest lies he shall not be deliberately and unfairly deceived by a lack of information he cannot remedy or by false information that he cannot reasonably be expected to check. Lying newspapers are at least as objectionable as false statements of the weight of soap powder in a King Size packet. Though there may be no objection to manufacturers attracting customers by putting small amounts of soap in large packets, the consumer who wants to make a reasoned choice between brands is entitled to know the weight of soap he is buying without the inconvenience of carrying his own scales or insisting on having the alternative packets weighed before he decides. Of far greater importance is his right to be told the truth in news reports, on which he has to base rational judgements on public affairs, and which he simply cannot confirm for himself. Of course, insisting that newspapers tell the truth is far more problematic and politically hazardous than insisting on the truth about soap powders. Since governments are interested parties there are no doubt good reasons for relying on newspapers to expose one another's lies, and for leaving it to the reader to check one against the other.

Applying the criteria to techniques which, designed to get under the consumer's guard, may be incompatible with his autonomy, is rather more complicated. A practice which simply exploits the consumer (or the voter) presents no theoretical difficulty; if it is both an infringement of the consumer's freedom and an attack on his interest, it is indefensible. But how firmly can the liberal turn down a plea that a manipulative technique is being used in the general interest,[12] or in the interests of the individual himself? *Pace* Mill, it is difficult to sustain unqualified the doctrine that 'the sole end for which mankind are warranted, individually or collectively, in interfering with the liberty of action of any of their number, is self-protection' and that 'his own good . . . is not a sufficient warrant'.[13] Mill's equivocation in the matter of the unsafe bridge[14] is evidence of his own uneasiness; and one can have legitimate doubts about his plea that poisons and dangerous drugs be freely available without medical prescription. What kind of an interest, however, would justify interference for a man's own good?

Consider a possible advertiser's argument that, by persuading a consumer to want G (which the consumer can afford and the manufacturer can supply) he makes it possible for the former to satisfy his wants; moreover, creating a want he can also satisfy, he is acting in the consumer's own interests by maximising his satisfactions. (If this be a man of straw, this particular kind of straw can still be illuminating.)

The argument would be mistaken, in my view, firstly in identifying the consumer's wants with his interests. Tobacco manufacturers who by advertising create tobacco consumers, may cultivate their customers' wants but are questionably serving their interests. And this is not because the experience might not be 'really satisfying'. For once the habit is formed smoking undoubtedly satisfies a craving, and deprivation is so unpleasant that many smokers accept the risk of lung cancer rather than give it up. One has to recognise that people often want what is conspicuously bad for them, and that what satisfies their desires may not be in their interests. Suppose, however, the desire were for something reasonably harmless; what value would we attach to satisfying it, once it were seen as the deliberate creation of someone else? If the advertiser succeeds in producing a mass demand for a product that no one wanted before, is his product valuable and his activity worthwhile, simply because it now meets a demand? Or are we entitled to look critically at the sorts of things that men are encouraged to demand, and to decide that some demands may be unworthy of satisfaction?

Writers in the empirical, liberal tradition, and most notably, of course, writers in the utilitarian tradition, have been inclined to treat as a reason in favour of any performance or provision whatsoever that someone wanted it. Though this reason might be overridden in a given instance by other people's wishes, or by the expectation of harmful consequences, these would weigh as reasons against doing something that would still have been intrinsically worth doing simply as satisfying a desire. Moreover, if the thing were not done, there would be a presumption in favour of saying that the person desiring it had been deprived of a satisfaction, that the result had been to his disadvantage, and that he would have been better off had he got what he wanted. So *ceteris paribus* a world in which many desires were satisfied would seem to be a better world than one in which fewer were satisfied, whether because some remained unsatisfied or because people had fewer desires.

Though this view is persuasive when stated generally, I have difficulty in extending this presumption in favour of satisfying desires to desires demonstrably contrived by someone else, especially if contrived for his own purposes. That is not to say that no contrived desire would ever be worth satisfying; one might properly claim that some kind of experience for which one had induced a desire in someone else, for whatever purpose, was worth having, and that he would consequently be better off if his desire for it were satisfied. But this would be to recognise a distinction between experiences which were worth having, for which the corresponding desires would be worth satisfying, and those which were not. This is quite different from allowing a residual kind of worth in the satisfaction of any desire, simply as such and irrespective of its object.

It might be objected, as a general negative reason for satisfying desires, that a desire unsatisfied is a source of suffering. Certainly, if a drug addict had no hope of cure, what he suffered from his unsatisfied desire would be a strong reason, perhaps a sufficient reason, for satisfying it. It is surely a mistake, however, to assimilate all desires to cravings; to be disappointed is not necessarily to suffer, or, at any rate, to suffer in the same sense in which deprived addicts suffer. Furthermore, there is something repugnant about saying that, in a case of deliberate torturing a saving factor in an otherwise totally deplorable situation is that the sadistic desires of the torturer have been satisfied. Malicious satisfaction makes a situation worse, not better.

The view I am challenging depends for its persuasiveness in part on a meaning shift in the word 'satisfaction'. I may get satisfaction from contemplating a picture or reading a novel, but this is not necessarily because a desire to look at a picture has been satisfied. On the other hand, if I desire X and get X my desire is satisfied but it may give me no satisfaction. I may discover that what I wanted was not worth having. And this may not be because I was misinformed about the nature of the thing; I may have got precisely what I desired and expected, yet still be no better off for having it. The quality of the life into which it enters may be no better for it—it may have no function in my life, and add nothing to me as a person. My wanting it may have been factitious, in the sense that the desire arose from no integral tendency in my nature, no search for a mode of expression, no recognisable need. I could have set my heart on almost anything else, or on nothing at all, and have been now worse off. Now, if my desires were simply the contrivance of persuaders, they might very well be like this. In that case one would be led to ask whether the mere fact of a desire could really be a reason for satisfying it or whether what gives value to the satisfaction of a desire is the quality of the life of which it forms a part and in which it has a function. Satisfying a desire would be valuable then if it sustained or made possible a valuable kind of life. To say this is to reject the argument that in creating the wants he can satisfy the advertiser (or the manipulator of mass emotion in politics or religion) is necessarily acting in the interests of his public. What their interests are depends now on some objective assessment of what constitutes excellence in human beings, not on what they happen, for whatever reason, to want. If this is true, advertising that presents consumption as a self-justifying activity, that attributes value to things, rather than to what they do to and for a person, is essentially corrupting in that it promotes a misconception of the nature of man. Misunderstanding what we are, we are misled about the nature of the enterprise in which as men we are engaged.

This does not mean we ought to repudiate the cautious liberal approach to protection 'in one's own interests'. For everything depends on what one takes to be the characteristic human excellences. The liberal conception of man, as sustained by Kant and Mill, places at the top of the list a man's capacity for making responsible choices among alternative ways of life, for striving no matter how mistakenly or unsuccessfully to make of himself something worthy of his own respect. This is a creative enterprise calling for experiment, intelligent self-appraisal, and criticism. Consequently, it cannot be fostered by denying men the opportunity to make false starts and to learn from experience. Men have an overriding interest in liberty itself.

This account of human interests suggests an important qualification to my earlier provisional statement, that there was no ground for objecting to persuasion that did not infringe the freedom of the persuadee, and constituted no threat to the interests of anyone else, since it was for him to determine whether his own interests would be served or impaired by falling in with it. For we can now suggest a case for protecting a man from any influence, irresistible or not, which if successful would lead to a condition like drug addiction in which his ability to make further rational choices would be permanently and irremediably impaired. For though the mode of persuasion might not itself be an interference, nevertheless, if successful, it would impair freedom, understood as rational self-mastery.[15]

I do not expect everyone to agree on the application of this criterion, on whether, for instance, it would rule out advertising by cigarette manufacturers, or advertising of the type mentioned earlier, which corrupts by promoting the worship of consumption for its own sake. It is arguable, on the one hand, that advertisements of this latter kind are not, taken severally, irresistible, nor would responding to them irremediably impair the individual's capacity for discovering for himself what kinds of things are valuable and why. Indeed, the very opposite might be the case. On the other hand, the cumulative influence of an environment filled with a variety of advertisements all with the same underlying message hidden by its very ubiquity may be more closely analogous to influences like subliminal suggestions that one cannot directly perceive than to a straightforward appeal to emotions.

The same basic principles on which I have relied for criteria justifying protection from persuasion also provide criteria for the use of irresistible manipulative techniques. Just as the sole ground for protecting a man from an influence which is not irresistible is that he should not risk impairing his capacity for choosing rationally and for making critical appraisals of his own experience and achievements; so the justification for manipulation must be that he is suffering from some impediment or handicap, which inhibits such activities, and which he could not remedy by his own efforts. This would justify, for instance, the use in psychotherapy of hypnosis and 'truth-drugs'; for the aim of the treatment is not to dominate nor to mould the patient, but to restore his capacity for making his own rational appraisals of his environment, and for deciding for himself what would be his appropriate adjustment to it. Here again one has to rely heavily on conceptions of normality; for to be handicapped is to lack capacities that a man normally enjoys.

I have said that these criteria are not easy to apply, and there would be plenty of argument about any particular application. Nevertheless since we are bound to make decisions of this kind, it is well that we should be conscious of what we are about in making them.

Notes

1 See, for instance, J. A. C. Brown, *Techniques of Persuasion*, Penguin, Harmondsworth, 1963. Joseph T. Klapper illustrates the confused state of the subject, with references in *The Effects of Mass Communication*, Free Press, Chicago, 1960, p. 3: 'In reference to persuasion, we have maintained that the media are after all not so terribly powerful, and yet we have reported very impressive successes in promoting such varied phenomena as religious intolerance, the sale of war bonds, belief in the American way, disenchantment with Boy Scout activities.'

2 Cf. Klapper, *op. cit.*, p. 13.

3 Cf. Isaiah Berlin, *Two Concepts of Liberty*, Clarendon Press, Oxford, 1958.

4 *Ibid.*, p. 6.

5 *Ibid.*, p. 7.

6 Of course, one may want to say that the gaoled objector is the victim of injustice, that punishing him infringes his rights or liberties. But that is another matter.

7 This is not sufficient on its own, of course, to make sense of the plea 'I was not free to do X'. One must also be able to conceive of the possibility of X detached from P, i.e. P must not appear as a natural consequence of X, but as one that follows only because someone chooses that it should. Our inability to leap from a cliff top without broken bones is not a limitation of our freedom. Similarly, since classical liberals regarded market limitations of choice as the social equivalents of natural laws, and therefore irremediable, they did not consider them as limiting freedom.

8 Mr Denis White of Monash University (whose helpful comments on this paper I gratefully acknowledge) has made the following point against this passage: 'If a very able arguer uses his skill in argument to persuade a dolt to do something, and he presents an argument that has some force, and which he knows the dolt will be unable to counter, then . . . we should have to say that rational persuasion was being used, regardless of the purpose of the arguer in using the argument, and of whether he himself thinks it valid. Yet this seems a bit odious. That is, I would think rational persuasion must also be circumscribed before it can be regarded as legitimate.'

I agree that someone who deploys persuasive arguments that he knows to be merely specious, or downright false, but which he is confident that someone else will not see through, is a manipulator, even though he appears to be using rational arguments, and even though the same arguments used in good faith would count as rational persuasion. This suggests either that rational persuasion is consistent with autonomy if, and only if, it is employed in good faith and with integrity; or that someone who, to persuade another man, uses an argument that has not persuaded himself is not arguing rationally after all; he is not giving reasons sufficient for the view he advocates, but is only pretending to be doing so. I incline to this latter account. But I do not think it matters for my present purpose which of these things one says.

9 A pleads, in his defence, that he yielded to an irresistible temptation. B objects that C, in the same situation, did not yield to it. A might reasonably reply, 'Yes, but C was a saint'. The force of this retort is that resistance to such temptation is too much to ask of ordinary (normal) men. It might, of course, be open to B to object that though A's excuse might come well enough from an ordinary man A, being no less of a saint than C, or being a clerk in holy orders and therefore obliged to set higher standards for himself than he would for ordinary men, is not entitled to use it: there is nothing out of the way in expecting saintly standards from saints. The move here would be to shift the norm: B would be arguing that the standard on which A was relying was inappropriate for evaluating what in this particular case had to be evaluated.

10 The democratic system puts its own special value on certain particular liberties, like freedom of publication, over and above these basic, prima facie freedoms. But there is no need to develop that argument here.

11 Mill equivocates on this point. He considers the possibility that where the public or the state considers conduct against an individual's own interest, it might be justified, not in prohibiting it, but in excluding 'the influence of solicitations which are not disinterested, of instigators . . . who confessedly promote it for personal objectives only', so that '. . . persons shall make their election, either wisely or foolishly on their own prompting, as free as possible from the arts of persons who stimulate their inclinations for interested purposes of their own.' While admitting that such arguments have force, Mill does not 'venture to decide whether they are sufficient . . .' On Liberty, Everyman edition, pp. 154-5.

12 I do not pursue the argument from 'the general interest' here. I have wrestled with the concept elsewhere, and hope to look in detail into its relation to the ethics of persuasion. It would be too elaborate an argument, however, to squeeze into this paper.

13 Ibid., pp. 72-3.

14 Ibid., pp. 151-2.

15 This is an extension of Mill's principle that the man who uses his freedom to sell himself into slavery 'defeats . . . the purpose which is the justification of allowing him to dispose of himself . . . the principle of freedom cannot require that he should be free not to be free' (op. cit., p. 158).

Select bibliography

Introductions to moral and social philosophy

Benn, Stanley I., and Peters, R. S., *Social Principles and the Democratic State,* Allen & Unwin, London, 1959.

Downie, R. S., and Telfer, E., *Respect for Persons,* Allen & Unwin, London, 1969.

Feinberg, J., *Social Philosophy,* Prentice-Hall, Englewood Cliffs, N.J., 1973.

Client self-determination and social work values

Foren, R., and Bailey, R., *Authority in Social Casework,* Pergamon Press, Oxford, 1968, ch. 2.

Plant, R., *Social and Moral Theory in Casework,* Routledge & Kegan Paul, London, 1970, ch. 2.

Timms, N., *Social Casework—Principles and Practice,* Routledge & Kegan Paul, London, 1964, ch. 3.

Younghusband, E. (ed.), *Social Work and Social Values,* Allen & Unwin, London, 1967, chs 2 and 6.

Self-determination and freedom

Berlin, I., *Four Essays on Liberty,* Oxford University Press, 1969, Introduction and ch. 3.

Bosanquet, B., *The Philosophical Theory of the State,* Macmillan, London, 1951, ch. 6.

Cranston, M., *Freedom, A New Analysis,* Longmans, London, 1953.

Marcuse, H., *Studies in Critical Philosophy,* New Left Books, London, 1972, particularly the last chapter.

Mill, J. S., *On Liberty,* several editions.

Milne, A. J. M., *Freedom and Rights,* Allen & Unwin, London, 1968, chs 1, 5 and 9.

Rights

The Monist, issue on 'Human rights', vol. 52, no. 4, 1968.
Vlastos, G., 'Justice and Equality', in *Social Justice,* R. B. Brandt (ed.), Prentice-Hall, Englewood Cliffs, N.J., 1962.

Self-determination and persuasion

Margolis, J., *Psychotherapy and Morality,* Random House, New York, 1966, ch. 5.
Snook, I. A., *Concepts of Indoctrination,* Routledge & Kegan Paul, London, 1972.

Determinism and free-will

Berofsky, B. (ed.), *Free Will and Determinism,* Harper & Row, New York, 1966.
Franklin, R. L., *Freewill and Determinism,* Routledge & Kegan Paul, London, 1968.
Hook, S. (ed.), *Determinism and Freedom in the Age of Modern Science,* New York University Press, 1957.
O'Connor, D. J., *Free Will,* Macmillan, London, 1972.

Index of names

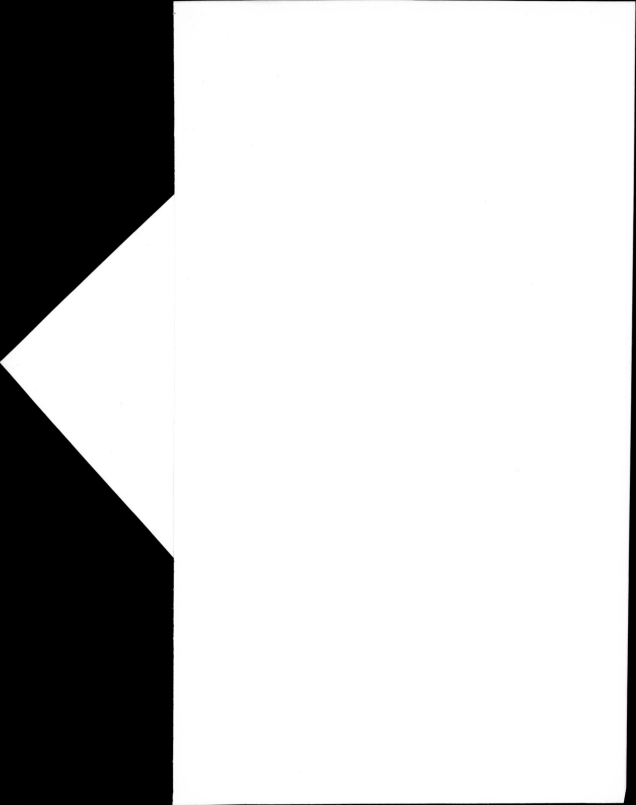

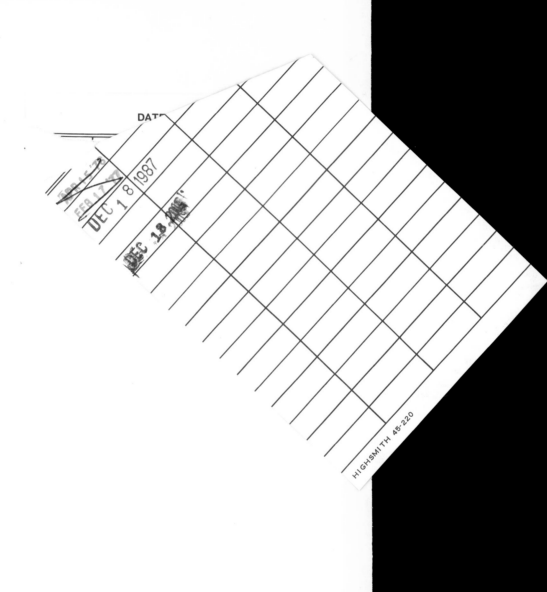